FACING THE APOCALYPSE

ARGUMENTS FOR ECOSOCIALISM

Published February 2019 by Resistance Books: www.resistancebooks.org
and International Institute for Research and Education: www.iire.org
Facing the Apocalypse is Issue No 63 of the IIRE Notebooks for Study and Research

Designed by Ed Fredenburgh
Typeset by First Touch
in 10/16pt Palatino and News Gothic

ISBN: 978-0-902869-91-2
EAN: 9780902869912

To those who stood strong against the odds

FACING THE APOCALYPSE

ARGUMENTS FOR ECOSOCIALISM

ALAN THORNETT

Contents

Part Two: The evolution of ecosocialism

Part Three: Important debates

Part Four: Debates

Foreword

This book is the result of three years of fascinating and rewarding work. I would not have thought, twenty years ago, that today I would be publishing a book on the ecological crisis and the need for ecosocialism.

I have been politically active for almost 60 years. Most of that time, however, was in the trade unions and in radical left politics. My working life was spent mostly as a worker (and shop steward) in a car assembly plant. I was involved in the militant trade union struggles in the car industry in Britain in the 1960s and 1970s, which I have recounted in my 2011 book *Militant Years – car workers' struggles in Britain in the 1960s and 1970s.*[1]

Since my belated commitment to the environmental struggle I have been writing on environmental issues, mostly for *International Viewpoint* and *Socialist Resistance,* that I have supported for many years. I have been active in a number of environmental campaigns, including the Campaign Against Climate Change (CACC) and its trade union group. I have worked with ecosocialist groups in Britain and internationally to promote ecosocialists ideas. I was on the ecology commission of Left Unity before I joined the Labour Party in 2017, though promoting ecological issues there was not easy.

I was involved in the International Ecosocialist Network (IEN), initially launched in 2001 by Joel Kovel, the late New York Marxist ecologist and editor of *Capitalism, Nature, Socialism: A Journal of Socialist Ecology,* and Michael Löwy, the French-Brazilian Marxist ecologist (and comrade) who has written extensively on ecological issues for many years. They were joined later by Ian Angus, the Canadian ecosocialist, and by Derek Wall, who was a Principal Speaker of the Green Party of England and Wales and a member of the Green Left at the time.

Today I am a member not only of Jeremy Corbyn's Labour Party but of SERA, Labour's Environmental Campaign.[2] I am also a supporter of the RedGreen Labour network, an ecosocialist current inside the Labour Party, dedicated to raising the profile of environmental and ecological issues and strengthening Labour's policies in this regard.[3]

Acknowledgements

I received invaluable help, in writing this book, from many comrades and friends, who read the manuscript at various stages and made many valuable comments and proposals.

These include Klaus Engert from Germany (now in Lagos) who read the manuscript at an early stage and made many important suggestions as well as providing valuable information on the history of the German Greens. Anders Ekeland from Norway also read the whole manuscript and made valuable suggestions (particularly around an exit strategy from fossil fuel) – as did Rob Marsden and Tony Richardson. I am in debt to Sheila Malone with whom I discussed some of these issues over 10 years ago. Also to Terry Conway who was endlessly helpful, read the manuscript several times, and made many valuable suggestions including for the title. Bill MacKeith edited and proof-read the whole manuscript and made numerous invaluable suggestions in regard to both content and presentation and overall structure of the book. Derek Wall made a critical assessment of each individual chapter as well as of the manuscript as a whole. He made many important, and indeed challenging, observations that I hope are reflected adequately in the final product. I am in debt to Michael Löwy, Hugo Blanco, and Derek Wall for their very generous endorsements for the back cover. I am also in debt to my children Julian and Charlotte who both made important contributions to the book. All remaining errors, of course, are entirely my own.

Books and papers

I also benefitted from the many books and papers I have been able to consult throughout, that are listed in the bibliography. I mention in particular Edward Wilson's *The Diversity of Life*, first published in 1992, Elizabeth Kolbert's 2014 book *The Sixth Extinction: An Unnatural History*, and Philip Lymbery's *Farmageddon: The True Cost of Cheap Meat*, published in 2014 and *Dead Zone: Where the Wild Things Were*, in 2017.

I owe a particular debt to John Bellamy Foster and his ground-breaking book *Marx's Ecology: Materialism and Nature*, published in 2000 [4] – without which I might not have made this ecological journey in the first place. Also his collaborator Paul Burkett and his book *Marx and Nature: A Red and Green Perspective*, first published in 1999, that expounds the same thesis.[5] J. B. Foster is, in my view, the most important Marxist ecologist of his generation. He has long been editor of the important journal *Monthly Review*.[6]

The thesis they have so ably pursued was that classical Marxism, contrary to prevailing opinion in the 20th century, particularly amongst greens and ecologists, had a remarkably strong ecological content. It had been lost during the first half of the twentieth century, and has now been resurrected and re-claimed by Foster and Burkett as the essential basis for an ecosocialist approach to the ecological struggle today.

Terminology

I use the term 'left' or 'socialist left' when referring to the whole socialist and social democratic spectrum, and 'radical left' when referring to the far-left and Marxist tradition in its many forms. I use the term ecosocialist as embracing both Marxists and socialists who strongly relate to the ecological struggle.

In some historical quotations I have used – with William Morris and Rachel Carson , for example – they have used the term 'men' as a collective reference rather than the gender neutral term 'people'. Whilst this is not terminology that I would use today, it reflects the language of its time.

If my lack of language skills has caused me to miss out on important works in languages other than English, I apologise. Fortunately (for me) many of the books on ecological and environmental subjects are either written in English or translated into it.

Alan Thornett, October 2018.

Introduction

.

For surely there is no square mile of earth's habitable surface that is not beautiful in its own way, if we men will only abstain from wilfully destroying that beauty...

William Morris [7]

The naturalist Philip Lymbery, in his book *Dead Zone: Where the Wild Things Were*, published in 2017, argues that we, as human beings (*homo sapiens*), have arrived at an 'almighty crossroads': a unique period in the history of the planet during which the future of life on it will be decided.[8][9] It is what I call in this book a 'civilisational wake-up call'. It is what the British naturalist Chris Packham, presenter of the BBC's flagship nature-watch programmes, called recently: 'an ecological apocalypse'.[10]

It is a picture that is fully supported by scientific opinion world-wide. Science has long warned us that a rise of more than 2°C in the surface temperature of the planet, above the pre-industrial level, will trigger fast feedback processes that threaten to take climate change beyond the point at which it could be reversed. We are already 1°C above the preindustrial level, and the rate of increase is accelerating.

As I write this introduction, in October 2018, the scientific community has just raised the stakes even higher with the publication of the IPCC's (Intergovernmental Panel on Climate Change) *Special Report on Global Warming* – more widely known as its '1.5°C Report'. It was commissioned at the 2015 Paris climate summit, and conducted by Earth scientists from around the world. The conclusion it has reached is that the existing UN target of limiting the rise in the global average surface temperature of the planet to 2°C above preindustrial levels, is now out of date and should be replaced by a new target of 1.5°C.

The Report insists, moreover, that humanity has just 12 years left to act on this, since a crucial tipping point could reached as soon as 2030. It goes on to call for serious action, and not just changes in the structure of society – which of course are fundamental – but for big changes in the way we conduct our own individual lives: what we eat, the travel choices we make, the way we organise our homes and activities.

The Report's existence is a huge victory for those countries directly threatened by rising sea level, who campaigned in Paris in the shape of the High Ambition Coalition and under the slogan '1.5 to stay alive', for the UN to adopt a limit of 1.5°C rather than the existing 2°C. 1.5°C. This they argued, with great passion, would give them a fighting chance of survival, whilst 2°C would give them no chance at all.

What is clear is that if the Report's advice is not taken seriously, if today's production and consumption models remain in place, particularly in the rich countries of the global North, climate disaster will be inevitable. In fact serious damage is already unavoidable since even a 1.5°C limit would not stop those global warming process that are already in the pipeline that cannot be immediately reversed. Our task today is to halt this process as quickly as possible and keep damage to a minimum. A failure to do so will see the most impoverished in the world pay the highest price.

The global ice sheets

In addition to the fast feedback processes dealt with in the Report we also face 'slow feedback' processes, that are taking place on a longer timescale but are no less devastating in their effect. These come in the shape of the longer-term melting of the land based global ice sheets. The West Antarctic ice sheet poses the most dramatic threat to date. The complete release of its ice into the ocean would raise the global sea level by 4 to 6 metres, causing significant coastal flooding worldwide. Major coastal cities around the world are under threat: New York, Mumbai, Shanghai, New Orleans, Miami, Venice and Amsterdam, for example, along with island communities and low-lying countries and regions. Over 50 per cent of Bangladesh is under medium-term threat. Now NASA scientists have discovered similar processes taking place in East Antarctica, where some of the biggest glaciers are found to be losing ice at a previously undiscovered rate.

The ocean, a key factor in the Earth's climate, is in serious trouble as well. The ocean covers 71 per cent of the Earth's surface and is a vast store of carbon, heat, and moisture. Evaporation from the sea provides most of the Earth's rainfall. Ocean currents transfer heat around the globe, preventing the land masses from becoming too hot or too cold. Without the warming of the Gulf Stream, for example, Western Europe would have a sub-arctic climate. As global warming takes place, the climate of the Northern Hemisphere is likely to change faster than that of the Southern Hemisphere, which is stabilised to some extent by its more extensive sea cover.

Nor is it just global warming. We are facing a multifaceted threat to the biosphere of the planet. Crucial resources are running out, including fresh water and arable land. Pollution is choking the planet. The oceans are now 30 per cent more acidic than in pre-industrial times; coral reefs are dying off at an unprecedented rate. There will soon be more plastic in the oceans than fish. Ninety per cent of all sea birds have plastic in their bodies, species are becoming extinct at a disastrous rate, and plastic particles have invaded the food chain. Global warming is a part of this, but far from the full picture.

Inconvenient truth

Lymbery goes on to remind us that life on Earth has thrived for billions of years. "Wonderfully diverse civilisations have evolved, powered by an abundance of natural riches. The world is now home to more than 7 billion people and a multitude of different plants and animals, all with parts to play in a complex web of life." In the "blink of an evolutionary eye", he insists, "one particular species has gone from newcomer to the dominant force in shaping the planet – us."[11]

In other words the actions of ourselves, modern humans, are set to determine, during the course of the current century, whether life will continue to exist on this planet, or whether it will die out. This 'inconvenient truth', as Al Gore entitled his 2006 documentary, is now staring us, as socialists, radical leftists and Marxists, full in the face.

It is what Rachel Carson, the American biologist and giant of the early post WWII environmental movement, warned us of in her stunning 1962 book *Silent Spring*.[12] It is what the ecologist and writer Michael McCarthy[13] warned about in his 2009 book: *Say Goodbye to the Cuckoo*.[14] Migrating birds, he reminds us, "pour into Britain each year in a multi-coloured singing cascade: cuckoos, swallows, martins, swifts, turtle doves, warblers, wheatears, chats, nightingales, nightjars, thrushes, pipits and flycatchers". These tiny creatures, he says, make scarcely believable journeys from south of the Sahara to get here.[15]

My memories, as a child in rural Oxfordshire in the 1940s, are of dozens of swallows nesting every year in the stables at the top of the road, and of house martins building their muddy nests under the eaves of the houses. When I started work as a farm labourer, in 1953, swallows and martins nested in the barns and cowsheds. Plovers flocked in vast numbers, and followed the tractors as we prepared the fields for autumn sowing. The populations of these species have now crashed.

It is what Elizabeth Kolbert addressed so effectively in her 2014 book *The Sixth Extinction: An Unnatural History.*[16]

Today climate records are broken routinely every year. Extreme weather events – droughts, storms, floods and wild fires – become ever more frequent and severe. Fourteen of the fifteen warmest years since records began have all occurred this century – no doubt soon to be updated to fifteen of the sixteen as data is compiled. Irreversible and catastrophic changes are already underway. One thing is clear: if we human beings continue living, consuming, and disposing of our waste the way we are today, the ecosystems of the planet will be damaged beyond repair within decades, and we – along with the 8 million other species with whom we are privileged to share it – will be in deep trouble.

The record of the left

So how has the left responded to what is an existential threat to the future of life on the planet on which we live? The answer is, unfortunately, bleak. With most organisations of the left – socialist, radical socialist, or Marxist – the ecological issue remains a low priority: often at the bottom of the heap, sometimes non-existent. Most formally recognise the important of the issue but fail to translate it into practice. There are individuals within the left organisations that do prioritise the environment in a serious way, and do important work in the movement itself. Overall, however, the situation is surely not acceptable. The time is overdue for the left to decide whether it intends to be seriously involved in this issue or not.

This book is, in part, therefore, a plea to the left, in its many forms, to radically reassess its commitment to the environmental struggle. It is true that there are many demands on the resources of the left. There always will be, and I am not arguing for the left to become a single issue campaign. But it is beyond time for the left to recognise that the ecology of the planet is a number one mainstream issue for the workers' movement. The old prejudices have to go. The environment is as much a working class issue as wages, working conditions, or health and safety. It is not an add-on, an optional extra. The unavoidable reality is that in the end we can't defend anything, or win anything, or build a socialist (let alone an ecosocialist) society, on a dead planet.

Change not easy

Such a change will not be easy, however. The left had a disastrous 20th century from an ecological point of view, particularly in the Global North, from which it has yet to recover. It was, in its organisational forms, absent from the environmental struggle for most of the century. It also, during that time, fully embraced the capitalist mantra of growth and productivism. In Britain the left supported these things uncritically, in both the unions and in the Labour Party.

In the car industry, where I worked in the 1960s and 70s, there were strong trade unions, and even elements of workers control. Productivism, however, was the order of the day, and the environment was, more or less, a total blind spot – which I unfortunately shared at the time. There was even a reluctance to accept it as a legitimate working-class issue; and this attitude remains to some extent today. The environment was seen as a middle-class diversion from the 'real' struggle for wages and working conditions. It was, in hindsight, a remarkable position to take. Why would the working class and the oppressed need a viable planet any less than the rich?

In the Stalinised countries of 'actually existing socialism' – the Soviet Union, Eastern Europe, and China – the ecological crisis was even worse than in the capitalist countries. These regimes continued to exert an influence on the Labour and trade union left, despite the Stalinist nightmare, and were never likely to encourage their Western counterparts to take the environment seriously. (The Stalinist legacy is discussed further in chapter 13).

This situation was compounded by the loss, in the first half of the 20th century, of the ecological content classical Marxism – something that has been reclaimed in recent years (as previously mentioned) by the work of John Bellamy Foster and Paul Burkett. Partly as a result of this loss, when the modern environmental movement emerged in the 1970s it was led mainly by ecologists and greens rather than by socialists and Marxists. (The ecological content of classical Marxism is discussed further in chapter 5.)

Fortunately (for us and the planet) not everyone on the left was prepared to abstain from the environmental struggle in this way. Both before and after World War II individuals, and small groups, conducted the ecological struggle against the odds and the rising tide of productivism. As a result of this they made important contributions, first to the emerging environmental movement itself, and then to the development of a new generation of Marxist ecologists and ecosocialists as it emerged in the late 1980s. This development was driven by an increasing public knowledge of the effect of escalating greenhouse gas (GHG) emissions on global warming, and by the campaigning activities of the NASA climate scientist James Hansen. Hansen famously made a high profile intervention in the US Senate, which catapulted global warming and climate change into the public arena, making it an important turning point in public awareness. (The rise of the post-war ecology movement is discussed further in chapter 6).

Overcoming the legacy

Today, breaking with the legacy of the 20th century will require big changes organisational and political. It means a new level of both commitment to and engagement with the ecological struggle and the wider environmental movement. It means a serious re-examination of the strategic conceptions that the left has being applying to the ecological struggle for the last three decades. It means developing an overall ecosocialist perspective, and from that point of view, seeking unity with green activists and ecosocialist organisations at every level of the struggle.

It also means getting the role of capitalism into perspective. Socialist have long pointed to the destructive role of capitalism in the environmental crisis.

This is true but not straightforward. It is true that capitalism, with its drive for profit and growth, is the most ecologically destructive system of society the planet has ever faced. As Marx points out, it alienates human beings not only from the results of their labour but from the natural environment as well.

The question, however, is a different one. It is whether the ecological crisis can be *reduced* to the role of capitalism or whether the crisis is truly anthropogenic: that is, driven by human impact. This book argues – uncomfortable as it might be for us as human beings – that in the end capitalism is itself a human construct. It is one of the forms of social organisation created by humans in the course of our evolution on this planet. Hopefully it will not be the final form we will devise.

Joel Kovel puts this very well in his 2010 book *The Enemy of Nature: The End of Capitalism or the End of the World*. The division into classes is, he says: "an essentially man-made category, without root in even a mystified biology". We cannot, he argues, "imagine a world without gender distinctions... But a world without class is eminently imaginable".[17] In other words, class is a human construct.

This means accepting that humans are unique as a species when it comes to environmental impact. We had already done extensive damage to the ecosystems of the planet long before capitalism existed, and will continue to do so post capitalism unless a fully sustainable alternative society is established.

Human impact

Since modern humans migrated out of Africa around 180,000 years ago, we have had a disproportionate impact on other species. We destroyed the planet's large animals, or megafauna (land animals over 10 kg), in what was a major global extinction event. The American Pulitzer Prize winning entomologist Edward O. Wilson spells this out very effectively in his landmark book *The Diversity of Life*, first published in 1992.[18] Human hunters, Wilson says, 'spared no species' as they arrived in new lands:

> As the human wave rolled over the last of the virgin lands like a smothering blanket, Paleo-Indians throughout America, Polynesians across the Pacific, Indonesians into Madagascar, Dutch sailors ashore in Mauritius (to meet and extirpate the dodo), were constrained by neither knowledge of endemicity or any ethic of conservation.

For them the world must have seemed to stretch for ever beyond the horizon. If fruit pigeons and giant tortoises disappear from this island, they will surely be found on the next one. What counts is food today, a healthy family, a tribute for the chief, victory celebrations, rites of passage, feasts. As the Mexican truck driver said, who shot one of the last two imperial woodpeckers left in the world, 'it was a great piece of meat'.[19]

More recently, as human maritime capability developed along with colonial expansion, sailors ate their way through vulnerable species such as the great auk, the giant tortoise, and flighted birds that had evolved with no fear of predation. Such species went from abundance to extinction in very short periods of time. The large and slow-moving Steller's sea cow, from around the Commander Islands in the Bering Sea, was hunted to extinction by human beings within 27 years of its discovery. In the 18th century between 30 and 60 million bison roamed North America's great plains. The construction of the railroad network and accelerated human settlement led to a remarkable mass slaughter of the bison, taking it close to extinction. Around 2 million bison were killed on southern plains in a single year: an average of 5000 a day over a three year period.

We are the only species to have invaded every habitat on earth and capable of destroying the planet many times over and by more than one method. We shaped the surface of the earth by deforestation (in Britain largely in the Neolithic period) and by the introduction of agriculture. Human activity has destroyed a tenth of Earth's remaining wilderness in the last 25 years and there may be none left within a century if current trends continue. We are the only species that can act consciously, and understand the consequences of our own actions. If we ignore the impact we are having on the planet, we will destroy all other species that live on it and ultimately ourselves.

Recognition of the human impact on the ecology of the planet has recently been taken to a new level by the decision of the global scientific community to propose an historic change to the definition of the current geological epoch through which the planet is passing. What was previously identified as the Holocene (or interglacial period) will now, if the proposal is accepted, be defined as the Anthropocene, or the 'age of modern humans'. (The age of the Anthropocene is discussed more in chapter 15).

An open and ongoing discussion

This book seeks to promote an ongoing discussion on these issues on the left. Some, it is true, are controversial; at least one is a taboo subject. But we are not going to be able to defend the planet and those that live on it, against the apocalypse by avoiding the difficult or uncomfortable issues. Only frank and open discussion around such issues will equip the left to play a more effective role in the environmental struggle in the 21st century than we managed in the 20th.

We have to discuss how to move from fossil fuel dependency to zero carbon within the 12 years that science is giving us. Calls to abolish global capitalism, important as they are, will not stop global warming by 2030. This book argues that as long as fossil fuels remain the cheapest way of generating energy they are going to be used. It is a massive challenge to the whole of human society. This raises the issue of high impact policies that can bring carbon emissions down to a safe level within the time-scale that has been left to us.

We have to discus strategies that can bring about rapid decarbonisation of our economies by methods that are socially just and economically redistributive, as well as popular and acceptable to millions of people. It is hard to see how this can be done in a restricted timescale without heavily taxing the polluters themselves. This book argues for a serious look at James Hansen's fee and dividend proposal as the best way on offer of approaching this problem. (The strategic challenges as well as an exit strategy from fossil fuel is discussed further in chapters 10 and 11).

We have to discuss economic growth and productivism, that is a key driver of ecological devastation. Whilst there is a greater awareness of the dangers of growth today on the radical left, it remains a no-go area in parts of the wider movement: in particular the trade unions and centre left political parties that still present growth as the goal to aim for.

Nor can we avoid the issue of the ongoing growth of the planet's human population, which is the other side of the same coin. This has tripled in the last 60 years – from 2.5 billion in 1952, when I left school, to 7.6 billion today. It increases every year by 70 million people, and this shows no signs of declining. Yet most on the socialist left continue to insist that it is not a problem for the ecology of the planet. (Economic growth is further discussed in chapter 12, and population in chapter14).

Simply feeding the current global population of 7.6 billion is an existential threat to the ecology of the planet. GHG emissions generated by agriculture are greater than those generated by the whole of the global transport system – land, sea and air. Today's global meat consumption is unsustainable in terms of water usage alone. It takes, for example, 24,000 litres of water to grow the feed to produce a single kilo of beef. The question, therefore, is not whether enough food can be produced to feed the existing human population, or indeed the 9 or 10 billion people expected to exist by mid-century. That might be possible if meat consumption was dramatically reduced. The question is whether it can be done without destroying the ecosystems of the planet. (Water is discussed in chapter 2 and food in chapter 16).

We are facing the biggest biodiversity crisis since the demise of the dinosaurs 65 million years ago. Species extinctions are running at 1,000 times the historical or 'background rate', which means around 200 species become extinct every 24 hours. This is increasingly recognised by scientists as the 'sixth mass extinction' in the history of the planet. The background extinction rate varies with the species. For mammals, it is one every 700 years, which means that a quarter of all mammal species are currently at risk. (The biodiversity crisis is discussed further in chapter 4).

We have to discuss the struggle for an international climate agreement – moves towards which began with the establishment of the IPCC under the auspices of the UN in 1988 and have continued ever since, recently with the Paris agreement. There are different views on whether to focus on this process or on direct action against the polluters themselves. This book argues for both. Whilst direct action remains crucial, we cannot ignore the struggle for an international agreement on an issue that is uniquely international. (The struggle for an international agreement is discussed in more detail in chapter 8).

The issue of lifestyle and individual responsibility, as mentioned in the IPCC report, is also important – though it remains controversial on the left. This book argues that while the principal responsibility lies at governmental level there must also be a responsibility on the individual to minimise his or her impact on the planet, where they are in a position to do so. And this must include reducing meat consumption because the production of it is now unsustainable. (Lifestyle and personal responsibility is discussed in chapter 17).

Meanwhile the most numerous categories of the refugees on the planet are now environmental refugees: those fleeing deserts, failed crops, flooding or wild fires fall foul of immigration controls and face the wrath of the police and the immigration services. The UN estimates that 50 million people are 'environmental refugees', forced to leave their regions of origin in the wake of climate change.

If this book can stimulate discussions on at least some of these issues, help the radical left to focus more clearly around the ecological struggle, it will have been more than a worthwhile project.

Alan Thornett, October 2018

PART ONE

THE SCOPE AND SEVERITY OF THE CRISIS

Planetary boundaries

Sooner or later, we will have to recognise that the Earth has rights too, to live without pollution. What mankind must know is that human beings cannot live without Mother Earth, but the planet can live without humans.

Evo Morales.[20]

A good way to get a grasp of the full extent of the ecological and environmental crisis is via the concept of 'planetary boundaries' – an approach developed by a team of Earth system scientists led by Johan Rockström from the Stockholm Resilience Centre, Will Steffen from the Australian National University, the Nobel prize-winning climatologist Paul Crutzen, and James Hansen.

They set out to identify those Earth system processes – or 'planetary boundaries' – that are critical to the stability of the planet's biosphere, and the most likely points at which catastrophic breakdown might occur. The conclusions they reached were contained in a paper entitled *'Planetary Boundaries: Exploring the Safe Operating Space for Humanity'* published in 2009 in *Ecology and Society*.[21]

The paper identifies nine such boundaries the transgression of which, they say, could result in deleterious or even catastrophic crossing of thresholds that will trigger non-linear, abrupt environmental change on a continental or even planetary scale.

The nine they identify are as follows.

Climate change

The first is climate change. On this they conclude the science behind it is sound. That it is caused by the release of greenhouse gases (GHGs) into the atmosphere, predominately carbon dioxide (CO_2) from the burning of fossil fuels – but also from methane (CH_4) which is 23 times more potent than CO_2

from nitrous oxide (N_2O), and from water vapour. Every tonne of fossil fuel that is burnt produces 3.7 tonnes of CO_2.

They note that since the industrial revolution, human activity has added 365 billion metric tonnes of CO_2 to the atmosphere and deforestation has added another 9 billion tonnes. Each year, this addition increases by a further 9 billion tonnes. As a result of this the CO_2 content of the atmosphere has increased from 275 parts per million (ppm) in pre-industrial times to a global average of 400ppm in 2016; and it continues to rise.

The most extreme warming is taking place in the Arctic region, which is now around 3°C warmer than preindustrial times. The tropics are around 1°C warmer. Middle-latitude warming is greater in the Northern Hemisphere than in the Southern Hemisphere because of the much larger land area in the North.

Rising sea level is the biggest single impact from global warming. The sea level is currently rising by 3 mm per year. This is generated by the melting of glaciers and land based ice caps and by ocean expansion – water expands as it warms up. (Climate change is discussed in more detail in many other parts of the book including in the Introduction and in chapter 8).

Ocean acidification

On ocean acidification the team points out that CO_2 dissolves readily into seawater to form carbonic acid, and as a result of increasing CO_2 levels in the atmosphere, the oceans are 30 per cent more acidic today than in pre-industrial times. By the end of this century, the oceans could well be 150 times more acidic than in pre-industrial times.

The consequences of this are severe since those species that are intolerant to this higher level will die-off. The ocean, like the biosphere, is an intimate, interwoven, and interdependent network of ecosystems, where the future of one species affects the situation and future of all, including our own. They point out that marine organisms secrete calcium carbonate primarily in the forms of aragonite (which is produced by corals, many molluscs, and other marine life) and calcite (which is produced by different single-celled plankton and other groups). Since aragonite is about 50% more soluble in seawater than calcite, with rising ocean acidity, aragonite shells are expected to dissolve before those made of calcite unless the organism has evolved some mechanism to prevent shell dissolution.

(Ocean acidification is discussed in more detail in chapter 4.)

Stratospheric ozone depletion

In 1985, a major hole in the ozone layer was discovered above Antarctica that threatened to spread rapidly around the Earth with catastrophic consequences. The appearance of the ozone hole, the team point out, was a textbook example of a threshold in the Earth System being crossed—completely unexpectedly.

The stratospheric ozone layer is a fragile band of gases in the stratosphere, or the upper level of our atmosphere, that shields us from the sun's damaging ultraviolet radiation. Stratospheric ozone filters out most of the sun's potentially harmful shortwave ultraviolet (UV) radiation. Exposure to higher amounts of UV radiation could have serious impacts on human beings, animals and plants. The ozone layer became depleted due to the release of such substances as chlorofluorocarbons (CFCs), allowing more UV rays reach the Earth and causing increased levels skin cancer and cataracts, and the development of malignant melanoma in humans. Ozone layer depletion also has negative effects on plant growth, on marine ecosystems and on biochemical cycles.[22]

Interference with the Global Phosphorus and Nitrogen Cycles

This involves the inflow of phosphorous into the oceans at levels higher than the natural background weathering. Phosphorus is an essential nutrient for plants and animals. P and N (phosphorus and nitrogen) cycles are the circulation of nutrients in the soil. Fertilisers containing nitrogen and phosphorus are widely used in modern agriculture. Eighty per cent of mined phosphorus is used to make fertilisers. Phosphates from fertilisers, sewage and detergents can cause pollution in lakes and streams. Excessive phosphate in both fresh and inshore marine waters can lead to massive algae blooms which, when they die and decay, lead to eutrophication of fresh waters only. An example of this is the Experimental Lakes Area in Ontario, Canada. The process can also trigger abrupt changes in the ecosystem, such as the dead zone in the Gulf of Mexico.

Rate of biodiversity loss

Today species are becoming extinct 1,000 times faster than the 'natural' or 'background' rate. The current rate of biodiversity loss, the team concludes, constitutes the sixth major extinction event in the history of life on Earth – the first to be driven specifically by the impacts of human activities on the planet

Currently around 50 per cent of all species of plants and animals are threatened with extinction. The IPCC predicts that a 1.5°C temperature increase could put between 20 and 30 per cent of the planet's species at risk – the bleaching out of coral reefs for example. But it is not just global warming that is doing the damage. It is habitat loss and pollution, including the acidification of the oceans, which is taking place at an alarming rate.

Today, a quarter of all mammal species are at risk, for example, compared with a background rate of one every 700 years. (Species extinction is discussed in more detail in Chapter 4).

Global Fresh Water Use

Fresh water is becoming ever scarcer, and increasingly the cause of international conflict. Ground-water aquifers are being depleted at an alarming rate. One in six people on the planet get their drinking water from glaciers and snowpack on the world's mountain ranges, which are receding. Twenty-five per cent of river water is now extracted before it reaches the ocean; many rivers run dry before they get there.

The fifteen thousand glaciers that flow from the Himalayan Mountains provide half of the water for the three main rivers in South Asia: the Ganges, Indus and Brahmaputra, on which a billion people rely.

(Fresh water use is discussed in much more detail in Chapter 2).

Land system change

Around 40 per cent of the Earth's land is now given over to agriculture. An area roughly the size of South America is used for crop production, while even more land – 7.9 to 8.9 billion acres (3.2 to 3.6 billion hectares) is being used to raise livestock. And with the world's population growing rapidly, the pressure is on farmers to find new land to cultivate. The question here is, how can we continue to produce food from the land while preventing negative environmental consequences, such as deforestation, species extinction, fertiliser run-off, water pollution, and soil erosion?

The use of land for agriculture has been increasing for centuries. In 1700, just 7 per cent of the world's land was used for farming. Today, figures from the Food and Agriculture Organisation of the UN suggest that the total farmland increased by 12.4 million acres (5 million hectares) annually between 1992 and 2002. In Brazil, for example, huge areas of rain forest have been replaced by soybeans, which are not a traditional crop in South America. Production has been fueled by demand for soy from China.

Aerosol Loading

The team found that human activities since preindustrial times have doubled the impact of aerosols on the environment by scattering incoming radiation back to space or indirectly by influencing cloud reflectivity. Aerosols they say can also influence the hydrological cycle by altering the mechanisms that form precipitation in clouds. Aerosols may also have a substantial influence on the Asian monsoon circulation. The absorption of aerosols over the Indo-Gangetic plain near the foothills of the Himalayas can also act as an extra heat source aloft, enhancing the incipient monsoon circulation.

The same aerosols lead to a surface cooling over central India, shifting rainfall to the Himalayan region. This "elevated heat pump" causes the monsoon rain to begin earlier in May–June in northern India and the southern Tibetan plateau, increases monsoon rainfall over all of India in July–August, and reduces rainfall over the Indian Ocean. Although the influences of aerosols on the Asian monsoon are widely accepted, there is still a great deal of uncertainty surrounding the physical processes underlying the effects and the interactions between them.

Chemical Pollution

The team found that primary types of chemical pollution include radioactive compounds, heavy metals, and a wide range of organic compounds of human origin. They confirmed that chemical pollution adversely affects human and ecosystem health, which has most clearly been observed at local and regional scales but is now evident at the global scale. Their assessment on why chemical pollution qualifies as a planetary boundary rests on two ways in which it can influence Earth System functioning: through a global, ubiquitous impact on the physiological development and demography of humans and other organisms with ultimate impacts on ecosystem functioning and structure and by acting as a slow variable that affects other planetary boundaries. For example, chemical pollution may influence the biodiversity boundary by reducing the abundance of species and potentially increasing organisms' vulnerability to other stresses such as climate change.

Chemical pollution also interacts with the climate-change boundary through the release and global spread of mercury from coal burning and from the fact that most industrial chemicals are currently produced from petroleum, releasing CO_2 when they are degraded or incinerated as waste. There could, they say, be even more complex connections between chemical, biodiversity, and climate-change boundaries. For example, climate change will change the distributions of pests, which could lead to increased and more widespread use of pesticides. (Pollution is dealt with in more detail on chapter 3)

Preliminary conclusions

The preliminary conclusions the team reached was that humanity has already transgressed three boundaries: climate change, the rate of biodiversity loss, and the rate of interference with the nitrogen cycle. There is significant uncertainty, they say, surrounding the duration over which boundaries can be transgressed before causing unacceptable environmental change and before triggering feedbacks that may result in crossing of thresholds that drastically reduce the ability to return within safe levels. Fast feedbacks (*e.g.* loss of Arctic sea ice) appear to already have kicked-in after having transgressed the climate boundary for a couple of decades. Slow feedbacks (*e.g.* loss of land-based polar ice sheets) operate over longer time frames.

Only one success

Since the planetary boundaries proposition was published in 2009, only one of the boundaries it identified – stratospheric ozone depletion – has been successfully dealt with, although a longer timescale will be needed for the effects to completely disappear. This was achieved as a result of the 1987 Montréal Protocol, which banned the manmade chemicals responsible for depleting the ozone layer. This was a planetary emergency averted as a result of international action by governments, and is rightly viewed as one of the greatest environmental success stories of modern times. As a result of this, the hole in the ozone layer over Antarctica has started to close and the ozone layer has started to thicken.

2 Fresh water

The water 'footprint' of western countries on the rest of the world deserves to become a serious issue. Whenever you buy a T-shirt made of Pakistani cotton, eat Thai rice or drink coffee from Central America, you are influencing the hydrology of those regions – a share of the river Indus, the Mekong or the Costa Rican rains. You may be helping rivers run dry.

Fred Pearce.[23]

The demand for fresh water has long outpaced its replenishment rate by precipitation – rain and snowfall. As a result of this we have been depleting underground reserves, in the form of aquifers, at an ever increasing rate. By 2025, an estimated 1.8 billion people will live in areas facing serious water shortages, with two-thirds of the world's population living in water-stressed regions.

During the 20th century, according to the UN, the demand for fresh water grew at more than twice the rate of the global population. In May 2000, the UN Environment Programme – the agency that coordinates its environmental responsibilities – concluded that the water crisis constituted 'the most important environmental issue of the twenty-first century'.

The water we drink today has been around for a long time – long before the dinosaurs. While the amount of fresh water on the planet has remained fairly constant – being continually recycled through the atmosphere and back into our taps – not only has the global human population risen dramatically, but as a result of changes in lifestyles and eating habits, the consumption of water per capita is going up sharply as well.

Availability

The science writer Fred Pearce, in his 2006 book *When the Rivers Run Dry*, presents a very useful overview of the availability of fresh water and its natural distribution.[24]

(This excellent book stands in sharp contrast to his later (2011) book *Peoplequake: Mass Migration, Aging Nations, and the Coming Population Crash,* in which he denies that the rising human population of the planet poses any kind of problem for its resources and ecology.)

The Earth, he notes, contains an awful lot of water. In fact, a staggering 1.4 billion cubic kilometres (yes, cubic kilometres!) of it. Seventy per cent, however, is sea water, and of the remaining 35 million cubic kilometres that is accessible, two-thirds is locked up in ice caps and glaciers. This leaves about one third, or 12 million cubic kilometres, in liquid form and potentially useable.

On the face of it, it's a lot. The problem, however, is its random and adverse location in relation to the human population. Pearce points out that just six countries have a half of the world's renewable water supply: Brazil, Russia, Canada, Indonesia, China and Colombia. On the other end of the scale is Gaza, with just 76 litres of contaminated water per person per day, as against 350 litres of clean water in Israel.[25] Many of the impoverished countries of the Global South, also missed out in this, and for them clean water is either desperately hard to come by or requires laborious work, or big investment, in order to obtain it. Vast quantities of water are impossible to transport unless gravity can be used to do it.

Most of the water we use on a day-to-day basis comes from rainfall – around 60,000 cubic kilometres a year. Some evaporates or is taken up by plants; whilst the remaining 40,000 cubic kilometres makes its way from the land to the sea each year – at least until we start diverting it. However, many of the rivers with the biggest flows run through impenetrable jungle or Arctic wastes, and in the end we are left with around 9,000 cubic kilometres to meet the needs of the human population for a year. Most of this, however, is contained in underground reservoirs or aquifers – much of it in sandstone rock. By chance, because of changing global climatic patterns, most of these aquifers are located in arid regions where rainfall is either minimal or non-existent – beneath the Sahara desert and the Arabian peninsula for example. Other big reserves lie beneath the Australian outback and the equally arid high plains of the American mid-west.

The Ogallala aquifer in the USA is one of the biggest in the world, stretching for 174,000 square miles beneath Colorado, Kansas, Nebraska, New Mexico, Oklahoma, South Dakota and Wyoming. It contains geological or 'fossil' water that has been there for at least 3 million years. Its replenishment rate is less than a half an inch a year, yet its level is dropping by between three and ten feet a year, as a result of extraction for human consumption. Many aquifers around the world are being depleted at up to 250 times their replacement rate – and when they are gone they are gone.

As Pearce puts it:

> Many of the world's greatest rivers are in regions where few people can or want to live. The three rivers with the greatest flows – Amazon, Congo and Orinoco – all pass through inhospitable jungle for most of their journey from headwaters to sea. These three alone carry almost a quarter of the water we have to survive on. And two more of the top ten – the Lena and the Yenisi in Siberia – run mostly through aridic wastes. A tenth of the word's river water flows into the Arctic. Take out these, and we are left with around 9,000 cubic kilometres of river water for our needs.[26]

This is still, he concludes, 1,400 cubic metres a year per person on the planet, which sounds a lot. But since he has calculated his own water consumption at between 1,500 and 2,000 cubic metres a year, we have a problem if everyone on the planet wants the same.

Agricultural usage

Agriculture devours around 70% of all fresh water extracted from rivers, glaciers, and underground reserves. While official statistics are sparse, Pearce says, the farmers of just three countries – India, China and Pakistan – pump out around 400 cubic kilometres of underground water a year, amounting for more than a half of the world's total use of underground water for agriculture.

For twenty years in India, tens of millions of small famers have been pumping underground water from beneath their fields, as cheap drilling technology allows them to reach far greater depths than their old hand-dug wells. In the Punjab, which produces 90% of Pakistan's wheat, the farmers compensate the diminishing deliveries of water from the river Indus by pumping from aquifers beneath their fields that, because they are not being fully recharged, are falling in level by one to two metres a year. They are, Pearce says, living on borrowed time.

Nor is it just industrialised farming involved. Farmers in India, he points out, have spent $12 billion dollars on boreholes and pumps in the last two decades, with the number of pumps rising by a million every year. At least a quarter of all Indian farmers are drawing on underground water reserves that cannot be replenished, and as a result of this 200 million people are facing a water stressed future. Tushaar Shah, the director of water management in Gujarat, told Pearce that in his view all this is a 'one way trip to disaster'. The underground water boom, says Pearce, is rapidly turning to bust.[27]

Every year, around 100 million Chinese people eat food grown with underground water that is not being replaced. Mexico, Argentina, Brazil, Saudi Arabia and Morocco are also significant users of underground water, as is sub-Saharan Africa. As rivers decline, underground water takes their place. Major cities, such as Beijing, Mexico City and Bangkok are increasingly resorting to underground water. In Arizona, underground water is being extracted at twice the replacement rate. California pumps out 15% more than is replenished – a deficit of 1.6 cubic kilometres a year. The combined annual over-pumping of the Ogallala, Central Valley and Southwest aquifers in recent years has been 36 cubic kilometres. And as the aquifers empty, they dry out and are crushed by the weight above, permanently reducing storage capacity.

Another cause of water depletion is the production of biofuels. In her 2008 book *Soil Not Oil: Climate Change, Peak Oil, and Food Insecurity*[28] Vandana Shiva points to a warning from the International Water Management Institute: that the plans of China and India to increase greatly their production of biofuels will undermine their ability to meet future food and feed demands, because of the impact on water supplies.

In many areas where water is already scarce, biofuel production could threaten river and underground water systems. China aims to increase its biofuel production by fourfold, from a 2002 level of 3.6 billion litres of ethanol to around 15 billion litres by 2010. India is pursuing a similarly aggressive policy. To meet their targets, China would need to produce 26% more corn and India 16 per cent more sugar cane. Doing so would require in China an extra 75 litres of irrigation water per person per day, and in India an additional 70 litres per person per day. This when the WHO's minimum supply of 20 litres per day per person remains unmet.[29]

Water wars

As rivers dry up, conflicts over water become more intense. Twenty countries get more than half of their water from their neighbours. The Israeli sequestration of the flow of the river Jordan, and of 80% of the 'mountain aquifer' beneath the occupied West Bank, has long been key to its oppression of the Palestinians.

Water has also been a central factor in the dispute between India and Pakistan. The Indus Water Treaty, which was brokered between the two countries in 1960, bound them to share the flow of the river, with each taking a share of water from three Indus tributaries. The flow of the Chenab, which flows through Kashmir, was allocated to Pakistan. This has since become the main source of water for the Punjab, the bread basket of Pakistan; but the flow is now threatened by the Baglihar Barrage. The Barrage is being erected in Indian Kashmir, just short of where the river crosses into Pakistan, and is now the subject of a bitter dispute between India and Pakistan.

This is just one of a number of disputes world-wide over the declining water flows of major rivers. Most big rivers pass through multiple countries, often with upstream countries threatening to grab more than their fair share of the water, and downstream nations facing serious ecological consequences.

In her 2002 book *Water Wars*, Vandana Shiva described the water supply as "the most pervasive, the most severe, and the most invisible dimension of the ecological devastation of the earth".[30]

In 1951, the average water availability in India was 3,450 cubic metres per person per year. By 1999 it had fallen to 1,250 cubic metres per person. When availability drops below 1,000 cubic metres per person, the health and economic development of a country is seriously compromised. By 2050, it is projected to fall to 760 cubic metres per person. When it drops below 500 cubic metres per person the survival of hundreds of millions of people is at stake.

In India, mass struggles against the damming of rivers have taken place historically and continue today. The Narmada Valley Sardar Sarovar Dam, inaugurated by Prime Minister Modi on 17 September 2017 is the biggest of 30 planned dams on the Narmada River and indeed one of the biggest dams in the world, at a height of 535 ft. Opposition to the project, has inspired decades of protests, making it one of the most important and controversial social issues of modern India.

Indian writer and activist Arundhati Roy puts it like this in *'The Greater Common Good'*, an essay reprinted in her book *The Cost of Living*,

> Big dams are to a nation's 'development' what nuclear bombs are to its military arsenal. They are both weapons of mass destruction. They're both weapons governments use to control their own people. Both twentieth century emblems that mark a point in time when human intelligence has outstripped its own instinct for survival. They're both malignant indications of civilisation turning upon itself. They represent the severing of the link – not just the link, the understanding – between human beings and the planet they live on. They scramble the intelligence that connects eggs to hens, milk to cows, food to forests, water to rivers, air to life and the Earth to human existence.

Vandana Shiva has witnessed the conversion of her country from water abundance to water crisis. In *Water Wars* she explains that she:

> saw the last perennial stream in my valley run dry in 1982 because of the mining of aquifers and catchments. I have seen tanks and streams dry up on the Deccan plateau as eucalyptus monocultures have spread. I have witnessed state after state pushed into water famine as Green Revolution technologies guzzled water. I have struggled alongside communities in water-rich regions as pollution poisoned their water sources. In case after case the story of water scarcity has been a story of greed, of careless technologies, and of taking more than nature can replenish and clean up.[31]

Huge dams, she says, are built to divert water from natural drainage courses to gain greater usage, and this often induces conflict with neighbouring countries. In India for example, every river has become a site of major and irreconcilable water conflicts. The Sutlej, Yamuna, Ganges, Narmada, Mahanadi, Krishna, and Kaveri rivers have all been, or continue to be, the subject of legal/political disputes between the governments of the countries through which they flow.

Bangladesh, like Pakistan, receives over 90 per cent of its water from India, which has built a barrage on the Ganges right next to the border.

The Danube, Rhine, Niger and Congo each pass through nine countries, the Zambezi through eight. Many downstream countries are dangerously dependent on upstream flows over which they have no control. Syria and Iraq rely for most of their water on the Tigris and Euphrates. Both originate in Turkey, which has full legal rights to the waters they contain and hence has built dams on both to hold it back – including the largest, the Atatürk Dam on the Euphrates.

The Nile, at 6,700 kilometres the world's longest river, flows through ten north-east African countries, with varying climates: Rwanda, Burundi, Democratic Republic of the Congo (DRC), Tanzania, Kenya, Uganda, Ethiopia, South Sudan, Sudan and Egypt.

Egypt gets 97 per cent of its water from upstream neighbours on the Nile, and has declared that it will wage war if the flow is interrupted. The current international treaty on the Nile, which dates back to British rule, gives the bulk of the water to Egypt, a small amount to Sudan, and nothing at all to anyone else, including Ethiopia.

There is a similar situation in West Africa. Mauritania gets 95 per cent of its water from beyond its borders, mostly from the river Senegal coming out of Guinea and Mali. Gambia gets 86 per cent of its water from Senegal. Botswana relies on other countries for 74 per cent of its water. The Limpopo rises in South Africa, and the Okavango rises in Angola and passes through Namibia before draining into the desert. Mexico receives virtually none of the water from the Colorado River which flows out of the USA and into Mexico before it drains into the Pacific Ocean.

Disputes could arise at any time from the many injustices that flow from this situation.

The exploitation of the Colorado

Phoenix Arizona, in the middle of the Arizona desert, is one of the most profligate cites in the USA for water consumption. It originally relied on water pumped from aquifers, but since there was so little rain to replenish them, water levels were falling fast. By the 1950s a new and more prolific source of water was needed. The answer was the Colorado River, which is 350 miles from Phoenix.

The Colorado is one of the principal rivers of southwestern USA and northern Mexico. It is 1,450-miles long with its headwaters in the Rocky Mountains. It drains an arid watershed that extends across seven US and two Mexican states, passing through the Grand Canyon and the Hoover Dam before emptying into the Gulf of California. The exploitation of the Colorado was the focus of the Central Arizona Project (CAP), designed to draw huge quantities of water to supply Arizona, primarily Phoenix and Tucson. The project was signed off by US President Lyndon Johnson in September 1968 (with construction to begin in 1973) after intensive, bipartisan pork-barrel lobbying on the pretext of providing Arizona with its 'fair share' of the Colorado River.

The backbone of the project was a concrete canal, or aqueduct, completed in 1993 and running for 336 miles from Lake Havasu (the southernmost of the four large Colorado reservoirs) to a terminus 14 miles southwest of Tucson. The new dams constructed as part of the project were completed by 1994. All non-Native American agricultural water distribution systems were completed in the late 1980s, as were most of the municipal water delivery systems.

The project cost $3.6 billion to construct and a further fortune to run. It extracts almost 2 cubic kilometres of water from the Colorado a year (around a fifth of the entire flow) and loses 7 per cent in evaporation during the journey. Since the project opened, climate change and drought have hit home, and the river is in crisis. For a number of years, none of the water flowing down the Colorado has reached the sea in the Gulf of California. In August 2016, the director and the general manager of the Central Arizona Project (CAP), which funded the project, issued an emergency Colorado River briefing:

> The Colorado River system has experienced extensive drought conditions for more than 16 years. As a result, water levels in Lake Mead, the primary storage reservoir for the lower basin, and the entire Colorado River system, have been rapidly declining; and projections indicate that this will continue into the foreseeable future. Lake Mead water levels are important because they determine whether a shortage is declared on the Colorado River.

All the states that share the river, [plus] the federal government and Mexico, previously agreed to shortage 'trigger levels' and resulting reduced delivery amounts in the 2007 Colorado River Interim Guidelines for Lower Basin Shortages and Coordinated Operations for Lake Powell and Lake Mead.

These were developed based on data that was available at that time, very early in the Colorado River drought. Now, nearly 10 years later it is apparent that those guidelines are not enough. New river flow projections indicate that Lake Mead levels could drop to the point of seriously impacting power generation and water availability, despite the Shortage Sharing Guidelines. So, the Lower Basin Drought Contingency Proposal (DC Proposal) has been drafted to protect Lake Mead in a way that improves the health of the river system and shares the burden of reductions among Arizona, California, Nevada and the United States, while still honouring the previous agreements.

3 Pollution

There are around 100,000 chemicals in commercial use today, many of them on a massive scale. The eventual effects of many of them on human and ecological health are as yet unknown. There are 10 substances that cause the most concern: Carbon Monoxide, Sulphur Dioxide, Carbon Dioxide, Volatile Organic Compounds (VOCs), Particulates, Nitrogen Oxides, Ozone, Chlorofluorocarbons, Unburned Hydrocarbons and Lead and Heavy metals. The best example of how chemicals can contaminate our environment enough to cause environmental problems is the state of the ozone layer, that is mentioned in Planetary Boundaries above. Global warming is caused by chemicals leaking into our atmosphere.

Over 2 million people globally are directly affected by mining and ore processing. The most hazardous chemicals that are found near these sites are lead, chromium, asbestos, arsenic, cadmium and mercury. Coal-fired power stations, many of them located close to large urban areas, generate sulphur dioxide (SO_2) and mercury pollution. Mercury is one of the most deadly toxins that can be carried in the air. It is highly damaging to the brain and the nervous system when inhaled or otherwise made contact with. Sulphur dioxide can cause lung cancer, asthma, emphysema, and bronchitis. Gold mining releases more mercury than any other global sector.

Lead smelting leads to the release into the air of toxic chemicals – primarily iron, limestone, pyrite and zinc from lead-smelting plants around the world. Lead smelting uses furnaces and other chemical agents to remove impurity from lead ores, putting approximately 2.5 million people at risk around the world.

Approximately 2 million metric tonnes of pesticides are used annually in agriculture, with a disastrous impact on ecosystems.

Dead Zones

Philip Lymbery, in *Dead Zone,* raises the frightening picture of a rapidly developing phenomenon arising from agricultural runoff – oceanic dead zones. He focuses on the dead zone in the Gulf of Mexico that forms every year from February to October, and is the second biggest in the world. Dead zones are generated by a lack of oxygen, creating a lifeless bottom layer of water which most creatures are unable to tolerate. Bottom-dwelling animals with no escape – crustaceans for example – are wiped out. I reviewed *Dead Zone* at the time of its publication. [32]

Lymbery points out that the number of dead zones around the world doubles every decade. There are now more than 400 dead zones covering some 95,000 square miles. Most are found in temperate waters off the coast of the USA and Europe. Some are also brewing in the waters off China, Japan, Brazil, Australia and New Zealand. There are about 40 dead zones around the coast of the USA. The biggest in the world is in the Baltic. The Gulf of Mexico dead zone stretches from the shores of Louisiana to the upper Texan coast, covering an area the size of Wales.

The responsibility for this dead zone, Lymbery says, is clear. It is the fertilizer used to produces the vast grain crops of the American Mid-West – an area of intensive corn and soya production where large amounts of nitrogen are applied to the soil every year to produce grain mainly for meat production. Whilst 160 million tons of nitrogen is produced every year for agricultural purposes, only a fraction of that which is spread on the fields ends up being absorbed by the crops: the rest ends up as run-off.

The run-off that feeds the Gulf of Mexico dead zone originates in the American Mid-West and arrives via the Mississippi River. The Mississippi drains from land in more than 30 states, making it by far the biggest drainage system in North America. Nitrogen applied to the vast cornfields of the Mid-West to increase the crop yield makes its way through the tributaries upstream into the Mississippi itself, and on into the Gulf of Mexico to fuel the dead zone. The more nitrogen is applied to the crops, the bigger the resulting dead zone.

The air we breathe

The air we breathe is becoming ever more polluted and today is responsible for 3 million premature deaths a year worldwide.

Some of the biggest cities in the world – such as Delhi and Patna in

India, Karachi and Rawalpindi in Pakistan, Narayanganj and Gazipur in Bangaladesh, Beijing, Xingtai, Shijiazhuang and Tangshan in China, Jakarta in Indonesia as well as major cities in the Global North such as London, Paris, and Los Angeles – are choking on air that is laden with life-threatening pollutants, including nitrogen dioxide from burning diesel, often restricting vision to a few hundred yards.

The situation is now so serious that even China, one of the world's biggest polluters, is being forced to take it seriously. China more than tripled its coal-burning capacity from 2000 to 2013, emitting billions of tonnes of climate-warming carbon dioxide. Its coal consumption peaked in 2014, however, and is now falling as a result of a major change of policy.

The throwaway society

Nor can the planet survive the kind of throwaway society that capitalism developed during the twentieth century, particularly in the Global North. Vast amounts of commodities are churned out, driven by the advertising industry, that go from factory to landfill in very short periods of time.

Today, the fashion industry is the second most polluting industry on Earth. The global clothing industry produced 150 billion garments in 2010, enough to provide twenty new articles of clothing for every person on the planet. Eighty per cent of all clothing, irrespective of the level of use, including baby clothes that are discarded very quickly, goes into landfill. Every year, consumers in the UK buy 2 million tonnes of clothes, of which more than half – 1.2 million tonnes – ends up in landfill. Religious and other popular festivals, like Christmas, result in the production of vast quantities of stuff that is used very little or even remains entirely unused before reaching a landfill site.

Plastic waste

Alongside the clothing industry goes plastic waste. A survey by Greenpeace found that single-use plastic bottles weighing more than 2 million tonnes are sold every year; another study has shown that that by 2050 there will be more plastic waste than fish in the sea. The stunning BBC documentary *Blue Planet II*, narrated by David Attenborough, told us that:

In January, a 6-metre-long Cuvier's beaked whale continually beached itself on the island of Sotra, near Bergen, in Norway. It was so ill that, after several failed attempts to guide it back out to sea, veterinarians were forced to euthanise the weak and emaciated animal. When they came to do a post-mortem examination, they were in for a shock. Its stomach was filled with about thirty large plastic bags, together with smaller bags that once contained bread, chocolate bar wrappers, and other human litter.[33]

Close to 70 per cent of all litter in the ocean is plastic. Off the coast of South Korea, for example, there are 10 billion pieces of litter per square kilometre.

In May 2017 researchers from the University of Tasmania and the Royal Society for the Protection of Birds from Britain, discovered that Henderson Island, a tiny uninhabited British possession in the South Pacific's Pitcairn group, 5,000 km from the nearest population and designated a World Heritage Site by the United Nations in 1988, was littered with an estimated 38 million pieces (18 tonnes) of plastic rubbish, and with 13,000 new items washing up every day.[34]

Blue Planet II reported that environmental researcher Lucy Quinn monitored albatross chicks on the remote Bird Island in the South Georgia archipelago:

We follow the chicks from when they are first laid as an egg, right through to when they fledge, and for a wandering albatross that can take a year…

Wandering albatrosses spend much of their life soaring across the ocean, so they are not so easy to study. However, what they feed their chicks is an indication of what they are finding during their time away from the nest.

Albatrosses have the ability to regurgitate the bit of food that they cannot digest, and from that we can work out what they have been eating. A healthy chick should have in its diet food such as squid and fish, so we can find squid beaks and fish bones in whatever they cough up, but from last season, the birds regurgitated bottle caps, wrapping, plastic gloves, and large pieces of plastic, and one bird brought up an intact light bulb![35]

Blue Planet II introduces us to the frightening world of micro plastics:

Plastic is broken down by ultraviolet light from the sun and wave action into smaller particles, with 92 per cent of all plastic in the ocean less than the size of a grain

of rice. This is entering the food chain at the lowest level. At the Plymouth Marine
Laboratory, scientists have videoed zooplankton ingesting not their more usual food
of phytoplankton, but minute pieces of plastic...

Another type of microplastic includes small particles from car tyres when
driving, and fibres from synthetic textiles when washing them. About two
per cent are microbeads from cosmetics. All told these microplastics account
for about a third of the notional 8 million tonnes of plastic released into
the oceans each year, and they make up 85 per cent of human-made debris
washed up on shores all around the world.[36]

Urbanisation

In parallel to all this is the rising global human population (currently 7.6
billion) and an even faster process of urbanisation. Thus when the global
population doubles – as it has (remarkably) since 1970 – the world's urban
population triples.

At the start of the nineteenth century, just 10% of the world's population
was urban. A century later the figure was between 20 and 25%. In 1990, 40 per
cent of the world's population were city dwellers and only two decades later it
had reached half. Today the World Health Organisation (WHO) predicts that
by 2030 some 60% of the world population will be urban and 70% by 2050.
Half of all urban dwellers live in cities with populations between 100,000 and
500,000 and fewer than 10% live in megacities of more than 10 million – cities
that suck the life out of a wide hinterland around them.

Almost all future population growth will be in towns and cities. The rate
of urban population growth will, however, be uneven. Among developing
countries, Latin America has the highest proportion of the population living
in urban areas. East and South Asia, however, are likely to overtake it in this
regard during the next 30 years. By 2014 the degree of urbanisation in North
America was 81%, in Latin America and the Caribbean 78%, in Europe 72%,
in Australia/Oceania 70%, in Asia 46%, and in Africa 40%.

The redistribution of the Earth's population on this scale is likely to
affect the natural systems of the Earth and the interactions between the
urban environments and populations. Urbanisation hastens the loss of

productive farmland, affects energy demand and modifies hydrologic and biogeochemical cycles. It creates serious food transportation problems as well as challenges over the disposal of rubbish and of human waste.

4 The 6th mass extinction of species

Each species around us is a masterpiece of evolution, exquisitely adapted to its environment. Species existing today are thousands to millions of years old. Their genes, having been tested by adversity over countless generations, engineer a staggeringly complex mix of biochemical devices that promote the survival and reproduction of the organisms carrying them.

Edward O. Wilson [37]

Today, as mentioned in Planetary Boundaries above, species are becoming extinct 1,000 times faster than the 'natural' or 'background' rate that has occurred naturally over millennia. This disaster is now recognised as the 'sixth mass extinction' – the biggest such event the planet has faced since the demise of the dinosaurs 65 million years ago. (Mass extinctions are defined events resulting in (or threatening) the loss of at least 75 per cent of all existing species).

The five previous such extinctions were: the Ordovician-Silurian Extinction 450 million years ago, which wiped out 86 per cent of life on earth; the Late Devonian Extinction 370 million years ago; the Permian-Triassic Extinction, (the most devastating of all) 225 million years ago; the Triassic-Jurassic Extinction 200 million years ago; and then, as mentioned above, the Cretaceous-Paleogene Extinction 65 million years ago, that destroyed 75 per cent of all species, including all non-flying dinosaurs.

Nor is it just iconic species that are at risk – the orangutan, the blue whale, the harp seal, the maul's dolphin, the vaquita porpoise, the polar bear, the snow leopard, the black rhino, the leather back turtle, and the mountain gorilla – important as they are both intrinsically and as living barometers. It is a vast range of less known creatures, some of which whole ecosystems depend. Many of them are also living barometers that chart the destruction we are bringing to the only planet we have and on which we live and rely.

Once a species is gone, it is gone. Species evolve over long periods of geological time – the average life-span of a species is well over a million years – and today, neither the biosphere of the planet, nor ourselves as a species, have the time or the conditions for such processes to be repeated.

Edward O. Wilson, in his landmark 1992 book *The Diversity of Life*, puts it this way in terms of the loss of insects:

> So important are insects and other land dwelling arthropods that if all were to disappear, humanity probably could not last more than a few months. Most of the amphibians, reptiles, birds, and mammals would crash to extinction about the same time. Next would go the bulk of the flowering plants and with them the physical structure of most forests and other terrestrial habitats of the world. The land surface would literally rot. As dead vegetation piled up and dried out, closing the channels of the nutrient cycles, other complex forms of vegetation would die off, and with them all but a few remnants of the land vertebrates... The land would return to approximately Paleozoic times, covered by mats of recumbent wind pollinated vegetation, sprinkled with clumps of small trees and bushes here and there, largely devoid of animal life.[38]

Today, three-quarters of world food production relies on bees and other insect pollinators such as bees and hover flies that are in deep trouble. A study published in June 2017 in *Science* magazine from the British Centre for Ecology and Hydrology established beyond doubt that honey bees and wild bees, crucial to pollination, are indeed under imminent threat from widely used insecticides called neonicotinoids.[39]

Bats, which are also in steep decline, control diseases though their diet of mosquitoes and other vectors that facilitate disease transmission. Earthworms, which are under threat from pollution and pesticides, transport vital nutrients and irrigation into the soil to maintain its fertility.

Human driven

What makes today's mass extinction unique is that it is not driven by naturally occurring phenomena, as in the past, but by human impact. This impact includes global warming and climate change, habitat loss, pollution, ocean acidification, the use of pesticides and herbicides, mono-culture agricultural methods, plus the introduction of alien species, parasites, and diseases.

It also includes some particularly barbaric (and totally unnecessary) human activities such as trade in endangered species, hunting for sport (which is massive), the poaching and slaughter of animal for animal parts for traditional medicine such as rhino horn and tiger parts. A 100 million sharks (a slow breeding species) are killed annually in the name of the shark's-fin soup industry. It also includes even the vast numbers of small animals and birds destroyed by domestic cat predation – up to a hundred million a year in Britain alone.[40] In the United States it is estimated that free-ranging domestic cats kill 1.3 - 4.0 billion birds and 6.3 - 22.3 billion mammals annually.[41]

Omaui, a tiny village in New Zealand, is planning to be the first to do something about cat predation. Under a regional pest management proposal all cats would have to be neutered, microchipped and registered so they could be tracked. Any noncompliant cats found would be euthanized, leading eventually to a domestic cat-free zone.

Today one of the most hunted (and least known) animals on Earth is the 80 million years old insect eating African pangolin. It is the only known mammal with a fully scaled body that protects it from all known predators – except, of course, humans. It is being hunted to extinction on the bazaar belief that its scales have medicinal qualities, and it could well be wiped out before most people have even heard of it.

Today, defending wildlife is a dangerous business. Over 200 people were killed in 2017 defending land, habitats, wildlife or natural resources. Brazil recorded the worst year on record anywhere in the world, with 57 murders in 2017 alone. According to the campaigning group Global Witness, these include the murder of Hernán Bedoya in Colombia, who was shot 14 times by a paramilitary group for protesting against palm oil and banana plantations on land stolen from his community. They include an army massacre of eight villagers in the Philippines who opposed a coffee plantation on their land, and violent attacks by Brazilian farmers, using machetes and rifles, which left 22 members of the Gamela indigenous people severely injured, some with their hands chopped off.[42]

Coral reefs

Coral reefs are the most sensitive indicators we have of environmental health. Many marine ecosystems, however, are being destroyed by a combination of bleaching from global warming and the acidification of the ocean. Bleaching occurs when a rise in ocean temperature disrupts the delicate balance between the coral polyps and the algae which interact to produce the coral. A study of three mass bleaching events on Australian reefs in 1998, 2002 and 2016, published in *Nature*, found coral was damaged by underwater heatwaves regardless of any local improvements to water quality or fishing controls.[43] The biggest back-to-back bleaching event ever recorded has affected two-thirds of the Great Barrier Reef over a 1,000-mile stretch that includes 800 individual reefs. The findings have alarmed scientists, who say that the damage is so serious that much of the reef will have little chance of recovery.

The oceans could within 50 years be too acidic to support such creatures, which would destroy the base of the food chain. Seagrass, which supports many forms of marine life, is declining at a rate of 7 per cent a year.[44] If you add to that the dumping of waste in the oceans and the run-off from fertilisers, the scale of the problem is clear.

At the same time the oceans are being overfished. According to the UN, a third of the fish stocks in the oceans are in danger. Stocks of tuna, swordfish, marlin, cod and halibut have been reduced by up to 90 per cent by overfishing, whilst at the same time they are under pressure from global warming and oceanic acidification.

The prospect of a dead ocean, something that is now a realistic prospect, is a direct threat to all life on the planet, since 78 per cent of the oxygen we breathe is generated not by the forests but by algae in the ocean itself.

A very good introduction to the biodiversity crisis can be found in Elizabeth Kolbert's 2014 Pulitzer Prize-wining book *The Sixth Extinction: An Unnatural History*.[45] [46] She argues that by the middle of this century, from global warming alone, between 38 and 52 per cent of species will be faced with extinction. An extinction rate of this scale, she says, ultimately puts at risk all species on the planet, including, eventually, our own.

Kolbert consulted scientists on the frontline of research. She visited the rain forest of the Manu National Park in the high Peruvian Andes, one of the planet's biodiversity hot spots, to meet forest ecologist Miles Silman. He was studying the effect of global warming by monitoring plants as they migrate up the mountain at rates of up to 100 feet a year in search of a higher, cooler, climate zone.

She visited the El Valle Amphibian Conservation Centre (EVACC) in Panama, which is dedicated to the survival of endangered amphibians, and linked up with its director Edgardo Griffiths for a scary look at what is happening to the planet's amphibian population. She found that amphibians are a group of species that has managed to survive most successfully everything the planet has thrown at them for hundreds of million years, but are now among the most endangered group of species – particularly over the past 40 years, when their plight has become catastrophic.

Amphibians

Amphibians, Kolbert points out, are facing be a mind-boggling extinction rate 45,000 times (yes 45,000) above the 'background' rate. They are not only affected by general habitat loss and pollution, but by the spread of diseases and invasive species as a result of the globalisation of travel and the mass transportation of goods, that now reaches every corner of the planet. All this produces a figure that is hard to grasp: the extinction rate among amphibians could

She went to the tiny island of Castello Aragonese, 30 kilometres west of Naples, to meet scientists studying the acidification of the oceans. She saw how underwater carbon dioxide vents raise the sea around the island to a level of acidity that is already the fate of some parts of the oceans, and could be the fate of their entirety if fossil fuels continue to be used at current rates. She describes a scene where the organisms that rely on calcification for their shells or body structure are in big trouble. Barnacles are bleached white and the shells of the mussels, snails, and sea urchins are being dissolved by acidification; small crustaceans have all but disappeared. She points out that the oceans are already 30 times more acidic than they were in 1800 and at the current rate by the end of the century they will be 150 times more acidic than at that time.

On One Tree Island in the Great Barrier Reef, she met scientists from the University of Queensland who were studying the health of the coral reefs –

and to witness the annual coral spawning. She discovered that the threat to coral reefs does not just come from acidification but also from overfishing and dynamite fishing, from algae growth, from deforestation and the resulting loss of water clarity, and most importantly from global warming and the resulting rise in sea temperature.

Invasive species

On invasive species she looks at the mass die-off of millions of bats in the northeast of the USA as a result of a fungus transported around the world by modern travel and trade. She notes the examples of Tristan da Cunha, where almost all of the unique land birds that had evolved there with no fear of predation were exterminated by pigs and rats, transported there by human agency. She notes the situation of the Hawaiian Islands, which lost their native plants and animals faster than almost any other place after the introduction of goats and other species. About the year 1513, she says, the Portuguese introduced goats onto the recently discovered island of St Helena, which had developed a magnificent forest of gumwood, ebony, and brazilwood.

> By 1560, or thereabouts, the goats had so multiplied that they wandered over the island by the thousand, in flocks a mile long. They trampled the young trees and they ate the seedlings. By this time, the colonists had begun to cut and burn the forests, so that it is hard to say whether men or goats were the more responsible for the destruction. But of the result there was no doubt. By the early 1800s the forests were gone. And the naturalist Alfred Wallace later described this once beautiful, forest-clad volcanic island as a 'rocky desert' in which the remnants of the original flora persisted in only the most inaccessible peaks and crater ridges.[47]

Today, she concludes, the problem is even worse. In any 24-hour period, some 10,000 different species are being moved around the world just in the ballast water carried by ships. In Hawaii today, a new invasive species is added every month. The advantage we have, she argues, is that whilst the damage done by modern humans was for most of the time unwitting, it is so no longer. We now have the ability to do it differently, should we choose – and it's about time we did so.

Living Planet Report

A similar picture was painted by the 2016 edition of the World Wildlife Fund's *Living Planet Report,* and its associated *Living Planet Indices* (LPIs).

The *Report* monitored over 10,000 species of mammals, birds, reptiles, amphibians and fish in both tropical and temperate regions: it concluded that in the last 50 years, human impact has done more damage to their habitats and survival systems than has been caused in any previous period in the history of the planet. [48]

Marco Lambertini, director general of World Wildlife Fund, put it this way:

> The richness and diversity of life on Earth is fundamental to the complex life systems that underpin it. Life supports life itself and we are part of the same equation. Lose biodiversity and the natural world and the life support systems, as we know them today, will collapse.[49]

The decline of species is steepest in the tropical regions – the regions where they are also the most abundant. The LPI index records a 56 per cent reduction in 3,811 populations covering 1,638 species over that period. Latin America shows a particularly dramatic decline, with a fall of 83 per cent. In the temperate regions, the report's temperate LPI shows a 36 per cent decline in the last 50 years in 6,569 populations covering 1,606 species.[50] In the Southern Ocean, the species in decline include marine turtles, many sharks, and large migratory seabirds such as the wandering albatross.

Madagascar is today a home to 11,138 native plant species, and of these 83 per cent are found nowhere else on the planet. In May 2017, Kew Gardens' scientists reported that Madagascar's special trees, palms and orchids, which provide habitats and food for dozens of species of rare lemur and other animals, are now facing catastrophic destruction caused by land clearances, climate change and the spreading of agriculture. The report, entitled *The State of the World's Plants,* revealed that almost half of these unique species are now at risk of extinction.[51]

The LPI index for freshwater species shows an average decline of 76% in the last 50 years. The main threats to freshwater species are habitat loss and fragmentation, pollution and invasive species, changes to water levels and freshwater systems connectivity – for example through irrigation and hydropower dams. These trends show no sign, whatsoever, of slowing down.

PART TWO

THE EVOLUTION OF ECOSOCIALISM

5 The ecological legacy of classical Marxism

"Labour is not the source of all wealth. Nature is just as much the source of use values (and it is surely of such that material wealth consists!) as labour, which itself is only the manifestation of a force of nature, human labour power." He goes on: *"a socialist program cannot allow such bourgeois phrases to pass over in silence the conditions that alone give them meaning."*

Karl Marx.[52]

In sharp contrast to the disastrous environmental record of the radical left in the 20th century, Classical Marxism – as developed by Marx, Engels and also by William Morris in the second half of the 19th century – took the ecology of the planet, and the relationship between human kind and nature, extremely seriously. An understanding of which, as mentioned above, we are in debt, in particular, to John Bellamy Foster and Paul Burkett. It is a heritage lost in the 20th century not least due to the impact of productivism and the Stalinisation of large parts the socialist movement.

Marx

Marx was one of the great materialist thinkers of the 19th century – although 'ecology' was not a word that he or they would have recognised at the time. His doctrinal thesis (in 1841) was on Epicureanism – a system of philosophy based on the teachings of the ancient Greek philosopher Epicurus' theory of (atomic) materialism. Epicurean philosophy had its roots in the 'principle of conservation' and therefore tended towards an ecological world view. [53] It represented a challenge to superstition and divine intervention, and although not denying the existence of a deity, it did deny its intervention into the material world.

When Engels read Darwin's *On the Origin of Species* on its publication in 1859 (having obtained a copy of the first edition), he wrote enthusiastically to

Marx about it.[54] Marx read it a year later and was equally impressed. In 1862, Marx attended a public lecture given by Thomas Huxley, a strong supporter of Darwin, defending the book.

In the early 1860s Marx also attended some lectures by the Irish physicist John Tyndall on the significance of the greenhouse effect on the atmosphere that Tyndall had recently discovered. Although Marx wrote mainly about labour power it was his interest in science that provided the basis for the ecological insights displayed by Marxism in its classical period. Thus Marxism was, as John Bellamy Foster and Paul Burkett point out in their highly influential studies of this period, remarkably ecologically advanced in the context of the 19th century.

This was reflected most clearly in the concept of a 'metabolic rift', an ecological dislocation between human activity and nature. This was developed by Marx in 1851 after studying the work of the German agricultural chemist Justus von Liebig, who had used the term in his book *Agricultural Chemistry*. Foster argues that Marx employed the concept of 'metabolism' to define the labour process as a process between man and nature, by which man, through 'his own actions', mediates, regulates and controls the metabolism with nature in a rational way, completely beyond the capabilities of bourgeois society.

In *The Ecological Rift: Capitalism's War on the Earth* (2010) by Foster, Brett Clark and Richard York, the authors argue that[55]:

> For Marx, there is a necessary 'metabolic interaction' between human beings and the Earth. Marx contended that 'man *lives* on nature' and that in this dependant relationship 'nature is his *body*, with which he must remain in continuous interchange if he is not to die'. Thus, a sustainable social metabolism is 'proscribed by the laws of life itself'. Labour is the process in which humans interact with nature through the exchange of organic matter.' In this metabolic relationship, humans both confront the nature imposed conditions of the process found in the material world, and alter these processes through labour (and the associated structure of production). [original emphasis]

Marx developed this further in the *Grundrisse* – written between 1857 and 1861, where he argued that:

> It is not the unity of living and active humanity with the natural, inorganic conditions

of their metabolic exchange with nature, and hence their appropriation of nature, which requires explanation or is the result of a historic process, but rather the *separation* between these inorganic conditions of human existence and this active existence, a separation which is completely posited only in the relation of wage labour and capital. [original emphasis][56] [57]

Engels

Engels also addressed ecological issues from the start in his early writings. His iconic work *The Condition of the Working Class in England*, published in 1845, was strongly focused on environmental and industrial pollution, the squalor and human degradation associated with the factory system, and its corollary, rapid urbanisation.

Writing jointly in the *German Ideology*, published in 1846, Marx and Engels said the following about industrial pollution and its effects on the environment:

> The 'essence' of the freshwater fish is the water of a river. But the latter ceases to be the 'essence' of the fish and is no longer a suitable medium for existence as soon as the river is made to serve industry, as soon as it is polluted by dyes and other waste products and navigated by steam-boats, or as soon as its water is diverted into canals where simple drainage can deprive the fish of its medium of existence.[58]

In the *Economic and Philosophical Manuscripts* of 1844, Marx wrote:

> Nature is man's *inorganic body* – nature, that is, in so far as it is not itself human body. Man *lives* on nature – means that nature is his *body*, with which he must remain in continuous interchange if he is not to die. That man's physical and spiritual life is linked to nature means simply that nature is linked to itself, for man is a part of nature.[59]

Marx also understood the importance of environmental sustainability, although he never used the term. When talking about the price of land in the third volume of *Capital* (1894), he said:

> From the standpoint of a higher economic form of society, private ownership of

the globe by single individuals will appear quite as absurd as private ownership of one man by another. Even a whole society, a nation, or even all simultaneously existing societies taken together, are not the owners of the globe. They are only its possessors, its usufructuaries, and like *boni patres familias*[60], they must hand it down to succeeding generations in an improved condition.[61]

Engels wrote the following remarkable passage in his book *The Dialectics of Nature* (not published until 1925). It displays a grasp of the relationship between the natural world and human kind that many on the left today have yet to understand:

Let us not, however, flatter ourselves overmuch on account of our human victories over nature. For each such victory nature takes its revenge on us. Each victory, it is true, in the first place brings about the results we expected, but in the second and third places it has quite different, unforeseen effects which only too often cancel the first. The people who, in Mesopotamia, Greece, Asia Minor and elsewhere, destroyed the forests to obtain cultivable land, never dreamed that by removing along with the forests the collecting centres and reservoirs of moisture, they were laying the basis for the present forlorn state of those countries. When the Italians of the Alps used up the pine forests on the southern slopes, so carefully cherished on the northern slopes, they had no inkling that by doing so they were cutting at the roots of the dairy industry in their region; they had still less inkling that they were thereby depriving their mountain springs of water for the greater part of the year, and making it possible for them to pour still more furious torrents on the plains during the rainy seasons. Those who spread the potato in Europe were not aware that with these farinaceous tubers they were at the same time spreading scrofula. Thus, at every step we are reminded that we by no means rule over nature like a conqueror over a foreign people, like someone standing outside nature – but that we, with flesh, blood and brain, belong to nature, and exist in its midst, and that all our mastery of it consists in the fact that we have the advantage over all other creatures of being able to learn its laws and apply them correctly...

And, in fact, with every day that passes we are acquiring a better understanding of these laws and getting to perceive both the more immediate and the more remote consequences of our interference with the traditional course of nature. In particular, after the mighty advances made by the natural sciences in the present century, we are more than ever in a position to realise, and hence to control, also the more remote natural consequences of at least our day-to-day production activities.[62]

Many on the radical left would do well to be thinking in such terms today.

William Morris

William Morris had already developed a strong ecological commitment by the time he became a Marxist. He had rejected industrialisation and productivism. He had been involved in socialist activity for many years, but it was not until he read *Capital* in 1883, a year after the death of Marx, at the age of 49, that he declared himself a Marxist and joined the Social Democratic Federation (SDF). He was an environmental campaigner and had been involved in opposing environmentally destructive developments in both Oxford and Epping Forest.

Morris had initiated the Arts and Crafts movement in the early 1850s with the philosopher and art critic John Ruskin (by whom he had been greatly influenced), together with his long-time friend Edward Burne-Jones, the architect Phillip Webb, and William and Evelyn De Morgan and others. They campaigned for a return to traditional crafts and to a simpler and more sustainable way of life. He saw the factory system as the alienation of workers from the commodities they produced and from the natural world around them – although he never used the word 'alienation' as such. It was a pointer to his future attraction to Marxism.

In his lecture *'Useful Work versus Useless Toil'* [63] first delivered in January 1884, he argued that factories should be human places where the work should be useful and sweated labour and long hours abolished. Workers should have access to social and intellectual activities such as the study of art and science. They should have access to the surrounding countryside, and the time to visit it.

He went on to point out:

Next there is the mass of people employed in making all those articles of folly and luxury, the demand for which is the outcome of the existence of the rich non-producing classes; things which people leading a manly and uncorrupted life would not ask for or dream of. These things, whoever may gainsay me, I will for ever refuse to call wealth: they are not wealth, but waste. Wealth is what nature gives us and what a reasonable man can make out of the gifts of nature for his reasonable use. The sunlight, the fresh air, the unspoiled face of the earth, food, raiment and housing necessary and decent; the storing up of knowledge of all kinds, and the power of disseminating it; means of free communication between man and man; works of art, the beauty which man creates when he is most a man, most aspiring and thoughtful – all things which serve the pleasure of people, free, manly and uncorrupted. This is wealth. Nor can I think of anything worth having which does not come under one or other of these heads. But think, I beseech you, of the product of England, the workshop of the world, and will you not be bewildered, as I am, at the thought of the mass of things which no sane man could desire, but which our useless toil makes – and sells?

In his lecture '*Art and Socialism*'[64] delivered in January 1884 in Leicester, he argued that:

The wonderful machines which in the hands of just and foreseeing men would have been used to minimise repulsive labour and to give pleasure – or in other words added life – to the human race, have been so used on the contrary that they have driven all men into mere frantic haste and hurry, thereby destroying pleasure, that is life.

In his lecture '*How We Live and How We Might Live*',[65] delivered in December 1884 in Hammersmith – he raised the issue of how to live dignified and fulfilling lives without the need for mass produced commodities and consumerism, and what kind of future society could best provide such an approach. Morris believed that capitalism generated profits by promoting demands that did not exist and persuading people to buy things they did not necessarily need. He argued that, in a socialist society, variety and pleasure would be no less essential than material wealth.

In his lecture '*Makeshift*',[66] delivered in Manchester in November 1894, Morris makes the following observation:

Mr Balfour was saying that socialism was impossible because under it we should produce so much less than we do now. Now I say that we might produce half or a quarter of what we do now, and yet be much wealthier, and consequently much happier, than we are now: and that by turning whatever labour we exercised, into the production of useful things, things that we all want, and not by refusing to labour in producing useless things, things which none of us, not even fools want. What a strange sight would be a great museum of samples of all the market-wares which the labouring men of this country produce! What a many of them there would be which every reasonable man would have to ticket as useless!

My friends, a very great many people are employed in producing mere nuisances, like barbed wire, 100 ton guns, sky signs and advertising boards for the disfigurement of the green fields along the railways and so forth. But apart from these nuisances, how many more are employed in making market wares for rich people which are of no use whatever except to enable the said rich to 'spend their money' as 'tis called; and again, how many more in producing wretched makeshifts for the working classes because they are so poor that they can afford nothing better? Slave-wares for wage-slaves I have called them before, and I call them so now again. In short in one way or another all the industry of the country is wasted, because the system we are undertaking, we one with another, just allows us to live, some honestly but miserably, some dishonestly and emptily, and no more.

This is also the theme of his iconic utopian novel *News from Nowhere*, published in 1890, which was ecosocialist in all but name. Written when industrial squalor and environmental pollution were at their height, it describes a form of society in which the overthrow of the world market has led to the demise of all forms of wasteful production geared to the drive for profit, and where society is reorganised in a way that 'nothing can be made but for genuine use'. It projects a vision of a society based on a sustainable relationship between human beings and nature. Free time must be made available because society had rejected its narrowly defined instrumentalist ends, and work itself was seen as serving the needs of both human creativity and the fulfilment of social needs.

News from Nowhere was serialised in *The Commonweal*, the publication of the Socialist League (SL) founded by Morris along with Eleanor Marx and others in 1885, after they split from the doctrinaire SDF. The novel presented a devastating critique of capitalism in a remarkably accessible way. In Chapter

2, for example, the historian Hammond is discussing the age of industrial capitalism which had preceded the utopia set out in the novel:

> It is clear from all that we hear and read, that in the last age of civilisation men had got into a vicious circle in the matter of production of wares. They had reached a wonderful facility of production, and in order to make the most of that facility they had gradually created (or allowed to grow, rather) a most elaborate system of buying and selling, which had been called the world market; and that world market, one set a-going, forced them to go on making and selling more and more of these wares, whether they needed them or not. So that while (of course) they could not free themselves from the toil of making real necessaries, they created a never-ending series of sham or artificial necessaries, which became, under the rule of the fore-said world market, of equal importance to them with the real necessaries which supported life. By all this they burdened themselves with a prodigious mass of work merely for the sake of keeping their wretched system going.[67]

We can't go back to the medieval village, of course, but the ideas of William Morris contain powerful insights into the implications of the capitalist mode of production and what it had in store for the future viability of the planet.

Edward Carpenter

Another socialist to make an important contribution to the environmental struggle in the latter part of the nineteenth century and the early part of the twentieth was Edward Carpenter (1844-1929). Although remembered mainly for his courageous defence of gay rights and women's emancipation – he was a gay man forced to conceal his sexuality to avoid persecution (he was denounced by George Orwell as a vegetarian smelling 'sodomite' for example)[68] – he was also, like Morris, a utopian socialist, a writer, a poet, a philosopher and environmental campaigner, as well as a pioneer of gay rights. He campaigned against pollution and for the protection of nature, and advocated living close to it. Like Morris, he was from a wealthy family and used his money to promote socialist, environmental and other radical causes.

Carpenter turned to Marxism, or an autonomist version of it, after reading Henry Hyndman, the eccentric founder of the Social Democratic Federation

(SDF). He first met William Morris in 1883, when he was invited by Hyndman to a meeting of the ruling committee of the SDF. Carpenter was regarded by Hyndman as a member after he had made a large donation to Hyndman's newspaper *Justice*. Carpenter stood by Hyndman when Morris led a split from the SDF, against Hyndman's authoritarian methods. He did, however, maintain a personal relationship with Morris and later joined the Socialist League.

The Bristol Radical History Group has recently produced (2017) an excellent publication on Carpenter's life that strongly draws out the ecological side of his work, which is sometimes under-estimated.[69] It reproduces a pamphlet Carpenter wrote in 1894 – just two years before the death of Morris – to promote his most prominent environmental campaign, which was around smoke and air quality. It was entitled *The Smoke-Dragon and How to Destroy It* and appeared as a five-part series in the popular socialist weekly *The Clarion* in 1896.[70] The pamphlet reflected Carpenter's experience of the fogs and filthy air in Sheffield, Manchester and London in the 1880s. The influence of Morris is unmistakable. The opening paragraph of the first part of the *Smoke Dragon* says the following:

> After a hundred years of commercialism we have learned to breathe dirt as well as eat it. Somehow, and by perceived degrees, in the pursuit of mere gain we have become callous and insensitive to matters even more important than money, and have habituated ourselves to evils that would shock the aesthetic sense of savages. Nearly six centuries ago, when coal first came to London from Newcastle, and supplemented the wood and charcoal before used as fuel, the Londoners, horrified by the smoke created, protested against it, and Edward 11 issued an edict forbidding the use of sea-coal. But today our manufacturers boldly make their boast in smoke, as a sign of prosperity and an advertisement of commercial success; and I have known cases where, being taxed with the creation of it as a public wrong, they quite ingeniously maintained that it was a good and right thing to do...[71]

Carpenter wrote an autobiography entitled *My Days and Dreams*, that was published in 1916. In 2008 the feminist and writer Sheila Rowbotham wrote a comprehensive 500-page biography of Carpenter: *Edward Carpenter: A Life of Liberty and Love*.[72]

6 Against the odds

In one sense, the earth is an experiment station, subdivided into many departments.
Man is an experimenter. Within his grasp are vast possibilities, both pluses and
minuses. He may use his position wisely or foolishly, to build and improve or to
degrade and destroy. Like any potentate, he may construct or tear down.

Scott Nearing [73]

There were, as mentioned above, both before and after World War II, important individuals and small groups of socialists who conducted the ecological struggle against the political tide on the left and the rising pressure of productivism.

They continued, through the darkest days of the 20th century, to prioritise the environmental struggle despite the Stalinist and productivist juggernaut. We owe them a very great debt, and it is to them I have dedicated this book. These pioneers were able to introduce into the ecological narrative of the day the impact of the capitalist mode of production – something on which the greens were extremely weak. They went on to form the basis of further ecosocialist developments in the 1990s.

In the Global North they were mostly, but not only, in the USA, Britain and Germany.

Scott Nearing

One remarkable example of such comrades was the American socialist, economist, and environmentalist Scott Nearing. Nearing was born in Pennsylvania just after Marx died in August 1883, and died in August 1983 just after his hundredth birthday. He was throughout his life an activist and a prolific writer, as was his wife and life-long companion, Helen. Nearing was influenced economically by John Ruskin.

He joined the Socialist Party of America (SPA) in July 1917 in the wake of the Bolshevik revolution in Russia, as a lecturer at the SPA's Rand School of Social Science. He wrote a series of pamphlets published by the Rand School, one of which, *The Great Madness: A Victory for the American Plutocracy*, resulted in his indictment under the Espionage Act for alleged 'obstruction to the recruiting and enlistment service of the United States'. The jury found Nearing not guilty, but the court fined the Socialist Party $3,000 – which was collected in New York City through small donations from socialists, labour groups, and civil liberty campaigners.

In the summer of 1919, the SPA split under the impact of the Russian revolution; one of the segments formed the Communist Party of the USA (CPUSA) – which rapidly surpassed the Socialist Party in size. Nearing remained in the Socialist Party until the end of 1923. He applied to join the Communist Party in December 1924 but was initially rejected. He finally gained admission in 1927 and worked on its newspaper, the *Daily Worker*. He was expelled from the Communist Party in January 1930, however, in a dispute over a study of imperialism that he had written and the *Daily Worker* had refused to publish.

Nearing's most important work by far was his *Economics for the Power Age* in 1952.[74] By then aged 69, he saw it as his life's work. By 'the power age' he meant industrialisation. It is a big-picture look at the industrial age and its implications for the working class and for the natural world. He sets out ten principles to confront it, which include: all subsistence originates with nature; subsistence should be apportioned according to need; the economy should be owned by those who use it.

Nearing was an advocate and pioneer of sustainable living – he and Helen sustained themselves for many years on a remote farmstead – and a campaigner for nature. He recognised the problems of a rising human population against the planet's finite and declining resources, and warned of the over-exploitation and degradation of nature that was taking place.

Nearing's over-riding concern was the impact of the industrial age on the natural world:

Men do not say to themselves and to one another: 'If we put our heads together and all lend a hand we can convert nature's stores into a moderately good living for every member of the human family.' Rather they say: 'if we can get title to the choicest part of nature's storehouse, and can make ourselves strong enough to hold our advantage against all comers, we can have more of the good things than anyone else and make others pay a tribute upon which we can live without doing any more work.'[75]

From this standpoint he was concerned by the rising human population of the planet, which had just reached 2.5 billion as he completed the *Power Age*. He thought that the basic point that Malthus was making should at least be taken seriously, although he was working from an incomplete picture. He did not support Malthus's proposed solutions, and recognised the need for a working balance between population increase and the means of livelihood available. Industrial society, he said, 'demands more and more goods from less and less natural resources' and that would in the end lead to disasters.[76]

Murray Bookchin

The work of Murray Bookchin was also important in this period. Bookchin (1921-2006) was a trade union militant, libertarian socialist, and environmental activist. He was born in New York from a Russian émigré heritage, and became politically active from an early age. In 1935 he joined the Young Pioneers, which was the children's section – for nine to fourteen year olds – of the Communist Party of the USA (CPUSA). He later joined its youth wing, the Young Communist League, and then the party itself. He broke with the CPUSA, however, shortly before the outbreak of WWII over the Moscow trials, and soon after joined the (American) Socialist Workers Party (SWP) eventually breaking with it at the end of the war.[77]

From 1947, having broken from Trotskyism, he worked with a group of other ex-Trotskyists who produced a periodical, *Contemporary Issues: A Magazine for a Democracy of Content* (there was a Movement for a Democracy of Content as well). The magazine published some of Bookchin's first articles, including his ground-breaking *'The Problem of Chemicals in Food'*, written in 1952. By this time he was already warning of the effects of climate change caused by fossil fuels, and campaigning against freeway construction.

In 1958, Bookchin defined himself as an anarchist, seeing, as he argued, parallels between anarchism and ecology. He developed what he called a theory of ecological decentralism. His first book, *Our Synthetic Environment*, was published under the pseudonym Lewis Herber in 1962.

Bookchin's 1964 essay '*Ecology and Revolutionary Thought*', one of his best works in my view, presented ecology as a component of radical politics. It is remarkable both for its understanding of the impact of human beings on the planet and for an early understanding of global warming and the role of CO_2 in the atmosphere. It says:

> Modern man's despoliation of the environment is global in scope, like his imperialism. It is even extra-terrestrial, as witness the disturbances of the Van Allen belt a few years ago. Today human parasitism disrupts more than the atmosphere, climate, water resources, soil, flora, and fauna of a region; it upsets virtually all the basic cycles of nature and threatens to undermine the stability of the environment on a worldwide scale.
>
> As an example of the scope of modern man's disruptive role, it has been estimated that the burning of fossil fuels (coal and oil) adds 600 million tons of carbon dioxide to the air annually, about 0.03 per cent of the total atmospheric mass – this, I may add, aside from an incalculable quantity of toxicants. Since the Industrial Revolution, the overall atmospheric mass of carbon dioxide has increased by 13 per cent over earlier, more stable, levels. It could be argued on very sound theoretical grounds that this growing blanket of carbon dioxide, by intercepting heat radiated from the Earth into outer space, will lead to rising atmospheric temperatures, to a more violent circulation of air, to more destructive storm patterns, and eventually to a melting of the polar ice caps (possibly in two or three centuries), rising sea levels, and the inundation of vast land areas. Far removed as such a deluge may be, the changing proportion of carbon dioxide to other atmospheric gases is a warning of the impact man is having on the balance of nature.[78]

Rachel Carson

The single most important contribution to the rise of the modern environmental movement was made by Rachel Carson. Carson graduated in 1935 as a biologist and joined the US Bureau of Fisheries as a writer. Her first big success, *The Sea Around Us*, was published in 1951. It sold a million copies and was translated into 28 languages. (Her first book, *Under the Sea Wind: A Naturalist's Picture of Ocean Life*, published a decade earlier, saw only limited sales.)

Carson was active in the movement against atmospheric nuclear weapon tests in the late 1950s, which had emerged in the shadow of Hiroshima and Nagasaki. She was interested, in particular, in the marine effects of nuclear fallout. She was one of an important group of environmentally committed scientists who could rightly claim to have been amongst the founders of the modern ecology movement.

It was her stunning book *Silent Spring*, published in 1962, that made the greatest impact. It was a frontal challenge to the impact of a new generation of pesticides (developed from wartime nerve gas) on the biodiversity of the planet. It sold over two million copies, became the single most influential ecological book of the twentieth century, and brought about important changes in public attitudes to chemical pollution.

Such toxins, she argued, affected the whole food chain. Creatures that ate poisoned insects were themselves poisoned, until eventually the whole ecosystem was affected. Carson, in fact, objected to the very term 'pesticides', which she considered to be an anthropocentric construct. A creature was only a 'pest', she argued, in consequence of a construct from a limited human perspective.

She summed this up in her final paragraph in the following way:

> The 'control of nature' is a phrase conceived in arrogance, born of the Neanderthal age of biology and philosophy, when it was supposed that nature existed for the convenience of man. The concepts and practices of applied entomology for the most part date from the Stone Age of science. It is our alarming misfortune that so primitive a science has armed itself with the most modern and terrible weapons, and that in turning them against the insects it has also turned them against the earth.[79]

Unsurprisingly *Silent Spring* incurred the full wrath of the agricultural chemical industry, which complained to the government that the book was damaging their profit margins. As a result, the book became the subject of investigation by the US government's Presidential Science Advisory Committee (PSAC).

Carson famously won the day in a televised confrontation with the agrochemical giants, as a direct result of which the PSAC concluded that her book was fully justified in bringing to public attention the toxicity of agricultural pesticides and the damage they were doing. The PSAC went on to call for major reforms of government regulation of pesticides.

Carson published four major ecological works before her life was cut short by cancer in April 1964 at the age of 57. These were: *Under the Sea* (1941), *The Sea Around Us* (1951), *The Edge of the Sea* (1955), and *Silent Spring* (1962). A fifth book, *Lost Woods*, was a collection of her writings discovered posthumously and put together by Linda Lear, who also wrote a monumental biography *Rachel Carson: Witness for Nature*, published in 1997.

Lost Woods includes a newspaper article from 1938 in which Carson looks at the devastation of wildlife taking place across the United States:

> The inescapable fact that the decline of wildlife is linked with human destinies is being driven home by conservation the nation over. Wildlife, it is pointed out, is dwindling because its home is being destroyed. But the home of wildlife is also our home.
>
> One of the most startling pictures painted by those who are fighting for conservation of natural resources is that of the speed with which the work of destruction has been accomplished. It is not necessary to go back to Colonial times for contrast. A scant hundred years ago, more than half of America was wilderness. Wild swans, geese and brant [geese] were to be found in every marsh and slough and prairie pot hole; slaves in the Chesapeake Bay country bay were fed on canvasbacks[80] until they are said to have been revolted at it. Wild turkey, grouse and other upland game birds were incredibly abundant. Antelope ranged the Western plains in numbers perhaps equalling the bison, and from coast to coast the bugling of the elk resounded in the forests.[81]

Three of Carson's books were serialised in the *New Yorker* and they were all translated into many languages. Carson had plans for other books had she lived longer, including one on climate change, which she had only just started to study. Her books can be said, without exaggeration, to have changed the way human beings see their place on Earth and their responsibilities towards the ecosystems that sustain life on it.

The changes *Silent Spring* brought about can be measured by developments that followed its publication. The first Earth Day and the US National Environmental Policy Act came in 1970. They were followed soon after by the Marine Mammal Protection Act (1972) and the Endangered Species Act (1973).

Roderick Frazier Nash

Another remarkable book was *Wilderness and the American Mind* (1967)[82] by the American environmentalist Roderick Frazier Nash, an environmental studies professor in Santa Barbara, California.

Like *Silent Spring*, it became a cornerstone text of the emerging environmental movement, and helped bring about a material change to public perceptions and attitudes to the environment in the USA and beyond.

The book chronicles the impact on the American wilderness – both the peoples and the natural world that inhabited it – of the arrival of European settlers in the early seventeenth century. It takes head-on the traditional 'frontiersman', 'wild West' mentality that shaped America and its people. This mentality saw the vast American wilderness – from the Everglades to the Great Plains, from the Nevada Desert to the Rocky Mountains – as a dangerous wasteland that had to be conquered, ravaged and exploited in the name of progress, civilisation and Christianity.

Nash details the long struggle to defend the American wilderness against the encroachment of human kind, as the population expanded and living standards rose, intensifying the demand for more land, water and raw materials – all available in abundance in the wilderness, if you were prepared to destroy it in the process. He includes in this the struggle against the damming of the great rivers to provide hydro-power, and water for the expanding cities, from the battles against the Hetch Heychy Valley dam project in California (to supply San Francisco) in the 1880s, to the struggle against the construction of the Colorado River Storage Project in the Grand Canyon National Park in the 1950s. He also gives an account of the struggle for the Wilderness Act in 1964 that he regarded as a major achievement of environmental campaigning in the USA.

Nash puts forward the idea that the preservation of wilderness is crucial to the preservation of the planet as an environment habitable for the biodiversity it supports, including ourselves.

He writes about the meaning of wilderness in the late twentieth century and takes a critical look at the somewhat oxymoronic notion of 'wilderness management'. He examines the significance of the American invention of national parks and legally protected wilderness.

He was interested in alternatives to the anthropogenic arguments that had anchored the early appreciation of 'wilderness'. Wild places had been valued and protected for people. Whether involving scenery, recreation or the economics of nature tourism, wilderness seemed to be all about us. He argued for a new ecocentric rationale, that valued wilderness rather as a symbol of the capacity for restraint on the part of a species with the capacity to destroy all else.

Wilderness and the American Mind has gone through a remarkable five editions over a 47-year period: 1967, 1973, 1982, and then two more twenty years later, in 2001 and 2014. Nor were these just reprints: Nash added to each version, taking into account new developments and new ideas.

Nash's other most important book – he has published many during a long life of activity – was *The Rights of Nature: A History of Environmental Ethics*, published in 1989.[83]

In a short annex to the fifth edition, he starts to raise some controversial solutions in terms of the defence of the wilderness, notably his proposal for 'island civilisations' that has an authoritarian connotation. However one might view this development, his contribution over so many years is remarkable.

Barry Commoner

Yet another remarkable contribution to the environmental struggle was made by the American biologist and committed socialist Barry Commoner. Commoner was one of the founders of the modern ecology movement and one of the world's most renowned ecologists from the 1960s to the 1980s. His best-known book, written from an ecosocialist standpoint, was *The Closing Circle: Nature, Man, and Technology* (1971).[84] He published five other books on the ecology of the planet over a twenty-year period: *Science and Survival* (1966), *The Poverty of Power: Energy and the Economic Crisis* (1976), *The Politics of Energy* (1979) – both of which were best sellers – and *Making Peace With the Planet* (1990), which was essentially an update of *The Closing Circle* and was also very successful.

After serving as a lieutenant in the US Navy during World War II, Commoner moved to St. Louis, Missouri, where he became a professor of plant physiology at Washington University. He taught there for 34 years and during this period, in 1966, he founded the Center for the Biology of Natural Systems, to study 'the science of the total environment'. Commoner was on the founding editorial board of the *Journal of Theoretical Biology* in 1961.

In the late 1950s, he became renowned for his opposition to nuclear weapons testing, and was part of the team which conducted the 'Baby Tooth Survey', demonstrating the presence of strontium-90 in children's teeth as a direct result of nuclear fallout. In 1958, he helped found the Greater St. Louis Committee on Nuclear Information. Shortly thereafter, he established *Nuclear Information*, which later became the *Environment Magazine*.

Commoner went on to write several books about the ecological effects of atmospheric nuclear testing. He could rightly claim to have been partly responsible for the Limited (*i.e.* atmospheric only) Nuclear Test Ban Treaty of 1963. He has described it since as 'the first victorious battle in the campaign to save the environment – and its human inhabitants – from the blind assaults of modern technology'.[85]

Along with Carson, he was one of the first to bring the idea of the looming ecological crisis and the need for environmental sustainability to a mass audience. He argued that the American economy should be restructured to conform to the natural laws of ecology, for example that polluting products such as detergents or synthetic textiles should be replaced with natural products such as soap or cotton and wool. He raised the issue of the polluting character of non-biodegradable products like plastic.

His remarkable *Four Laws of Ecology*, which he set out in *The Closing Circle*, form the essential basis of an ecosocialist relationship between human beings and nature. They can be summarised as follows.

- Everything is connected to everything else: *i.e.* there is only one – intricately interconnected – ecosphere containing all living organisms, and what affects one thing affects all.
- Everything must go somewhere: *i.e.* matter is indestructible and ultimately there is nowhere to which things can be 'disposed of'.
- Nature knows best: *i.e.* one of the most pervasive features of modern technology

is the notion that it is intended to 'improve nature'. Stated baldly, however, any major man-made change in a natural system is likely to be *detrimental* to that system. (original emphasis)

• There is no such thing as a free lunch: *i.e.* with every gain will come a cost. Nothing can be gained without loss, anything extracted for human gain must be replaced. Payment for this cannot be avoided, it can only be delayed.[86]

These are powerful and perceptive points for their day. The second and third points in particular are the basis of any sustainable relationship between modern humans and the rest of nature. The second could hardly be more relevant today when we contemplate the oceans filling up with plastic waste and the atmosphere with CO_2.

At the beginning of *The Closing Circle*, Commoner explained the current relationship between human kind and nature this way:

Biologically human beings *participate* in the environmental system as subsidiary parts of the whole. Yet human society is designed to *exploit* the environment as a whole, [in order to] produce wealth.[87] (original emphasis)

Commoner saw not only the dangers in the drive for profit, but also the implications of the economic growth that he (rightly) identified as inherent to the capitalist system, and in total contradiction with the limitations of environmental sustainability. In fact, he was a pioneer in recognising this. He put it this way:

Thus, there must be some limit to the growth of the total capital, and the productivity of the system *must* eventually reach a 'no growth' condition. At least with respect to the accumulations of capital goods designed to exploit the ecosystem, and the products they yield.[88] (emphasis original)

When Commoner died in November 2012, at the age of 95, Ralph Nader called him the greatest environmentalist of the twentieth century. Like Rachel Carson he was a leading figure in the anti-nuclear weapons testing movement in the early 1950s. He observes in the *The Closing Circle* that he learned about the environment from the Atomic Energy Commission of the USA in 1953.[89]

In Britain

In Britain, important ecosocialist, or eco-Marxist, contributions were made in both the immediate pre-war and post-war periods, though they never achieved the public impact of Carson, Frazier Nash or Commoner in the USA.

They were, however, also rooted in the history of the Communist Party (CP) as much, possibly more than, in the USA. The Kinder Scout mass trespass movement in 1932, for example – a campaign for working class access to the Derbyshire Peak District moorland – was led amongst others by Benny Rothman, a member of the CP. CP members were also involved in the origins of the National Trust, which arose out of the demand for the defence and conservation of the countryside. E. P. Thompson's, post-war, biography of William Morris played a role as well.

Christopher Caudwell

A brief but spectacular contribution was made by Christopher St. John Sprigg, better known by his pen name (his mother's maiden name) Christopher Caudwell.

Caudwell left grammar school at fifteen because his parents could not afford university, and after several brief journalistic jobs he and his brother launched an aeronautics and applied science magazine. He also studied engineering, and designed gearboxes for cars.

After volunteering as a scab driver during the General Strike of 1926, he moved sharply to the left in the early 1930s in reaction to the rise of Mosely and the Black Shirts. In 1934 he joined the CP in Poplar, East London, and in December 1936 he drove an ambulance to Spain and joined the International Brigades. He trained as a machine-gunner at Albacete before becoming a machine-gun instructor and group political delegate, for which he edited a wall newspaper.

He was killed in action in January 1937, at the age of 29, after only a few weeks at the front, whilst serving with the British battalion of the International Brigade at the disastrous battle of Jarma in defence of Madrid. He and his fellow gunner refused orders to retreat in an attempt to cover the withdrawal of the battalion, but were overrun when their Soviet-supplied machine gun jammed in the heat of the battle.

His brother Theodore had attempted to have him brought back by the CP by showing Harry Pollitt, its General Secretary, the manuscript of Caudwell's book *Illusion and Reality*.

Caudwell's writings including physics, literature, psychology, economics, poetry, novels and politics. He defended the historical and materialist conception of nature as advocated by Darwin and Marx against their contemporary detractors.

All of his major political works had been written – unknown to the CP at the time – during the two short years between joining the CP and going to Spain, and were never published during his lifetime. They include *Studies and Further Studies in a Dying Culture, Illusions and Reality, The Concept of Freedom, Heredity and Development, The Crisis in Physics, Romance and Reaction*, and a volume of poems.

He would write during the day and do routine political work – selling the *Daily Worker* and going to meetings – during the evening. His manuscripts were published posthumously by Lawrence and Wishart, the CP publishing house, some in first draft form.

His most important work, in ecological terms, was *Heredity and Development*, which was initially suppressed by the CP because of its explicit critique of Lysenkoism, which challenged the official line. They eventually published it in 1986 – 50 years later.[90]

Lysenko, a Soviet agronomist in the Stalin era, claimed, in 1928, to have developed an agricultural technique, which he termed vernalisation, that could triple crop yield by exposing wheat seed to high humidity and low temperature. By 1948, Lysenkoism had become the party line. With Stalin's support, he became a Hero of the Soviet Union and a vice president of the Supreme Soviet. Many Soviet scientists were executed or sent to labour camps for challenging Lysenko's theories, which in the end proved fake.

A very good Marxist critique of Lysenkoism can be found in the *The Dialectical Biologist*, published in 1985 by the American Marxist biologists Richard Levin and Richard Lewontin.[91] They point out that, far from overthrowing traditional genetics and creating a new science, Lysenkoism cut short the pioneering work of Soviet geneticists that had already taken place and set it back a generation, while its own contribution to contemporary biology was negligible.

The 'Caudwell controversy'

A fascinating sequel to Lysenkoism took place in the British CP in the early 1950s, when what became known as the 'Caudwell controversy' broke out. It started when a leading member of the Soviet Communist Party and the hero of the defence of Stalingrad, A.A. Zhdanov, wrote an article in the British CP journal *Modern Quarterly*, denouncing Caudwell as an 'idealistic sheep in Marxist clothing'.

Maurice Cornforth, the head of Lawrence and Wishart, supported him, arguing that Caudwell's views were reactionary and metaphysical since they relied on 'a basic changelessness in the human genotype as the foundation of society'.[92]

Caudwell received more support than the CP leadership expected, however. He was supported by George Thompson, a member of the party's executive committee and of its cultural commission. Thompson had been the only member of the CP executive to vote against the adoption of *The British Road to Socialism*, the reformist programme of the CP that had been signed off by Stalin. He was then supported by E.P. Thompson, the most important member of the party's influential Historians Group, by J.B.S. Haldane, the evolutionary biologist who wrote for the *Daily Worker* on popular science, and by Margot Heinemann, a leading member of the party. It was a formidable line-up.

Edward (E.P.) Thompson

E. P. Thompson was strongly influenced by Caudwell. Christos Efstathiou, in his study *E.P. Thompson: A Twentieth-century Romantic*, puts it this way:

> For Thompson, Caudwell was the 'most original communist critic of the 1930s'; an exceptional figure who defied 'the usual stereotypes of the literary Left of the Thirties' and ventured 'a new and conjectural aesthetics, science, philosophy and politics within Marxism...'[93]

Thompson's epic 900-page study of William Morris – *William Morris: Romantic to Revolutionary* – was published in 1955.[94] A much revised second edition was published 21 years later in 1976. His equally epic work, *The Making of the English Working Class*, was published in 1963.

Whilst the Morris biography reflected Thompson's genuine admiration of Morris, it was also an attempt to reclaim Morris from those who had sought to promote his artistic achievements and obscure his socialist politics – something that the book admirably achieves. Morris was, he argues, in the foreword to the second edition, 'an outstanding member of the first generation of European Communist intellectuals, the friend of Engels, and the comrade and peer of Bebel, Liebknecht, Eleanor Marks, and Eduard Bernstein'. In a postscript, he describes Morris as 'an original socialist thinker whose work was complementary to Marxism'.[95]

The biography was also an attempt by the Historians Group to establish some home-grown roots for Marxism in Britain at a time when the CP was under attack for its ultra-slavish adherence to the Moscow line and 'Uncle Joe' Stalin.

The Historian's Group, founded in 1946, was a talented and influential group of mostly, but not only, academics. It had come together in the course of discussions on the English Revolution of the 17th century, around material being developed by Christopher Hill—a specialist in the subject.

Membership of the group (according to Christos Efstathiou) were: Maurice Dobb, Christopher Hill, Rodney Hilton, Eric Hobsbawm, Victor Kiernan, Arthur Leslie Morton, George Rude, Raphael Samuel, John Saville, Dona Torr (who worked with Thompson on Morris), plus Dorothy and Edward Thompson. The group promoted the idea of history from below: by which they meant looking at social conditions and not just 'great men'.

The CP split over Hungary

Some of the Historians Group's members, including Thompson himself, were to become the driving force behind the split in the CP over the suppression of the Hungarian uprising in 1956, when many thousands left the party. The Group lost most of its prominent members as the full implications of the uprising, and Khrushchev's secret speech, broke into the public domain.

The split was, Thompson argued, a rejection of the 'mechanical materialism of the Stalinism era in favour of the historical materialism of true Marxism'. Many group members went on to become prominent in the emerging New

Left, including Samuel, Saville and Edward and Dorothy Thompson. Others, most notably Hobsbawm, remained in the party.

After his resignation from the CP, Thompson dedicated himself as he saw it to ridding Marxism of the Stalinist legacy. In 1957, along with John Saville, he began publishing a new journal called *New Reasoner* in order to promote the battle against Stalinism. In an article entitled *'Through the Smoke of Budapest'* he described its purpose as: 'the re-discovery of our traditions, the affirmation of socialist values, and the undogmatic perception of social reality'. *New Reasoner* later became a component part of *New Left Review*.

The impact of the split is reflected in the second edition of Thompson's William Morris biography published in 1976, in the sense that it now reflected not only his (Thompson's) resignation from the CP and his consequential re-appraisal of the politics of the CP and the brand of 'Marxism' that it espoused, but the impact that Morris had had on Thompson himself. He puts it this way in his usual understated style:

> It is true that in 1955 I allowed some hectoring political moralism, as well as a few Stalinist pieties, to intrude upon the text. I had then a somewhat reverent notion of Marxism as a received orthodoxy, and my pages included some passages of polemic whose vulgarity no doubt make contemporary scholars wince. The book was published at the height of the Cold War. Intellectual McCarthyism was not confined to the United States...[96]

He makes this explicit in the last paragraph of the postscript to the second edition, where he says the following:

> When, in 1956, my disagreements with orthodox Marxism became fully articulate, I fell back on modes of perception which I'd learned in those years of close company with Morris, and I found, perhaps, the will to go on arguing from the pressure of Morris behind me. To say that Morris claimed me, and that I've tried to acknowledge that claim, gives me no right to claim him. I have no license to act as his interpreter. But at least I can say now that this is what I've been trying, for twenty years, to do.[97]

That William Morris played such a significant posthumous role in splitting the CP over Hungary should be no surprise. It was clearly difficult for

Thompson to spend many years studying the libertarian communism of William Morris and at the same time accept the worst excesses of the Stalinist monstrosity. The CP never recovered, and the New Left continued to grow – as did organisations to the left of the CP. Some prominent members of the CP went over to the radical left including to the Socialist Labour League (SLL).

The longer-term impact of Thompson's writings on William Morris, beyond the WEA, however, is more difficult to quantify. The unions were growing and industrial militancy was on the rise. On the other hand, the Cold War was at its height and anti-communism was rife. Ecological consciousness in Britain was still in deep freeze, particularly on the left.

When I joined the CP youth organisation, the Young Communist League (YCL), in 1959, three years after the Hungary split (shame on me), I saw no evidence of a Morris legacy at all. Not a single mention of Morris or of the environment the whole seven years I was in the party. Nor was it just the CP: it was the bulk of the left, including the SLL that I joined soon after, that was oblivious to both the legacy of William Morris and the environmental issues.

Raymond Williams

Raymond Williams, the Welsh literary critic, novelist, socialist and environmentalist, joined the CP in 1939 under the influence of Eric Hobsbawm, and worked increasingly with the Historians Group and with Edward Thompson.

He enlisted into the British army in 1941 in defiance of the party line but was rehabilitated a year later, after Hitler invaded the Soviet Union and Stalin and the CP changed sides. He finally became disillusioned with the CP in the early 1950s over the suppression by the Soviet Union of the East German uprising. He maintained a connection with the Historians Group for several years after that, at least until the 1956 split. He later joined Plaid Cymru.

Raymond Williams was a prolific writer, reflecting the traditions of John Ruskin and of William Morris in particular. He published six novels and numerous political writings, including *Culture and Society 1780-1950* in 1958, three years after Thompson's study of William Morris. This was followed by *The Long Revolution* (1961), *The Country and the City* (1973), *Marxism and*

Literature (1977) and *The Politics of Modernism* (published in 1989, a year after his death). *Problems in Materialism and Culture: Selected Essays,* (1980) was reissued as *Culture and Materialism* in 2005.

Edward Thompson held Williams's *Culture and Society* in high regard. He made numerous references to it in the postscript to the second edition of his William Morris biography, where he debates with Raymond Williams the nature of Morris's utopianism, over which they had some subtle difference.

In 1982, Raymond Williams raised the banner of ecosocialism in a booklet entitled *Socialism and Ecology,* published by the Labour Party's ecological grouping, the Socialist Environment and Resources Association (SERA), in which he was active. The pamphlet strongly reflects William Morris' attitude towards industrialization and the relationship between human beings and nature. Williams argued in particular for a convergence between ecology and the trade union movement, and he challenged productivism and economic growth, which were dominant on the left at the time.

On economic growth and productivism, he said the following in *Socialism and Ecology*:

> As socialism, from around the middle of the nineteenth century, began to distinguish itself from a whole body of associated and overlapping movements, there was a tendency to make a quite different emphasis: to say that the central problem of modern society was poverty, and that the solution to poverty was production and more production. Although there would be incidental costs of this production, including changing and perhaps to some extent damaging the immediate environment, nevertheless poverty was the worst evil. Poverty had to be cured by production as well as by the more specific policy of changing the social and economic relations. Thus socialists for three or four generations, with only occasional exceptions – and this we still find to be the main tendency within socialism today – made the case that production is an absolute human priority, and that those who object to its effects are simply sentimentalists or worse...[98]

In fact, SERA was playing quite a radical role at this time. In 1980, it had published highly effective book in a cartoon format, entitled *Eco-Socialism in a Nutshell,* by Stan Rosenthal.[99] It sets out, as it says on the back cover, to address 'one of the most significant developments in contemporary politics – the blending of the traditional concerns of the labour movement with those of the fast growing ecological lobby into a new concept: ecosocialism'. The booklet is a sustained critique of maximalism and a defence of a transitional approach. In the introduction Rosenthal says:

> For some time now respected academics have been alerting us to the dangers of diminishing natural resources, mounting environmental pollution and uncontrolled technology. Until recently the labour movement in this country has tended to regard these warnings as being at best irrelevant or at worst hostile to working class interests.
>
> However, the post-1973 energy crisis has brought home to even the most diehard growth-at-all-costs fanatic, the finite nature of one vital resource and there is a growing realisation that other raw materials are in short supply in relation to the needs of a world population expected to increase from 4 billion to 6 billion by the 21st century.[100]

It reflected another important book in the same idiom published two years earlier, *Nuclear Power for Beginners*, by Stephen Croall and Kaianders Sempler, which demolished the case for nuclear power.[101]

These writers – Caudwell, Edward Thompson (in his work on William Morris), Raymond Williams, and Stan Rosenthal, together with the development of SERA – provided an important reference point for the establishment of an agenda for the left in Britain based on an eco-socialist standpoint.

The rise of the greens

The birth of the modern ecology movement – and the rise of the greens – can be dated from around the first internationally recognised Earth Day, that was held on 22 April 1970 – the first day of spring in the Northern Hemisphere. It has been celebrated on that date ever since.

In Britain, Greenpeace and Friends of the Earth emerged in 1971, and green parties started to be established in other parts of Europe soon afterwards. The Green Party of England and Wales has its origins in the People Party, which was founded in 1973. It became the Ecology Party in 1975 and then in 1985 the Green Party.

The strongest green movement in Europe in the 1970s was in West Germany. It emerged initially in the form of independent action groups.[102] The West German Green Party (Die Grünen) was established in 1980, when a number of green electoral lists and organisations – that emerged at the end of the 1970s around opposition to nuclear power – came together to form it. It became the strongest green party in Europe, particularly in terms of elected representation.

The first leader of the Green party was a former Christian Democrat Bundestag deputy, Herbert Gruhl, who split from his party over the environmental question. In the 1970s he published a book called *Ein Planet wird geplündert* (a planet plundered).

Some Marxists in West Germany were discussing ecosocialism in the framework of the Green Party in the 1970s. They called themselves ecosocialist and later left the party, due to its shift to the right. At the beginning of the 1980s, a large group from the German section of the Fourth International (FI) split and joined the Green Party, but were later pushed out by the likes of Joschka Fischer, who went on to become the German foreign minister.[103]

Die Grünen had some remarkable electoral success. It won elected positions in the south-western state of Baden-Württemberg with 5.3 per cent of the vote. It went on to win seats in the state parliaments of Lower Saxony, West Berlin, Hamburg and Hessen. 1981 and 1982 were the years of the peace movement's rise across Europe, against the NATO decision to deploy Pershing 2 and cruise missiles in Western Europe.

In their book *The German Greens: Paradox between Movement and Party*, the American writers Margit Mayer and John Ely describe the way the German Green Party was formed:

From the outset, the process was strongly influenced by former leftists and independents intent on utilising environmentalism as a new unifying force to transcend political divisions. Throughout the 1970s, independent Marxists and socialists, including former student protesters like Rudi Deutschke and the Czech emigrant Malan Horacek, debated the possibility of founding a 'free, independent, and undogmatic' socialist party. In the spring of 1977, Horacek explored the possibilities of uniting various leftist circles and ecologists, but with little success. In meetings at Vlotho (1977), Troisdorf (1978), and Kassel (1978), a diverse group formed around Horacek, Haussleiter, Gruhl, the artist Joseph Beuys, Petra Kelly, Ossip K. Flechtheim, Rudolf Bahro; these and others continued the effort to create an alliance of environmentalists spanning the political spectrum from right to left, from 'Gruhl to Dutschke'. With anthroposophists and ecologists from Northern Germany, this group established the Political Association of Greens which received 3.2 per cent of the vote to the European Parliament in 1979.[104]

In the Federal elections of March 1983, the Greens won 5.6 per cent of the vote and 28 seats in the Bundestag. The European Parliament elections in June 1989 saw Green Parties in many countries of the European Community gaining very good results. The British Greens won 14.5 per cent, but the electoral system denied them a single seat. A new parliamentary group was established in the European Parliament, consisting of Green and Green-related MEPs elected from five countries: Portugal, Spain, France, West Germany, and the Netherlands. The Greens had by now established a presence in the national parliaments of Sweden, Finland, West Germany, the Netherlands, Belgium, Luxembourg, Austria, Switzerland, Italy and Portugal.

Despite this, in Germany today the first Green Party Ministerpräsident of a federal state in the history of Germany, in Baden-Württemberg, is defending 'his' car industry in the context of the scandal over the notorious faked diesel cars emission tests, and is opposing effective measures to reduce air pollution in the towns and cities.

The greens and direct action politics

In Britain an important surge in the green movement came in the latter part of the 1980s and into the 1990s with the rise of direct action around road building. Derek Wall in his 1999 book *Earth First! – and the anti-roads movement* records that in the late 1980s Green Party membership rose to 20,000, Friends of the Earth grew from 31,000 to 150,000 and members of Greenpeace from 150,000 to 281,000. In the 1989 elections for the European Parliament the Green Party won 14.9 per cent of the vote.[105]

The 1990s also saw the launch of an important direct action movement in Britain against the remorseless rise of the car, and the expansion of the road and motorway network to accommodate them. It was initiated by Earth First, that had its origins in the USA. There had been some road protects in the 1970s but these were on a much larger scale.

The protests started at Twyford Down in Hampshire in 1991, against the completion of a section of the M3 motorway from London to the south coast of England. These were followed by a major protest against the M11 link road in Leytonstone, London, in opposition not only the destruction of houses for the construction itself, but also against the car culture that drove it.

The M11 protests were followed by Solsbury Hill on the outskirts of Bath, that started in February 1994 and became the biggest and most high profile of the road protests to date. There is a very good account of it is Derek Wall's book *Earth First! – and the anti-roads movement* and indeed of the whole anti-roads movement at that time. Like its predecessors, the protests were about not just cars and car culture, but the defence of nature against the human juggernaut. The protesters argued that the new road would damage an area of outstanding natural beauty, destroy numerous badger setts and a pond with newts, and would turn one of the most important water meadow eco-systems into mud and rubble.

Although these protests were unsuccessful in stopping the roads being built, they raised the issue of the defence of nature in a very effective way. As that phase of road building declined, they morphed into the Reclaim the Streets movement and guerrilla gardening protests.

The protestors were comprised of green and autonomist activists with little involvement by the left.

7 The indigenous struggle

The modern inhabitants of the forest have been hugely influenced by their ancestors' culture. They knew how to build their houses on stilts so that they were not affected by floods. They learned from them how to eat the palmito (the heart of the palm), the yucca and the pijuayo. They memorised how to how to prepare the quintessential forest drink the masato. They knew how to sail on the Amazon's rivers. They knew the healing properties of many of the plants.

Hugo Blanco.[106]

Across the world – in the Global North and the Global South – indigenous peoples have been and remain in the front line of the struggle for land and rights, and against environmental destruction. Their struggles often combine with those of peasants and rural communities, and assume an ecosocialist dynamic.

According to the UN there are around 370 million indigenous people on the planet. They exist in around 90 countries and speak about 7,000 languages. They have long been the most effective defenders of the planet's ecosystems and wildernesses, and the best guardians of its integrity and its biodiversity. Such struggles go alongside their own ongoing battles for sovereignty over their own lands, territories, and resources, and for self-determination.

Many indigenous peoples struggled historically against colonisation, and continue to combat all forms of imperialism and racism. Many live on resource-rich territory, partly because they have protected and preserved such resources for future generations. This now makes them prime targets for extractive industries and land grabs.

Indigenous and First Nation peoples from Canada and the northern United States have been in the forefront the battle against exploitation of the Alberta tar sands. They have opposed the construction of pipe lines to facilitate extraction of the sands. In 2016 fifty indigenous peoples organisations signed up to an agreement to oppose tar sand extraction. They included the Standing

Rock Sioux tribe that had opposed construction of the North Dakota access pipeline, designed to facilitate shale gas exploitation in the Bakken shale oil fields in Western North Dakota.

Many First Nation peoples support the Idle No More movement, an ongoing protest campaign founded in 2012 by three First Nations women and a non-First Nation ally. It is a grassroots movement comprising the First Nations Métis and Inuit peoples and their supporters in Canada and internationally. It has become one of the biggest mass movements of indigenous peoples in Canadian history.

Hugo Blanco

A towering figure of the indigenous struggle for over 50 years has been the legendary Peruvian Marxist and campaigner for ecosocialism, Hugo Blanco. Blanco was the leader of the revolutionary struggle of the indigenous peoples of Peru and of the Latin American revolutionary left. A contemporary of Che Guevara, he grew up in Cuzco, in the Peruvian highlands, the city that had been the capital of the Inca empire in the pre-Columbian period.

After studying agronomy in Argentina he joined a revolutionary socialist organisation. He returned to Peru in 1958 where he played the decisive role in strengthening peasant unions and in developing the rural struggle – specifically the drive for agrarian reform – resisting the repression of the state and the local bosses, including with armed actions.

In the early 1960s, he led the Quechua peasant uprising in the Cuzco region, and was the first to build a bridge between Spanish speaking intellectuals and the Quechua speaking agricultural workers and peasants. He set up a peasant trade union in the valleys of Convención and Lares. He organised occupations of the big landed estates, and then the physical defence of those occupations against the police and the landowners. The Chaupimayo insurrectionary movement he led controlled an independent region where governmental control did not exist, and they were able to put into effect the agrarian reform they had fought for. It had its own government, public law, popular justice, defence and education – a situation Blanco defined as dual power.

Blanco was arrested and jailed in May 1963, along with most of his Trotskyist comrades. He was held without trial until 1966 when he was tried by a military court. He was convicted and sentenced to death, but saved by a world-wide campaign organised by the Fourth International, of which Blanco was a central leader. His death sentence was eventually commuted to 25 years in prison, to be served on the prison island of El Frontón. During his imprisonment, he wrote his first book *Land or Death: The Peasant Struggle in Peru*, which remains the authentic record of the peasant struggle in that country.

In 1968, a group of reform minded military officers, led by General Juan Velasco Alvarado, took power in a coup d'état, and Blanco and other peasant leaders were eventually released from jail in 1970 after an international campaign by Jean Paul Sartre and others.

Three years later, in 1971, he was arrested and deported to Chile. When Pinochet's coup took place in September 1973, he survived by taking refuge at the Swedish embassy. He was smuggled out of the country under dramatic circumstances in 1976, following an international solidarity campaign led by Jean-Paul Sartre, Simone de Beauvoir, and Bertrand Russell, eventually becoming a political refugee in Sweden. After several years of exile in Sweden, Mexico and Chile he returned to Peru in 1978 and became a founding member of the Workers Revolutionary Party.

In 1980 he was elected to the Peruvian Senate as a part of a wider left-wing slate, the Partido Unificado Mariateguista. He served on the Senate from 1980 until 1992, joining the Senate's Environmental Commission in the early 1990s, where his interventions and writings led to the development of environmental justice movements, and later to the concept of ecosocialism.

Blanco's 1991 essay *'The Environmentalism of the People'* contrasted the elitist approach of some conservationists with the environmental concerns of poorer communities, noting that the cloud forests 'have been inhabited for thousands of years by people who know how to coexist with, and be part of, their environment.'[107]

After the Alberto Fujimori coup later that year, and the declaration of a state of emergency, he discovered that both the Peruvian intelligence service and the Shining Path guerrilla movement had sentenced him to death. He fled to Mexico, together with two of his children and his partner, where he was granted asylum and worked closely with the Zapatistas, returning to Peru in 1997.

Pachamama

Today Hugo Blanco remains fully active and committed, particularly around the ecological struggle in all its forms. He has been, since 2000, director of the Cusco-based newspaper *Lucha Indígena,* and a member of the editorial board of *Sin Permiso.* He argues that the inhabitants of the Andes, along with other indigenous peoples globally, play a crucial role in the ecological struggle and the defence and understanding of nature. They embody, he argues, a great respect for the environment, as reflected in the concept mother Earth, or 'Pachamama'.

In 2017 a collection of his political writings were published by Merlin and Resistance Books under the title *We the Indians: The Indigenous Peoples of Peru and the Struggle for Land.* In it he sets out what he sees as the relationship between the indigenous peoples of the Andes and the natural world in which they live, in terms of what he calls 'the age of Pachamama':

> The inhabitants of the Andes felt great respect for nature, for Pachamama. We are not referring to the non-use of agrochemicals, which did not exist, but to other aspects, such as the care for the arable soil: by making terraces known as *andenes*, leaving fringes of grass on the hillsides to contain the earth, giving the canals a certain course so they cause less land erosion, making the furrows on the hillsides with the necessary inclination depending on the degree of rainwater, so that the rain erodes the smallest possible quantity of soil. Some of these techniques still exist.
>
> The land was enriched with the excrement of sea birds, wano (guano in its distorted Spanish form), and of llamas and guinea pigs. A typical example of their ecological sense is that before the European invasion, vicuñas were not hunted; rather, they were surrounded, kept alive, sheared and then released.
>
> During the Inca period there was, and still is now, full understanding and use of biodiversity. An average sized community had one group of people raising alpaca in the uplands and another cultivating coca in the low part. When a community member is asked what his land produces and he answers proudly that it produces 'complete', he is indicating that it has various ecological terrains. As a boy, I took potatoes from the high ground to exchange for tuna from the mountain streams; as a youth I exchanged coca (before the empire ordered the sacred leaf to be

exterminated) from the forest edge for *ch'arki* (cured meat) and cheese from the cold mountains.[108]

This year, 2018, saw the publication of Derek Wall's excellent biography *Hugo Blanco: Revolutionary for Life*. Wall brings to life, from pages of *Lucha Indigena*, some of the environmental struggles Hugo has been involved in over recent years:

> One of the most important and dramatic struggles covered by *Lucha Indigena* occurred in 2009, when the indigenous peoples of the Peruvian Amazon rose up to oppose gas and oil exploitation of the forests. Alan Garcia, once again President of Peru representing APRA, continued to move right. He was committed to neoliberal policies, including accelerating mining and other forms of extraction in the country. As elsewhere in Latin America, the state claimed ownership of land below the surface, thus Garcia sold the rights to prospect for gas and oil to various foreign corporations as part of a free trade agreement with the USA (Blanco 2018a: 96).[109]

Asked in 2017 about his most recent struggles, Hugo focused on environmental issues:

> My fight now is for water. I am also with the Amazonians who fight in defense of the rainforest, which are the lungs of the world. I am also against agro-industry, because it practices monoculture that is impoverishing the earth, because they put chemical fertilizers on the land. They also use insecticides and herbicides that are killing nature, they do not worry about killing the land because after killing the land cultivated here, the multinationals can go to Asia and Africa, to continue killing the land. They also produce for export, growing artichokes and asparagus that suck up a lot of water, taking away the water that should be for Peruvians. (Zevallos 2017).[110]

Vandana Shiva

In Asia too there is a long tradition of environmental protests, for example against the so-called 'green revolution' based on productivism; these are often led by peasant movements for whom a harmonious relationship with nature is literally a matter of life or death.

In India, mass struggles against the damming of rivers took place in the post-Independence period, and they continue today. I have already recounted the resistance to the Narmada Valley Sadar Sarovar project in Chapter 2.

Vandana Shiva has spent much of her life supporting such struggles and working in the defence and celebration of biodiversity and indigenous knowledge. She is the author of numerous books. She has worked to promote biodiversity in agriculture to increase productivity, nutrition, farmers' incomes and food sovereignty. Her work on agriculture started in 1984, after the violence in Punjab, and the gas leak in Bhopal from Union Carbide's pesticide manufacturing plant.

In Shiva's 1993 book *Ecofeminism*,[111] authored jointly with the German feminist Maria Mies, she relates powerful stories of community struggle, often under the leadership of women, to defend Mother Earth; in particular she recounts the remarkable struggle of the Chipko women in 1987 to resist illegal mining activities that were destroying the environment, including the water courses in Nahi-Kals village in the Doon Valley, in the Thano region of India. The Doon Valley is within the Shivalik Hills in the Lesser Himalayas.

In her 2002 book *Water Wars*, Shiva describes the 1983 struggle of farmers in Karnataka against the spread of a eucalyptus monoculture to provide pulp for the paper industry. The farmers marched *en masse*, she says, to the forest nursery, uprooted millions of eucalyptus seedlings, and planted tamarind and mango in their place. The book also describes the struggle, over several decades, against the damming of the Narmada Valley and the Ganges. The project involved construction of 30 large dams, 135 medium-sized dams and 3,000 minor dams on the Narmada river and its tributaries. It resulted in the loss of 350,000 hectares of cultivatable land and the displacement of a million people. Shiva puts it this way:

> The Narmada protest, which once was a fight for a just settlement for the displaced people, has rapidly evolved into a major environmental controversy, calling into question not only the method of compensation for the evictees but the logic of large dams altogether. The movement has taken inspiration from the struggles that led to the withdrawal of two major dam proposals: Silent Valley and the Bodhghat dam.[112]

Chico Mendes

Chico Mendes (Francisco Alves Mendes Filho), the Brazilian rubber tapper, environmentalist, and socialist, led the epic struggle of the rubber tappers in the 1970s and 1980s. He was born into a liberationist Christian culture and was won to Marxism (or we should say eco-Marxism) in the 1960s. In 1975 Chico, with his comrade Wilson Pinheiro, founded the Rural Workers Union of Xapuri (where he was born), and organized mass actions against the big logging companies engaged in deforestation. In the course of this, Mendes received many death threats, and in 1980 Wilson Pinheiro was murdered by the death squads.

Mendes responded by forming the Forest Peoples Alliance: for the first time, indigenous peoples and rubber tapers united against a common enemy in order to defend the Amazon rain forest – the last great rain forest in the world and the lungs of the planet – against logging, deforestation, and the excessive introduction of rubber plantations. In 1988, Mendes himself was assassinated by a gunman hired by the big landowners.

Michael Löwy, in his tribute to Mendes in *Capitalism Nature Socialism* in 2010, said the following of the assassination:

> But Chico in his combination of socialism and ecology, in agrarian reform and the defence of the Amazonian forest, in peasant and indigenous struggles, in the survival of humble local populations, and in the protection of a heritage of humanity: the last great tropical forest not yet destroyed by capitalist 'progress' … His struggle will continue to inspire new struggles both in Brazil and far from Brazil, in other countries and on other continents.[113]

Dorothy Stag

Many have died since Chico Mendes in the struggle to defend the Brazilian rain forest from the big landowners and the big timber companies. In the 1990s, deforestation intensified in the Amazonia region and many struggles have taken place. One of the campaigns that should be mentioned here is that of Dorothy Stag, a Roman Catholic nun.

Stag was born in Dayton, Ohio, but was a naturalised Brazilian citizen, having arrived in Brazil as a missionary in 1966. She worked as an advocate for the rural poor, beginning in the early 1970s and helping peasants make a living by farming small plots, and extracting forest products without deforestation. She was often seen wearing a T-shirt with the slogan: 'The death of the forest is the end of our life.'

Dorothy's involvement with land conflicts began in 1982, when she moved to the small town of Anapu on the Transamazonian Highway – a deprived area with a long record of misery and land conflicts. There, along with many other activities, she sought to protect peasants from criminal gangs who worked on behalf of ranchers to steal their plots of land.

In June 2004, she testified before a parliamentary Commission of Inquiry on Rural Violence, where she denounced the impunity which big landowners enjoyed and which enabled them to continue with their violent activities. In February 2005, at the age of 73, she was gunned down by a death squad and killed.

8 The struggle for an international climate agreement

The world at present is fast approaching a climate cliff. Science tells us that an increase in global average temperature of 2°C constitutes the planetary tipping point with respect to climate change, leading to irreversible changes beyond human control... The paleoclimatic record shows that an increase in global average temperature of several degrees means that 50 percent or more of all species—plants and animals— will be driven to extinction. Global food crops will be negatively affected.

John Bellamy Foster[114]

Moves towards an intergovernmental response global warming and climate change began in 1988 with the establishment of the International Panel on Climate Change (IPCC) as a scientific body under the auspices of the UN, comprising 2,500 scientists from 130 countries. Its terms of reference were to provide the world with an objective, scientific view of climate change and its political and economic impacts. Its first major international initiative was the UN Conference on Environment and Development held in Rio de Janeiro, Brazil, in 1992, known as the Earth Summit.

The outcome of the Summit was the establishment of the UN Framework Convention on Climate Change (UNFCCC) the terms of reference of which was to establish an international agreement that would 'stabilise greenhouse gas concentrations in the atmosphere that would prevent dangerous anthropogenic interference with the climate systems'. It set a voluntary target, to come into force in March 1994, of reducing GHG emissions from the developed countries to 1990 levels by 2000. The targets set at the 1992 Rio Summit ended in failure, however, when most countries pledged to them failed to meet them.

The Kyoto Protocol

This led to the Kyoto Protocol (to the Framework Convention) of 1997 which went beyond Rio in that rather than the voluntary principle, it would commit its participants by setting internationally binding emission reduction targets. It would do this whilst 'recognizing that developed countries are principally responsible for the current high levels of GHG emissions in the atmosphere as a result of more than 150 years of industrial activity'. The Protocol therefore placed a heavier burden on developed nations under the principle of 'common but differentiated responsibilities.'

This was an important step forward. Unfortunately, when it came to implementation, however, the Protocol recommended a series of unsupportable market-based mechanisms.

Article 17 of Kyoto allowed industrialised countries to trade their allocation of carbon emissions amongst themselves – known as 'cap and trade'. The idea was that GHG emissions are capped (a target set), with every country in the world allocated a fixed quantity of emissions that it must not exceed. If the limits are tight enough, emissions will fall. The trade part of this the 'cap' means that if countries reduce their emissions enough they will be able to sell their 'savings' to other countries. This allows countries to appear green abroad but pollute at home, under what was called the clean development mechanism (CDM). Businesses could purchase the right to continue polluting, provided that they funded projects that claimed to reduce green-house gas emissions in the Global South. The scheme was easy to manipulate so that governments could 'show' that they were doing something.

It allowed industrialised countries to invest in carbon-mitigation projects in so-called developing countries which, in effect, allowed them purchase the right to emit GHG in their own countries whilst polluting elsewhere. The deal was signed by Bill Clinton, on behalf of the world's biggest polluter, and then rejected by the US Congress – after which the whole thing fell apart.

The Stern Review

The influential (and monumental) 700 page *The Economics of Climate Change – The Stern Review*, commissioned by the British Labour government under

Gordon Brown, was published in 2006. Stern was the World Bank Chief Economist from 2000-2003.[115]

The Report is important in that it defends the science and rebuts the deniers. His overall conclusion is that delay in seriously tacking climate change will end up being a lot more costly. He puts it this way:

> The scientific evidence that climate change is a serious and urgent issue is now compelling. It warrants strong action to reduce greenhouse gas emissions around the world to reduce the risk of very dangerous and potentially irreversible impacts on ecosystems, societies and economics... Reversing the trend to higher temperatures requires an urgent, world-wide shift towards a low-carbon economy. Delay makes the problem worse much more difficult and action to deal with it much more costly.[116]

He goes on to define the climate crisis as the greatest market failure in all history. He puts it this way:

> In common with many other environmental problems, human induced climate change is at its most basic level an externality. Those who produce green-house gas emissions are bringing about climate change, thereby imposing costs on the world and on future generations, but they do not face directly, either via markets no in other ways, the full consequences of the costs of their actions.

Much economic activity involves the emission of greenhouse gases (GHGs). As GHGs accumulate in the atmosphere, temperatures increase, and the climate changes that result impose costs (and some benefits) on society. However, the full costs of GHG emissions, in terms of climate change, are not immediately – indeed they are unlikely ever to be – borne by the emitter, as they face little or no economic incentive to reduce emissions. Similarly, emitters do not have to compensate whose who lose out on climate change. In this sense, human induced climate change is an externality, one that is not 'corrected' through any institution or market, unless policy intervenes.[117]

Remarkably, despite such remarks Stern goes on to base his conclusions entirely on market forces. He concludes not only that the best way to tackle the climate crisis is via market mechanisms – i.e. more bankrupt Kyoto-type market solutions along the lines of cap and trade and the clean development mechanism (CDM) – but that the ecological crisis can be resolved in the context of an overall policy based on economic growth. Over 180 countries signed up to his proposals. (This is covered in more detail in chapter 12 on growth and productivism.)

In 2008 Stern announced that his report had underestimated the speed and scale of some of the climate impacts and increased his recommendation for expenditure on emissions reductions to 2% of global GDP.

Derek Wall in his book *The Rise of the Green Left*[118] makes a very good critique of market based schemes. He quotes a *Financial Times* report of April 2007 that exposed the widespread abuse of carbon offset and included many examples of people and organisations buying worthless credits that did not yield any reductions in carbon emissions, or gaining carbon credits on the basis of efficiency gains from which they had already benefitted substantially.[119] [120]

Indigenous Peoples Global Summit

An Indigenous Peoples Global Summit was held in Anchorage, Alaska in April 2009 – in advance of the Copenhagen summit to be held in December of that year. It was attended by 500 delegates, representing 80 nations from the Arctic, North America, Latin America, Africa, the Caribbean and Russia.

It allowed indigenous peoples from across the world to respond collectively to the impacts of climate change, and to develop the key message they wanted to deliver in advance of the COP 15. The issues discussed included the effects of climate change, from the rising sea level on coast lines, drought, melting Arctic ice, and extraction projects that further exacerbate the effects of climate change. The Anchorage Declaration that emerged from the conference said the following:

> We express our solidarity as indigenous peoples living in areas that are the most vulnerable to the impacts and root causes of climate change. We reaffirm the unbreakable and sacred connection between land, air, water, oceans, forests, sea ice, plants, animals, and our human communities, as the material and spiritual basis for our existence.
>
> We are deeply alarmed at the accelerating climate devastation brought about

by unsustainable development. We are experiencing profound and disproportionate adverse impacts on our cultures, human and environmental health, human rights, wellbeing, traditional livelihoods, food systems and food sovereignty, local infrastructure, economic viability, and our very survival as Indigenous Peoples.

Copenhagen COP15

The job of picking up the pieces from the collapse of Kyoto fell to the Copenhagen COP15 in December 2009. Despite an international mobilisation demanding that it take serious and effective legally binding action this broke up in disarray and acrimony after a group of 25 countries, including some of the world's greatest polluters – the USA, China, Canada and Australia – rejected a binding agreement and proposed instead a voluntary pledge to limit global warming to no more than a 2°C increase. This pledge was called the Copenhagen Accord; it was drafted by the USA, China, India, Brazil, and South Africa, and was 'taken note of', but not adopted by the conference itself. It was a major defeat for the climate movement, from which it would take some years to recover.

Cochabamba

Following the collapse of the Copenhagen summit, the Bolivian president Evo Morales called a Peoples' Conference on Climate Change and the Rights of Mother Earth, in Cochabamba, Bolivia, in April 2010 to ensure that the voices of the indigenous peoples were heard. This was a conference led by indigenous people, whose key role in the environmental struggle was increasingly recognised by other climate activists.

Over 35,000 people attended the conference despite international travel being disrupted by the eruption in Iceland of volcano Eyjafjallajökull, which prevented many thousands more from attending. The conference adopted the Universal Declaration of Rights of Mother Earth, the preamble of which said:

We, the peoples and nations of Earth:
• considering that we are all part of Mother Earth, an indivisible, living community of interrelated and interdependent beings with a common destiny;
gratefully acknowledging that Mother Earth is the source of life, nourishment and

learning and provides everything we need to live well;

• recognising that the capitalist system and all forms of depredation, exploitation, abuse and contamination have caused great destruction, degradation and disruption of Mother Earth, putting life as we know it today at risk through phenomena such as climate change;

• convinced that, in an interdependent living community, it is not possible to recognise the rights of only human beings without causing an imbalance within Mother Earth;

• affirming that to guarantee human rights it is necessary to recognise and defend the rights of Mother Earth and all beings in her and that there are existing cultures, practices and laws that do so;

• conscious of the urgency of taking decisive, collective action to transform structures and systems that cause climate change and other threats to Mother Earth;

• proclaim this Universal Declaration of the Rights of Mother Earth, and call on the General Assembly of the United Nation to adopt it, as a common standard of achievement for all peoples and all nations of the world, and to the end that every individual and institution takes responsibility for promoting through teaching, education, and consciousness raising, respect for the rights recognised in this Declaration and ensure through prompt and progressive measures and mechanisms, national and international, their universal and effective recognition and observance among all peoples and States in the world.

Paris COP21

The COP21 summit, held in Paris in December 2015, was another landmark climate event. It took place not only against rapidly worsening climate chaos – with severe heat waves in India, Pakistan, Europe, East Africa, East Asia, and Australia – but in the shadow of the failures of Kyoto and Copenhagen. It was make or break in terms of doing something between governments, at the international level, that could avoid major irreversible developments.

In the run up to the summit mass mobilisations took place around the world demanding decisive action. London saw its biggest climate demonstration ever, with 70,000 people on the streets. There were demonstrations and protests in Paris itself during COP, despite the imposition of a state of emergency by the French Government under anti-terrorism laws.

The main proposal put to the COP was to seek to restrict global warming to a maximum temperature increase, over the preindustrial level, of 'well below a 2°C'. This was an advance of the Copenhagen target which had been to seek restrict the increase to not more than 2°C'.

The proposal, however, was bitterly resisted by those countries and island states at greatest risk from the already rising sea level, some under imminent threat of submergence. They were organised (as mentioned above) into what they called the High Ambition Coalition, which was led by the Marshall Islands. They put up a ferocious fight for a maximum increase of 1.5°C rather than 2°C'around the slogan '1.5°C to stay alive'.

In the end both proposals were accepted, though not with equal status. The main target would be 'well below a 2°C' with a further limit of 1.5°C accepted as an 'aspiration' rather than a target: 'recognising that this would significantly reduce the risks and impacts of climate change'.[121]

Although this was a compromise the importance of the 1.5°C breakthrough that had been made should not be underestimated. It was the most important gain made in Paris. Once adopted, even in the terms it was, it would not go away. It set a new benchmark against which the struggle to reduce carbon emissions would have to be measured in the future. It was a signal – though will be ignored by the industry today – that the writing is on the wall for fossil fuels.

The Paris agreement was an important landmark in that it was the first unanimously agreed accord of its kind in 21 years of UN organised conferences and summits. Also for the the first time there was unanimous recognition of what climate scientists and climate campaigners have been saying for many years: that there is a real and urgent threat from anthropogenic climate change, that will have catastrophic consequences for hundreds of millions of people if the burning of fossil fuels is not brought to an end. For the first time, neither the scientific basis of global warming, or its anthropogenic character, was disputed at a COP. The climate sceptics were a non-existent – a big change since Copenhagen.

Deeply flawed

Although hailed as a great victory by the governments involved, the agreement was deeply flawed – despite the gains outlined above.

The biggest flaw by far was that the agreement was based on none-legally binding pledges to reduce emissions – called Intended Nationally Determined Contributions (or INDCs). These were submitted by each country in advance of the COP in order to provide a baseline for the agreement. They would then be subject to a five year auditing process, starting in December 2018 at COP24 in Poland, aimed at tightening the UNDCs up each year to make them increasingly effective – 'ratcheting them up' is the terminology used. During this process each country will be expected to provide new INDCs designed to 'ratchet up' their targets towards the levels necessary. The Paris agreement will ultimately be judged against the success or otherwise of this process.

The problem, however, and it's a big one, was and is that if they remain unchanged, they will collectively result in, not in global temperature increase of 2°C – far less of 1.5°C – but of 3.4°C. A rise on this scale would not only impact disastrously on the lives of hundreds of millions of people, but would bring into play dangerous feedback processes that could irreversibly destabilise global climate systems.

Whether a binding agreement was ever going to happen in Paris is another matter. Noam Chomsky points out in his new (February 2015) book *Who Rules the World* that as far as the USA was concerned, whatever position the Obama administration took, any binding agreement on climate change would be dead on arrival on Capitol Hill with its Republican-controlled Senate stacked out with fanatical hard line climate deniers. In any case fighting to enforce the full implementation of the Paris agreement is now an important part of the work of the climate and ecology movement.

An international agreement, of course, is far from the only level at which the struggle to defend the planet needs to take place. It is, however, an indispensable component of the overall struggle and can set the framework for the struggle at a national level. It also reflects the reality that global warming and the ecological crisis are the ultimate international issues – there is only one atmosphere and only one biosphere.

The Global South

Another highly controversial aspect of Paris summit was the situation of the impoverished countries of the Global South, who pollute the least but suffer the most from climate chaos. Eventually, as a result of a struggle by these countries themselves, the conference accepted that they will need help if they are to adopt sustainable (non-carbon) models of development and eradicate poverty at the same time. The wealthy countries are consequently 'strongly urged', within the agreement, to provide a $100 billion a year (from 2020) to help them in this. This grossly inadequate figure is to be progressively raised in future years by negotiation at climate summit meetings.

The agreement consequently resolves to:

> ...enhance the provision of urgent and adequate finances, technology and capacity building support by developed country Parties in order to enhance the level of ambition of pre-2020 action by Parties, and in this regard *strongly urges* developed country Parties to scale up their level of financial support, with a concrete roadmap to achieve the goal of jointly providing USD 100 billion annually by 2020 for mitigation and adaption while significantly increasing adaption finance from current levels and to further provide appropriate technology and capacity building support.

Member states were not required to sign-up to the new agreement there and then in Paris, but could do so the following year, at COP22 in Marrakesh, when the agreement would be finally ratified.

Movement stronger

Importantly, the climate movement emerged far stronger from Paris than from Copenhagen. This was partly because the climate crisis was more urgent and dangerous, but also because the movement had gone into the campaign for Paris with a more thought-through (*i.e.* political) approach from the outset than had been the case in Copenhagen. This time it was a case of prepare for the worst but build the movement at the same time; make sure that the movement comes out stronger than it went into the campaign for the COP. To build, as was said, not just for Paris but through Paris towards higher levels of activity in 2016 and beyond.

This reflected an important radicalisation of the movement, including the big NGOs, that had been taking place in the run up to Paris and thereby breaking the impact of Copenhagen.

And this was indeed reflected at a higher level in the first half of 2016. During the first two weeks of May, a global wave of action took place around the world, with the demand: 'Break free from fossil fuels – keep the coal, oil, and gas in the ground'.

Anti-fossil fuel activities – both demonstrations and direct actions – took place across the world at that time: in Australia, Brazil, Canada, Ecuador, Germany, Indonesia, New Zealand, Nigeria, Philippines, South Africa, and Turkey, as well as in Britain. In the USA, protests took place in Denver, Los Angeles, Washington DC and Chicago, as well as in the North West and the North East.

In Britain, the Reclaim the Power network mobilised several hundred people at the UK's largest opencast coal mine at Ffos-y-fran, near Merthyr Tydfil. Activists blockaded the mine and brought it to a halt in the biggest ever mass action at a coal mine in Britain. In London, the Campaign against Climate Change organised a march from Trafalgar Square to Downing Street – marching backwards in order to symbolise the direction of government policy on climate change.

This was the biggest international wave of actions against the fossil fuel industry outside of the mobilisations for the COP conferences. Naomi Klein said:

> The global climate justice movement is rising fast. But so are the oceans. So are global temperatures. This is a race against time. Our movement is stronger than ever, but to beat the odds, we have to grow stronger.[122]

It is true that the Paris agreement is framed within the parameters of the capitalist system, with its productivism, growth, and drive for profit. It could not be otherwise. The COP was comprised of 195 capitalist governments (194 if we discount Cuba) led by the UN. It was never going to produce the anti-capitalist solution to the climate crisis – based on social and climate justice – that is needed. If we judge it – and dismiss it – on that basis, we will miss the point.

The issue at stake in Paris, however, was not just whether a deal, if reached, would be the ultimate solution. Few, I imagine, expected that it would. The objective for most was to fight for the best deal possible that would create a new dynamic from which a new round (or stage) of the struggle could be launched. This much, at least, was achieved.

Marrakesh COP22

Held a year after the Paris agreement, this was the first a series of summits to be held with the aim of consolidating and strengthen the Paris agreement. Whist it was able to record that the Paris agreement had been ratified by the required number of countries – it needed to be ratified by at least 55 Parties to the UN Framework Convention on Climate Change, accounting in total for at least an estimated 55 per cent of the total global greenhouse gas emissions – other progress was hard to come by.

This was particularly the case given that the conference was rocked to its foundation only a day after it opened by the election of Trump to the US presidency.

Whilst the conference was licking its wounds, and speculating as to whether Trump (who has said that climate change was a Chinese hoax aimed at damaging the US economy) would carry out his campaign pledges to pull out of Paris, to maximise fossil fuel extraction and to start drilling in the national parks, China stepped up and made a bid for the moral high ground.

There had also been a shift in China's position, however, since Copenhagen, when it supported the proposal that wrecked the conference. In Marrakesh they spoke of the importance of the implementation of Paris despite any position taken by Trump. The *Guardian* of 26 November 2016 put it this way:

> This time, rather than seeing the announced US departure from the climate stage under a Trump administration as an excuse for others to slacken their efforts, Chinese officials made clear that this latest act of US self-harm would not deter China from pursuing its own interests, and that those interests lie firmly in a vision of a low-carbon future. As Liu Zhenmin said in Marrakesh, any change in US policy 'won't affect China's commitment to support climate negotiations and also the implementation of the Paris Agreement.

This is a view that is widely shared in China's circles of experts and policymakers. While this latest turn in the US administration's climate policy might be disappointing for the global effort, China's policy at this point has a standalone logic and an internal coherence that makes a change of direction highly unlikely. China plans to be the supplier of low-carbon goods to a carbon-constrained world: It already boasts the world's biggest installed capacity of wind and solar power, and its climate policies are built in to its current five-year economic plan.

The struggle for an effective international agreement to take control of GHG emissions, however, has been long and hard and remains unresolved. There is no alternative, however, to the struggle for such an agreement, which has to be fought out alongside many other battles to defend the environment including direct action against the polluters themselves and the methods they use, fracking, opencast coal mining, coal fired power stations and many other forms of CO_2 generation. The alternative is to let them simply get on with it on their own terms and without challenge – which would be ineffective and counterproductive.

A useful way of gauging the scale of this inequality is provided by the Maplecroft Climate Change Environmental Risk Atlas (CCERA).[123] It provides comparative risk data on climate change for every country in the world; it identifies, in its Climate Change Vulnerability Index (CCVI) 2015, the 32 countries that are at the highest risk and their governmental capacity to adapt to climate change over the next 30 years. Those are: Bangladesh, Sierra Leone, South Sudan, Nigeria, Chad, Haiti, Ethiopia, Philippines, Central African Republic and Eritrea. Others also classified as at high risk are the growth economies of Cambodia, India, Myanmar, Pakistan and Mozambique.

A common feature of these countries is that they are extremely vulnerable. They depend heavily on agriculture: with 65 per cent of their combined working population employed in that sector. Changing weather patterns are already impacting on food production, and consequently on poverty, migration and social stability.

PART THREE

STRATEGY AND TACTICS

9 Ecosocialist developments

The past is not dead, but is living in us, and will be alive in the future which we are now helping to make.

William Morris

The opening paragraph in Raymond Williams 1982 pamphlet *Socialism and Ecology*[124] says the following:

> In recent years some of us have been talking about ecological socialism – though it's a bit of a mouthful. But in many countries and at a growing pace there is an attempt to run together two kinds of thinking which are obviously very important in the contemporary world; yet the attempt to run them together is by no means simple. There are a number of questions which we have to look at both in practical contemporary terms and also in the way in which the different bodies of ideas have developed.[125]

There was still not, however, a common understanding, even on the radical left, of what ecosocialism is and what it is not – particularly in the Global North. Some have seen it simply as taking ecological crises more seriously, or as a convergence of socialism and ecology – 'you have to be green to be red and you have to be red to be green'. Others stress that in the twenty-first century it is no longer enough simply to call yourself a socialist (or a Marxist), given the scale of the ecological crisis and its consequences for life on the planet. There has been progress, but there remains a long way to go.

Towards the end of the 1980s, however, as the ecological crisis intensified, a new level of interest began to emerge around the idea of ecosocialism and red-green unity, that reflected Williams's observations in his pamphlet. More books began to emerge, from a Marxist standpoint, addressing the ecological issues in general and ecosocialism in particular.

There remained, however, indeed important obstacles to be overcome before red-green unity could become a reality. Ted Benton summarised this very well in an article in an article in *New Left Review* in 1989 entitled *'Marxism and Natural Limits: An Ecological Critique and Reconstruction'*. He put it this way:

> Five themes recur in the 'traditional' socialist critiques of ecological politics. The first, my focus here, equates the ecological perspective with neo-Malthusianism and rejects it as a 'natural limits' conservatism. The second sees in green politics a generalised and reactionary opposition to industrialism and technology as such, thus deflecting attention from the specifically capitalist character of environmental destruction. The third theme, closely connected with the second, accuses the ecologists of deflecting attention from class and regional inequalities in resource use and environmental destruction, in the name of a universal 'human interest' in environmental sustainability. Fourthly, this, like all 'general interest' ideologies in class societies, is a mask for *particular* interests: in this case an alliance of technocrats with affluent rural middle-class activists who share vested interests in ecological scare-mongering, and/or in the defence of a privileged minority life-style. Finally, ecological priorities are sometimes seen as elite preferences, matters of aesthetics or taste, which privileged minorities impose on the rest of a population, many of whom lack fulfilment of their more basic needs...[126]

The critique of the socialists by greens and ecologists, on the other hand, unsurprisingly, focused on the weakness of the left's involvement in the struggle itself, and the disastrous environmental record of the 'actually existing' socialist societies of eastern Europe (as set out later in this chapter), and/or the record of the western social democratic parties in governmental office. Socialism is widely condemned for its 'productivist values'. As Jonathon Porritt put it in his 1984 book *Seeing Green: Politics of Ecology Explained*: 'Both are dedicated to industrial growth, to the expansion of the means of production, to a materialist ethic as the best means of meeting people's needs, and to unimpeded technological development'.[127] [128]

The problem for the left is that this critique is substantially correct – see chapter 12, for example on growth and productivism and 13 on The Stalinist Legacy. If we are to take the issue of red-green convergence seriously – and we should – we have to address the ecological failures of the left in the 20th century, and not sweep them under the carpet. This means basing an ecosocialist project today, not on the failures of the 20th century but on the ecological achievements of classical Marxism in the second half of the 19th century – as developed and elaborated by Marx, Engels and William Morris.

It means that the old models (as far as they existed) of a future post-capitalist/socialist society, envisaged by socialists during the twentieth century, are entirely inadequate today – even if we discount the Stalinist monstrosities. Even the models discussed by the opponents of Stalinism did not begin to address the essence of the problem. It means the development a model of a post-capitalist ecosocialist society, based not only on economic and social justice, but on ecological sustainability and the ability to remain that way.

It also means an end to the use of fossil fuels and a complete changeover to renewables. It means an end to productivism and built-in obsolescence. It mean production for use values rather than exchange values. It means an end to factory farming and a big reduction in the consumption of meat. It means developing a relationship with nature based on human kind seeing itself as a part of nature, rather than being in conflict with it and existing at its expense.

Martin Ryle

A thoughtful contribution on the issue of red-green unity was made by Martin Ryle with his 1988 book *Ecology and Socialism*,[129] This was an attempt to define an ecosocialist perspective from within the Green Party. He points to the need to inject more specifically socialist ideas concepts into the environmental movement.

He argues that there has been a dearth of political discussion about the desirability of growth, and that even on the left growth has been repeatedly advocated: 'when what we clearly need is a more differentiated and complex debate about what kinds of economic development would promote social and ecological well-being'.[130] Nonetheless, he argues:

> '...the Greens do represent something new: a negative but essential recognition of ecological limits—and also, positively, one channel for the 'new social movements' (also courted by the left) to find political expression and a new mode of political

activism and activity which tries to avoid hierarchy and leader-fixation and is critically aware of processes as well as goals. Nobody active on the left, or engaged in radical politics, can neglect their advent.'[131]

1988 also saw the launch of the ecological journal *Capitalism, Nature and Socialism: A Journal of Socialist Ecology,* with James O'Connor as its first editor-in-chief, that was to play such an important role in the development of environmental politics.

1992 saw the publication of Yrjö Haila and Richard Levins' book *Humanity and Nature: Ecology, Science and Society,* which dealt with the impact of the ecological crisis in the post-war period. Yrjö Haila was a research fellow in zoology at the Academy in Finland, and Richard Levins – best-known as a co-author of *The Dialectical Biologist* – was professor of public health at Harvard Medical School.

The earlier works of Rudolf Bahro – the East German dissident, critical Marxist, and environmentalist – are also interesting. He became a leading figure on the left of the West German Green Party after his expulsion from East Germany in 1979, and wrote a number of books on the ecological crisis. He raged against industrialisation (East and West), which he called the 'Big Machine'. His books included *Socialism and Survival* (1982), *From Red to Green* (1984), *Building the Green Movement* (1986) and *Avoiding Social and Ecological Disaster* (1994). He eventually moved away from Marxism altogether – *From Red to Green'* was already a clue.

There were other dissidents in East Germany (the GDR) who also addressed ecological issues. One such was Wolfgang Harich, member of the Communist Party of Germany (KPD), and later the Socialist Unity Party, which became the ruling party of the GDR in 1946. Harich – who was imprisoned for ten years – argued for something between Stalinism and capitalism based on ecological principles, and developed a Marxist/Hegelian approach to the environmental question.

The 1990s

Edward O. Wilson's *The Diversity of Life,* already mentioned above, was published in 1992. David Pepper's controversial, eco-autonomist, but interesting book *Eco-socialism: From Deep Ecology to Social Justice* was published in 1993. Ted Benton's thought-challenging *Natural Relations: Ecology, Animal Rights and Social Justice* appeared the same year, exploring not only the relationship between human beings and nature (and non-human beings) but also the emerging red-green debate.

Ted Benton was involved in the Red Green Study Group established in 1992 and still functioning today. In 1995, the Group published a booklet entitled *What on Earth is to be Done?* – which explores the possibilities of red-green unity. It has a freshness about it that makes it particularly relevant to today's debates.

Most important from a Marxist standpoint, the 1990s saw the emergence of John Bellamy Foster and Paul Burkett, along with Fred Magdoff and others, around the journal *Monthly Review* in the United States. Foster and Burkett in particular would go on to make a huge contribution to dragging Marxism out of the twentieth century, as far as the ecology of the planet was concerned, and reconnecting it to the ecological heritage of classical Marxism itself.

The first of John Bellamy Foster's many important books on ecological issues – *Ecology Against Capitalism* – was published in 2002. In 1996 *The Sixth Extinction* was published, written by the Kenyan paleoanthropologist and conservationist Richard Leakey and Roger Lewin. It was ground-breaking in showing the sheer scale of the biodiversity crisis, and was the fore-runner of Elizabeth Kolbert's later work.

Paul Burkett's already mentioned *Marx and Nature* was published in 1999, followed by Foster's *Marx's Ecology* in 2000, which further shifted the debate on the ecological left. His *Ecological Revolution* was published in 2009; *What Every Environmentalist Needs to Know about Capitalism* in 2011, with Magdoff; and his latest book, with Paul Burkett, *Marx and the Earth* in 2016. These writers give a powerful voice to a consistent ecosocialist alternative – particularly Bellamy Foster's highly acclaimed *Marx's Ecology*.

This new generation brought to the table not only a better understanding of global warming, due to the ongoing efforts of Hansen, but also of the destructive capacity of capitalism as a global system, and the debates around ecosocialism as a key strategic response to it.

Globalised capitalism

By the end of the 1990s, the ecological struggle intersected with the rising struggle against globalisation. The great demonstration for global justice in Seattle in 1999 against the World Trade Organisation (WTO) had an important ecological content to it, and saw the coming together of ecologists and trade unionists – the 'Teamsters and Turtles' phenomenon.

In the Global South, where the ecological crisis had its greatest impact, there was already a much stronger ecosocialist dynamic – particularly in the indigenous movements, with socialists and Marxists such as Chico Mendes in Brazil, Hugo Blanco in Peru, and Vandana Shiva the socialist, feminist and ecological activist in India.[132]

The World Social Forum (WSF) in 2001 saw the mass participation of activists from the Landless Workers Movement, demanding global and climate justice and protesting about the commodification of the planet and the trashing of its ecology.

The second edition of Joel Kovel's already mentioned *The Enemy of Nature: The End of Capitalism or the End of the World* was published in 2007, and *The Global Fight for Climate Justice*, edited by Ian Angus, in 2009. Derek Wall's *The Rise of the Green Left* was published in 2010 with a foreword by Hugo Blanco. The English edition of Daniel Tanuro's *Green Capitalism: Why It Can't Work* (*L'impossible capitalisme vert, 2009*) came out in 2013, and the second edition of Paul Burkett's *Marx and Nature* in 2014, with a major introduction by John Bellamy Foster.

During the first decade of the twenty-first century, it became increasingly clear, to me at least, that major issues remained to be resolved for Marxism and the ecological struggle, in terms of both analysis and response, if Marxism was to have an impact on the struggle itself – particularly in the Global North.

The Ecosocialist International Network (EIN)

An important initiative in promoting the idea of ecosocialism was taken at a meeting of the EIN in 2001, when Michael Löwy and Joel Kovel drafted what they termed an ecosocialist manifesto. It received a good response and played a useful role in defining and popularising an ecosocialist world view.

A second and wider meeting was called in the spring of 2007, called by Joel Kovel and Michael Löwy jointly with Ian Angus and Derek Wall. It was held in Paris and attended by 60 people from a dozen countries. It called for an Ecosocialist International Network to be launched in Belém, Brazil, at the World Social Forum in January 2009. It appointed a committee of three – Joel Kovel, Michael Löwy and Ian Angus – to draft a Second Ecosocialist Manifesto that would be discussed and edited and then brought to Belém for adoption. Whilst this meeting took the project forward, its weaknesses were that the great majority of those present were from Western Europe, and very few were women. Much of the discussion focused on ways of overcoming these weaknesses.

The second version of the Ecosocialist Manifesto, known as the Belém Declaration, was signed by hundreds of people – including a few from the global South, and some women. It was distributed at the World Social Forum in Belém. (It is an appendix of this book.)

The EIN, however, has failed to make progress in recent years, and ecosocialism remains a minority position on the radical left today. The only far left organisations in Britain, for example, that define themselves as ecosocialist today are Socialist Resistance (SR), the Alliance for Green Socialism, and the Green Left inside the Green Party. Socialist Resistance took the decision to define itself as ecosocialist in 2007, with the adoption of a text entitled *Savage Capitalism*.[133] The British SWP did have some involvement in the EIN at one stage, but appears to have set its face against an ecosocialist identity, on the basis that no change is necessary.

Ecosocialism on the ground

Today the only international radical left current to declare itself ecosocialist is the Fourth International (FI), which did so in 2010. The strongest advocates of this were its supporting organisations from the impoverished countries of the Global South – those that are the most impacted by extreme weather events. Some of these sections were already in effect ecosocialist.

In Mindanao in the Philippines, for example, a region facing ever more frequent and powerful typhoons, FI supporters have long been involved in the defence of their communities against extreme weather events. They are also involved in the development of agricultural methods based on food sovereignty, and the exclusion of genetically modified seeds from multinationals like Monsanto. Instead they are harvesting their own seeds and producing organic food for the local communities.

Bangladesh, one of the most vulnerable, low-lying, and most impacted countries in the world in terms of climate change, is already suffering from rising sea levels and the salinification of vast areas of the country. The FI supporters there are heavily involved in the struggle against climate change and rising sea level. It is centrally involved in major peasant movements, which are campaigning both against climate change and for land redistribution, along the lines of the MST in Brazil. Along with *La Via Campesina* and other organisations, it is campaigning for food sovereignty, the rights of peasant producers, and for land redistribution. It has been heavily involved since 2011 in organising climate caravans, which have campaigned throughout Bangladesh and into Nepal and India against climate change and global warming.

In Pakistan, FI supporters have also been on the sharpest end the climate struggle. In 2010, devastating floods submerged a fifth of the country and left millions homeless. Twenty million people were affected; 2,000 lost their lives, 12 million people had their homes damaged or destroyed, half a million livestock were lost, and 10,000 schools destroyed.

Five FI supporters were jailed for defending villagers after a landslide blocked the Hunza River in the Gilgit-Baltistan region of Pakistan, sweeping homes away and killing nineteen people. The slide formed a 23 km-long lake that submerged three villages, leaving 500 people homeless and 25,000 stranded. The five comrades are still in jail today, seven years later, and campaigns continue for their release.[134]

In Brazil, FI supporters have campaigned in defence of the Amazon and promoting self-organization of indigenous communities. In Ecuador, comrades have been involved in defence of the Yasuní national park against oil drilling. In Latin America as a whole, the organisations of the FI have been involved in mobilisations around the People's Summit at Cochabamba.

In Europe and North America, FI supporters have been increasingly involved in climate mobilisations – whether around COPs in Copenhagen and Paris, or around more localised struggles – against fracking in Britain, against the tar sands in the Canadian state, or against the Keystone Pipeline in the US and Canadian state.

Some radical left parties, Europe-wide, have defined themselves as ecosocialist, including the Red-Green Alliance in Denmark, the Left Bloc in Portugal, the Socialist Left Party in Norway and, formally at least, the Parti de Gauche in France.

10 The strategic debate

The ecological issue is, in my opinion, the great challenge for a renewal of Marxist thought at the threshold of the twenty first century.

Michael Löwy. [135]

The radical left has, in my view, a major issue to resolve in terms of its response to global warming and climate change – and indeed the wider ecological crisis. This is nothing less than its overall strategic response to the crisis.

The standard 'solution' advanced by most on the radical left in this regard, is the revolutionary overthrow of global capitalism – by implication within the next 12 years because that is how long we have to do it. It is what I call 'one solution revolution'. This is the idea expressed across the writings of socialist, Marxist, or radical left environmentalists. Capitalism is the problem and its overturn is the solution – and not just as a long-term perspective, which is a different matter – but as an immediate solution to global warming. Such an approach is maximalist, leftist, and useless. We can all, as socialists, vote to abolish capitalism with both hands, and this is indeed our long-term objective. But as an answer to global warming within the next 12 years it makes no sense.

It amounts to a 'credibility gap': while catastrophic climate change is indeed just around the corner, the same can hardly be said with any credibility of global socialist revolution – unless I have been missing something. It may not be impossible, but it is far too remote a prospect to provide an answer to global warming and climate change.

The SWP placard on the pre-Paris COP demonstration in London on 29 November 2015 carried the slogan: 'System change not climate change – One solution revolution', with the second phrase highlighted in red.

Put bluntly, if the overturn of global capitalism in the 12 remaining years is the only solution to global warming and climate change, then there is no solution to global warming and climate change.

Joel Kovel, reflects it in his 2002 book *The Enemy of Nature: The End of Capitalism or the End of the World*. He put it this way: [136]

> But we should not lose sight of the whole picture in attending to particulars. There is a single world-dominating order, capitalism; and even though it still has not reached everywhere, it cannot be reformed, cannot be satisfied with less than everything, and has the institutions in place for its purposes. No set of individual reforms can encompass what capital means, nor drive it out by the root. Therefore, no matter how meritorious or necessary a particular reform may be, the fact remains that it is capital as a whole that has to be confronted and brought down, daunting as that prospect may be. [137]

Fred Magdoff and Chris Williams take a similar position in *Creating an Ecological Society – towards a revolutionary transformation,* published in 2017.[138] They argue that pressing for reforms under capitalism is not only pointless but is an obstacle to advocating a revolutionary road. They offer the following anecdote:

> A few years ago, Fred was speaking to a professor of environmental studies at a liberal art college in midwestern United States. The professor agreed with Fred's contention that a whole new system, having new ways of relating to one and another and the environment, was needed. But the professor went on to explain that he did not talk to his students about it because any such change was so far off that he felt it was more important to talk about what might be done within the system in the near future to make things better. Realising the necessity for system change, his students might become discouraged and immobilised by the enormity and long-term nature of the project. Fred's response was that if we don't begin thinking about what a new society might look like, how it might be organised, how it might work... it will put the project off for the indefinite future...
>
> This is the crux of the issue: if we can't even imagine a different way of interacting with one another, the economy, and the resources we use and depend upon, then the struggle for a just and ecologically sound world recedes into the realm of utopian fantasy. And without a vision of a plausible, genuine alternative, people understandably set their sights on reforms that will never add up to the immense changes that are needed.[139]

Even John Bellamy Foster, who has done more than anyone else to drag the radical left (including me) out of its ecological dark ages, is not immune from this either. In his 2009 book *The Ecological Revolution: Making Peace with the Planet* he says the following:

> My premise in this book is that we have reached a turning point in the human relation to the Earth: all hope for the future of this relationship is now either revolutionary or it is false.[140]

Foster accepts that this is based more on hope than expectation, and has nothing to say as to how it could be achieved – a point that Ted Benton identified in his review of the book in March 2010:[141]

> If we are set on a course to socio-ecological catastrophe on a global scale, and if the principal dynamic taking us there is a capitalist juggernaut incapable of effective reform, then the only possibility of avoiding destruction of human civilisation and much of life on Earth is a revolutionary overthrow of the prevailing world-system. Foster is clear at the outset of the book that it is grounded in the 'principle of hope': on the face of it, this is not a very hopeful conclusion! It has been said, with some justification, that it is easier to imagine the end of the world than the end of capitalism.

In response, Foster argues the following:

> Ironically, one common criticism that has been directed against the revolutionary environmental outlook offered here is that it is devoid of hope, since it requires going beyond the existing capitalist system. However, the view that the historical journey of humanity is over and that the prevailing mode of production is inviolable – even when faced with an impending collapse of the world's ecosystems and of human civilisation, placing in question the continued existence of humanity itself – can only lead to despair, since it offers no conceivable way out of today's closing circle.[142]

The practical upshot of a maximalist approach of this kind is to deprioritise the struggle for changes in the here and now, and so to demobilise the left.

Interestingly, most on the radical left do not propose maximalist solutions in relation to other major arenas of struggles. In the women's movement, for example, the left has generally engaged in the struggle (often with success) for social change in the here and now, whilst capitalism still exists. Very few say today (as they often did in earlier decades) that we have to abolish global capitalism before anything can be done about the oppression of women. Rather the struggle for immediate gains is seen as a part of the overall struggle against capitalism. The same is the case with the struggles against poverty and for a decent standard of living, against racism and homophobia, and for civil and human rights.

Reforms and reformism

There are some misunderstandings here that need to be discussed. Rejecting maximalism is not in contradiction to the need to go beyond the existing capitalist system. Reforms are not necessarily reformist. On the other hand we cannot go beyond the existing system just by calling for it – however often we do so. The road to revolutionary change is forged in the struggle for reforms – such as opposing fossil energy and demanding renewables. In fact the struggle for reforms can offer the only real road to revolutionary change. It depends on the framework and situation in which they are advanced, and the dynamics of struggle they generate.

The strategic task we face today, therefore, if we are to halt global warming and defend the ecology of the planet, is to force capitalism to make major changes as an integral part of the struggle for a future socialist or ecosocialist society. In the end, only this kind of struggle can get us beyond the parameters of the capitalist system.

The task today, therefore, is not first and foremost whether we can overturn capitalism in next 20 years, but whether we can force it to introduce major measures to protect the planet as a part of an ongoing struggle for the eventual overturn of capitalism and its replacement by an ecosocialist society. If we are unable to build the kind of movement capable of forcing major change under capitalism, how are we going to build a movement capable of overturning it?

The most effective way to cut carbon emissions quickly and democratically is by making fossil fuels much more expensive than renewable energy, by means that are socially just, economically redistributive, and capable of commanding popular support – and in the two or three decades that remain to us.

I would argue that the best proposal on the table is Hanson's fee and dividend proposal that is outlined in chapter 11.

Nor is it true, as many on the left imply, that capitalism cannot be forced to take such measures. If that were case we would indeed be in deep trouble. There have already been important changes won while capitalism continues to exist – over airport expansion, for example, and against nuclear power in Germany and Japan. The international campaign to save the whales in the 1970s and 1980s resulted in the 1986 moratorium on commercial whaling and massively reduced the rapacious slaughter that had been taking place since the middle of the nineteenth century. Currently, Japan, Russia, and a number of other nations continue to oppose this moratorium.

The hole in the ozone layer has also been repaired, for now at least, by an 80 per cent reduction in the use of CFCs since the signing of the Montréal Protocol in 1987. The recent decision (in England) to impose charges on plastic bags can make a huge difference in terms of plastic pollution. Just look at the impact of BBC TV's *Blue Planet II* on the plastic pollution and biodiversity debate. Even the current inadequate level of renewable energy now being generated would not exist but for decades of campaigning by environmentalists. In fact, the chance to make fundamental change is created in the course of the struggle for partial and immediate change.

A transitional approach

Maximalism, we can conclude, is taking us nowhere. We need instead what Michael Löwy in *Ecosocialism: A Radical Alternative to Capitalist Catastrophe* terms a transitional approach. He puts it this way:

Not having illusions about 'ecologising' capitalism does not mean that one cannot join the battle for immediate reforms... The struggle for ecosocialist reforms can be the vehicle for dynamic change, a 'transition' between minimal demands and the maximal programme' – in other words, a transitional approach.[143]

Derek Wall also advocates such an approach in *The Rise of the Green Left*, where he puts it this way: 'developing transitional policies is especially important so that real progress towards ecosocialism can be made, rather than reforming an unsustainable and unjust system so that it can continue a little longer.'[144]

With this approach each small victory and partial advance contributes to the growth of an ecological and socialist consciousness, and can take us to a higher and more radical stage of the struggle. Such advances, such victories, promote the kind of self-organisation that is a decisive precondition for the kind of radical transformation of the world that we are struggling for in the longer term. In fact revolutionary transformation is only possible through the self-emancipation of the oppressed and the exploited: workers and peasants, women, indigenous communities, and all those stigmatised because of their race, religion or nationality, sexuality or impairment.

This approach will allow us to propose a new form of living, richer in human qualities – a new society based on the values of human dignity, solidarity, freedom and respect for 'Mother Nature'.

A good example of a transitional demand today is the 1.5°C limit recommended by Paris and now adopted by the IPCC. The contradiction for the UN, and its member states, is that despite the proposal being made within a capitalist framework, the 1.5°C and its implementation is a challenge to the logic of capitalism and its profit motive. It is at the same time a key demand around which the movement can organise. The task for ecosocialists, and indeed for the wider movement, is therefore to demand its full implementation, and to build the movement and advance the struggle in the process. Anything less would be to deny the movement its best chance to take the struggle forward.

The real choice is not between forcing major change whilst capitalism still exists or socialist revolution. The choice, actually, is between forcing capitalism to make major change in the course of the struggle for socialism, or capitalism doing things its way by repressive and regressive means. This means, crucially, the development of an exit strategy from fossil energy that offers a solution in the time scale of mere decades – a solution that is open to us as discussed above.

Should the polluters be taxed?

Most of the fossil fuels must the left in the ground. That is the explicit message that science provides.

James Hansen.[145]

O ne thing is clear when it comes to carbon emissions, that is that as long as fossil fuel remains the cheapest way to generate energy it is going to be used. An important mechanism, therefore, for bringing about big reductions in carbon emissions in a short period of time must be carbon pricing – making the polluters pay. This means levying heavy taxes or fees on carbon emissions, as a part of a strongly progressive and redistributive taxation system, that can win mass popular support.

Major carbon taxes already exist in most countries in the form of taxes on petrol and diesel for road usage that is not part of such an agenda, or not sufficiently so. It is important that the left defends the need for carbon taxes and presents them in the context of a redistribution of money from the rich to the poor.

Unsurprisingly the fossil fuel producers and the governments behind them, such as the USA, Russia and China, are strongly opposed to carbon taxes and fight to keep them to a minimum. They have already successfully excluded key carbon generating sectors from such taxes. There is a whole lobbying industry – led by the right-wing free market Cato Institute in the USA – devoted to opposing carbon taxes. When Al Gore, as vice-president to Bill Clinton, tried in 1993 to introduce a mild form of carbon tax, they ensured it never happened.

Aviation and maritime fuels, as a result, remain completely untaxed, although they account for a rising share of global energy-related carbon emissions (currently at 4 per cent). These fuels were explicitly excluded from the Kyoto Protocol and they are not subject to the taxes widely applied to road transportation fuels. There have been some important campaigns around this, led by Oxfam and the World Wildlife Fund (WWF) for example.

Carbon taxes and the left

It might be expected that the left would support such measures – but this is not the case. In fact most on the radical left oppose such taxes with a ferocity that is hard to understand. Interestingly, most of those who hold this position don't call for the repeal of the already existing carbon taxes on petrol and diesel, for example. This is presumably because they don't want to be associated with what is in fact a right-wing climate denialist agenda.

The Australian Marxist, Dick North, is the author of *Environment, Capitalism and Socialism*, a document of the Australian Democratic Socialist Party (DSP) published by Resistance Books in 1999. In his appendix, North strongly opposes carbon taxes, arguing that little or nothing can be done to curb carbon emissions whilst capitalism exists – so what is the point of carbon taxes? He puts it this way:

> Those who call for such taxes have to explain exactly how a system that has consumed more resources and energy in the last 50 years than all previous human civilisation can be made to stabilise and then reduce its rate of resource depletion and pollution emission. How can this monstrous wasteful, poisonous and unequal economic system actually be made to introduce the technologies, consumption patterns and radical income distribution without which all talk of sustainability is a sick joke.[146]

Daniel Tanuro, writing in *Green Capitalism: Why It Can't Work* (2010), takes a similar view, and points out why carbon taxes offer no solution:

> Let us suppose for a moment – a hypothesis from political fiction – that a strong global power were able to impose an overall price for CO_2 related to climate constraints. It is obvious that the large corporations would pass the cost on to the end-users.[147]

Energy producers would indeed pass carbon taxes on to their customers and the price would go up – in the end that is what reduces demand. This would be the case, however, whatever form of restriction was placed on fossil fuels: by government decision or by some form of rationing. Just saying 'Keep the oil in the soil and the coal in the hole', as is (rightly) demanded by environmentalists, would also imply that the price of fossil fuel would be driven up. Rationing would also see the rise of a black market. The question is how to place such measures in a progressive/redistributive framework. The same thing arises with economic or health taxes. Not every carbon tax is progressive or supportable, of course. But taxing pollution as a general principle is a necessary and effective weapon in our armoury against global warming and climate change.

Such taxes have to go alongside a range of other measures, of course, such as a complete changeover to renewable energy, a major programme of energy conservation, an end to waste and obsolescent production, a big reduction in the use of the internal combustion engine, both diesel and petrol, the localisation of food agricultural production, fresh water conservation, a big reduction in meat consumption, a shorter working week – the list could go on. Carbon taxes, properly applied, however, can be the driving force that can bring down carbon emissions rapidly and open the door to wider change.

It is an approach that has the potential to generate the level of popular support that would make such a reduction possible to achieve. It is an exit strategy from fossil fuels that does not require a global socialist revolution as a prerequisite but rather would be a part of an ongoing struggle towards socialist, or ecosocialist, revolution.

The left should – in fact already does – support general taxation that is economically progressive: *i.e.* redistributive. Why therefore oppose carbon taxes when they are equally progressive, in other words bring about emissions reduction whilst ensuring that the poor and the worse-off are fully protected?

Carbon taxes can indeed be regressive if they are framed in the wrong way, but the job of the left and environmental activists is to ensure that the opposite is the case, that they are introduced as a part of an overall taxation system that is socially progressive that compensates the poorest people when they are disproportionately affected by a particular tax. It is perfectly possible to do this; it is a political choice.

Carbon taxes are not 'greenwash'

Nor are carbon taxes 'greenwash', as often claimed on the radical left, and nor should they be confused with or associated with carbon trading as promoted by Kyoto and the UN: schemes such as the Clean Development Mechanism, the Joint Implementation Mechanism, and the EU Emissions Trading Scheme. These initiatives are at best window-dressing and at worst, a license to pollute under cover and make a profit at the same time.

Carbon taxes can be successful at many different levels. According to Britain's Department for Environment, Food and Rural Affairs (Defra) the 5p charge introduced in Britain in 2016 on single-use plastic bags resulted in an immediate 83 per cent reduction in plastic bag usage. More than 7 billion bags were handed out by seven main supermarkets in the year before the 5p charge – some of which goes to charity – but this plummeted to slightly more than 500 million in the first six months after the charge was introduced.

Britain wasn't the first country to take action against single-use plastic bags – Bangladesh imposed a complete ban on such bags in 2002. Some countries have issued partial bans and others have schemes similar to that in Britain. Those that have taken action include South Africa, Rwanda, Kenya, China, Macedonia and Italy. Action in terms of the wider issue of plastic waste is also now urgently needed.

British Columbia

There have been several examples in recent years of governments either introducing new or higher revenue neutral carbon taxes, or attempting to do so. One was the introduction of a carbon tax scheme in Canada's British Columbia (BC); another was the proposal for such a scheme in the neighbouring Washington State in the USA. Both were controversial on the left and amongst climate campaigners.

In 2008, the government of British Columbia announced its intention to implement a carbon tax of C$10 per tonne of carbon dioxide equivalent (CO_2e) emissions (2.41 cents per litre at the pumps) beginning in July 2008. The tax was to increase each year until 2012, reaching a final price of C$30 per tonne (7.2 cents per litre at the pumps). Government spending was to be kept revenue neutral, by reducing corporate and income taxes by an equivalent amount.

The main problem with the scheme – however you evaluate the principles that were involved – was that the maximum figure adopted, of 30 Canadian dollars a tonne, was never going to be enough to make any real difference to anything. Norway, for example, has carbon taxes at a much higher level – around $65 per tonne.

Washington

In 2016 a measure similar in broad principle was proposed for ballot in the neighbouring state of Washington in the USA – which became known as People's Initiative 732. It also imposed a steadily rising levy on carbon emissions, while offsetting the consequent price rises by cutting the state's sales and increasing the state's tax credit for low-income families.

Still, it was a far more substantial proposition than the British Columbia example, and had been put forward by a group of environmentalists called CarbonWA, led by Yoram Bauman, an economist and stand-up comedian. It was also controversial, and opposed by the left but also by most of the other climate groups in the state – who were grouped within the Alliance for Jobs and Clean Energy. They sought, unsuccessfully, to promote their own proposition on to the ballot paper. A useful account of all this has been written by eco-journalist David Roberts.[148]

People's Initiative 732 would have introduced a carbon tax on emissions starting at $15 per tonne in 2017, rising to $25 per tonne in 2018, and then rising every year thereafter at 3.5 per cent plus inflation, topping out at $100 a tonne. The price itself would have nudged the economy towards clean energy by making prices tell the truth about the cost of pollution.

In terms of CO_2 emissions reductions, Dave Roberts points out that the US Energy Information Administration's modelling suggested that a levy of around $60 per tonne by 2040 would slash electricity-sector pollution by two-thirds; and that the thinktank Resources for the Future predicted that a pollution levy on a path to reach $100 by 2050 would cut electricity-sector emissions by more than half by 2035. Roberts points out that:

> Researchers have also approached the problem of global warming pollution from the
> other direction, trying to calculate how much each ton of pollution costs us in damaged

health, reduced productivity, increased risk of flood and fire, and increased costs for air conditioning. They call this the 'social cost of carbon' and the estimated damages per ton of pollution are remarkably similar to modelling of the price per ton needed to cut pollution: the social cost of carbon rises to about $100 per ton in 2050.

Although CarbonWA obtained the necessary 300,000 signatures to get the proposition on the ballot paper – a prodigious effort in itself – the proposition was narrowly defeated in the ballot. Whether opposition from the left or from other climate campaigners tipped the balance, is difficult to tell.

The People's Initiative 732 embodied two important redistributive measures to offset the price rises and protect low income people. There would be a working families' tax rebate that would have provided up to $1,500 a year for 460,000 low-income households, and there would be a 1 per cent reduction. This was important because Washington has no personal income tax, which means it relies on the sales tax which is socially regressive – *i.e.* it hits low income people the hardest.

Far more controversially, the proposition would have cut the Washington State business and occupations (B&O) taxes for manufacturers by about $450 million per year, in an attempt to prevent manufacturers from relocating outside Washington as a result of the carbon tax. It would also have been revenue neutral, which was a gesture to those opposed to 'big government'.

The disputes that arose, then, were the priorities on which the money raised from the tax should be spent – disputes that were never resolved and no doubt had a negative impact on the vote.

In the event the proposition fell, although it won 41 per cent of the vote.

Such schemes were not wrong in principle, but in the specifics of the proposal. The devil, in other words, was in the detail.

Hansen's fee and dividend proposal

The best proposal currently on the table in this regard, in my view, is James Hansen's fee-and-dividend proposition. This seeks to provide an effective framework for a very big reduction in fossil fuel emissions, here and now whilst capitalism still exists.

Hansen's starting point is that, from a scientific point of view, a rapid reduction in greenhouse gas emissions is a non-negotiable necessity. He spells it out this way:

> Global phase-out of fossil carbon dioxide emissions is a stringent requirement. Proposed government policies, consisting of an improved Kyoto Protocol approach with more ambitious targets, do not have a prayer of achieving that result. Our governments are deceiving us, and perhaps conveniently deceiving themselves, when they say that it is possible to reduce emissions 80 per cent by 2050 with such an approach.[149]

Hansen argues that simply slowing down the rate of carbon emissions is far from enough; and that if the climate cliff is to be avoided, the rising carbon content of the atmosphere does not just have to be halted, but has to be taken back to 350ppm by the end of the century. Most fossil fuels, first and foremost coal, he therefore argues, must be left in the ground. That, he insists, 'is the explicit message that science provides.'

If coal emissions can be phased out rapidly, he argues – which is 'a tall order but a feasible one' the climate problem is solvable. Theoretically, he argues, this could be done by carbon capture and storage; but since from a scientific point of view that concept of 'clean coal' is an oxymoron, fossil fuel, particularly coal which is the dirtiest, will have to stay in the ground. If fossil fuels are phased out by 2030, he argues, CO_2 levels in the atmosphere could be held to a level of 'only' 425 ppm (parts per million) by 2050.

Hansen first launched his fee-and-dividend proposal as the practical conclusion of his remarkable 2009 book *Storms of my Grandchildren: The Truth About the Coming Climate Catastrophe and the Last Chance to Save Humanity.* (Note: 'the Last Chance to Save Humanity').

Despite Hansen's record as the world's pre-eminent climate scientist and the person who triggered the climate movement at the end of the 1980 with his game-changing confrontations with the US Senate, most socialist and Marxist environmentalists are either actively opposed to his proposal or indifferent to it. This is because, I presume, it does not explicitly call for the end of capitalism. It is, however, in my view, strongly in a transitional framework.

Hansen rejects carbon trading as a useless con, and advocates instead what he calls a fee-and-dividend system to facilitate the transition to a carbon-free economy. His proposal is to make CO_2 emissions prohibitively expensive and provide an alternative based on renewables, whilst fully compensating the majority of the population – by definition the poorest sections of society – for the cost of the scheme.

His proposal provides an exit strategy from fossil fuel based on the principle of making the polluters pay, and with the potential for mobilising the kind of popular support that would be necessary for such rapid change. It would need, as Hansen recognises, to go alongside many other measures, such as crash changeover to renewable energy, a major programme of energy conservation, an end to waste and obsolescent production, a big reduction in the use of the internal combustion engine, both diesel and petrol, the localisation of food agricultural production, a big reduction in meat consumption, fresh water conservation, a shorter working week.

He also calls for a ban on fracking and tar sand extraction, as well as the closure of all coal and gas production that is not subjected to carbon capture and storage; and since the technology does not exist, this means an all-out ban. He also says that it would have to go alongside measures such as reusing, recycling, rationing, energy reduction and retention measures. It would mean the ending of all subsidies to fossil fuel companies, for a global transition to sustainable farming practices, and for substantial aid to developing countries for the implementation of these measures.

It is not easy, but it is radical, and it can be done.

How it works

Hansen's proposal involves placing a uniform fee (or levy) on the fossil fuel production, at the pithead, the wellhead or at the port of entry, for each ton of carbon produced. The fee would start low and increase annually until renewable energy is competitive with fossil fuels. It would be easy to collect and hard to evade. The result would be to increase the price of goods that had been manufactured or transported by fossil fuel, along with fossil fuel used for domestic purposes.

The revenue generated from the fees would be distributed as dividends to the population as a whole on an individual (per capita) basis – with half shares for children up to two children per family (though restricting this to two children seems problematic). Those who reduce their carbon footprint the most would stand to benefit the most. Consumers would be motivated to spend the money they receive as dividend on increasing cheap and available renewable energy (and its derivatives) rather than on increasingly expensive fossil fuels and their derivatives.

They could do this by changing over to energy efficient lighting and appliances, upgrading their insulation, replacing energy inefficient boilers, switching to green energy sources, and buying fossil free or fossil light goods and services and methods of transport. Equally with businesses, the incentive would be to become more energy efficient and convert to green energy, otherwise they would become uncompetitive.

The dividend would be transferred directly into each person's bank account or onto an electronic card if they do not have a bank account. Hansen gives the following example of how it would work:

> As an example. Consider the point in time at which the fee will reach the level of $115 per ton on carbon dioxide. A fee of that level will increase the cost of gasoline by $1 per gallon and the average cost of electricity by around 8 cents per kilowatt-hour. Given the amount of oil, gas, and coal sold in the US in 2007, $115 per ton will yield $670bn. The resulting dividend will be close to $3,000 per year, or $250 per month, for each adult resident. A family with two or more children would receive in the range of $8,000 to 9,000 per year.[150]

Some 60 per cent of the population would receive net economic benefits from this: the dividends they received back would exceed the increased prices paid – and these net benefits would increase if they were to reduce their carbon footprints further. And since this is a fee imposed on companies who are among the biggest users of fossil fuels, it would give them the incentive to develop alternative energy sources and keep the fossil fuels in the ground.

It would, Hansen argues, be a form of progressive taxation, since those with the most expensive lifestyles will pay out a lot more than the $9,000 they will get back in dividend. He calculates that the results of the scheme should be that the 40 per cent of richer people should end up paying more whilst the 60 per cent would directly benefit. Low-income people can gain by limiting their emissions, he argues. 'People with multiple houses, or who fly around the world a lot, will pay more in increased prices than they obtain in the dividend.'

He says that he prefers this system rather than normal government taxation procedures is because he does not trust governments to do it. They are, he argues, not only politically suspect but are 'virtually arms of the fossil fuel industry'. If the fees are distributed directly to the public, he asserts, people will be prepared to allow them to rise to high and effective levels, unlike the ineffective cap and trade schemes.

The further advantage is that, because of its socially progressive nature, it would generate mass popular support, which other methods of carbon reduction could not achieve. A tax imposed by government without this progressive element would simply push up prices and cause resentment. Rationing, which is another possibility, would be difficult to administer and would generate a black market.

Economic modeling for the USA, Hansen argues, 'shows that [even] a mere $10 per ton CO_2 fee, rising by $10 each year, would reduce emissions by 30 per cent after a decade – more than a factor of 10 greater than the oil carried by the proposed Keystone XL pipeline, rendering that pipeline superfluous.' A crucial principle of this approach, he argues, is that there must be no way around the scheme or of avoiding the fee; or in the jargon of the industry, no 'offsets'. He says:

> A successful new policy cannot include any offsets. We specified the carbon limit based on the geophysics. The physics does not compromise – it is what it is. And planting of additional trees cannot be factored into the fossil fuel limitations. The plan for getting back to 350 ppm assumes major reforestation, but it is *additional* to the fossil fuel limit, not *instead* of.[151]

Hansen bases his proposal on the assumption that other major changes will be necessary to stabilise the climate of the planet, in addition to introducing fee and dividend on fossil fuels. This needs to involve changes to lifestyle, tackling the issue of rising human population, and introducing renewable energy systems – though unfortunately he argues for the inclusion of nuclear power in the mix of technologies that should be used.

In terms of rising human population, he says the following:

> I do not want to wander far into these subjects, but it would be inappropriate not to mention the connection between population and climate change. The stress that humans place on the planet, and on other species on the planet, is closely related to human population growth. Stabilisation of atmospheric composition and climate almost surely requires a stabilisation of human population.
>
> The encouraging news is that there is a strong correlation between reduced fertility rates, increased economic well-being, and women's rights and education... The substantial funds that will necessarily be generated by an increasing fee on fossil fuel carbon should be used to reward the places that encourage practices and rights that correlate with sustainable populations.[152]

The only exception to this is Hansen's fee and dividend proposal, that would reduce the production of fossil fuel by reducing the demand for it.

Nor is Hansen's proposal dependent on an international agreement; it can be fought for through the national political arena in every country.

Important support

Not all Marxist ecologists, however, oppose Hansen's proposal. It has been strongly supported by John Bellamy Foster, Brett Clark and Richard York, no less, in their jointly authored book *The Ecological Rift: Capitalism's War on the Earth*, published in 2010. In the chapter 'Transition Strategies' they argue that Hansen's proposal is especially noteworthy:

> Hansen's emergency strategy, with its monthly dividends, is designed to keep carbon in the ground and at the same time appeal to the general public. It explicitly circumvents both the market and state power in order to block those who desire to subvert the process. In this there is the hope to establish a mass popular constituency for combatting climate change by promoting social redistribution of wealth towards those with smaller carbon footprints (*i.e.* the greater part of the population) ...[153]

They go on:

Such a proposal would mean that the rich nations would have to reduce their carbon emissions very rapidly by levels approaching 100 per cent, and a massive global effort would be needed to help countries in the global south to move towards emission stabilisation as well, while not jeopardising sustainable human development.[154]

And they conclude that:

In reality, the radical proposals discussed above, though ostensibly transitional strategies, present the issue of revolutionary change. Their implementation would require a popular revolt against the system itself. A movement (or movements) powerful enough to implement a full-scale social ecological revolution.[155]

John Bellamy Foster

John Bellamy Foster returned to the issue three years later in a *Monthly Review* article entitled 'James Hansen and the Climate Exit Strategy'.[156] He argued that:

The advantage of Hansen's fee and dividend scheme from a climate change standpoint is that it is directly aimed at making the fossil-fuel companies – those who take the fossil fuels out of the ground – pay, while increasing the price of carbon to decrease consumption in every nook and cranny of the economy. It also makes it possible to raise carbon prices to the extent required for a rapid phase out of fossil fuels, while garnering the necessary mass support. 'The public will only allow an adequate rising price on carbon,' he contends, 'if the system is simple and transparent with the proceeds distributed to the public'.

He goes on to say that

Hansen's climate-change exit strategy represents what is clearly a calculated attempt to push through the maximum plan that the regime of capital could conceivably accept, and the minimum necessary to avoid complete disaster. It represents a heroic effort to promote the formation of political-economic conditions that will prevent the world from crossing a catastrophic climate tipping point.

He says, however, that it does not

> address the question of capitalism and the accumulation imperative that drives
> such a system, which has obvious implications for any long-term strategy of climate
> or environmental stabilisation.

By the end of the article, however, he is arguing that Hansen's proposal is objectively revolutionary:

> What is objectively revolutionary in Hansen's proposal is its root in a shared sense of
> emergency and crisis that can be readily communicated at the center of the system
> in the monopoly-finance capital economies themselves. The greatest potential
> of Hansen's steadily increasing carbon fee and dividend is that its results would
> reverberate in every aspect of the society and economy. It would make clear, as
> never before at the level of everyday life, the class nature of carbon footprints and the
> increasing destruction of the planet as a place of human habitation. And it would soon
> be evident that the radical kinds of changes that would need to be introduced into the
> whole constellation of production, distribution, and consumption relations could not
> 'be effected except by means of despotic inroads on the rights of property, and on the
> conditions of bourgeois production; by means of measures, therefore, which appear
> economically insufficient and untenable, but which, in the course of the movement,
> outstrip themselves, necessitate further inroads upon the old social order, and are
> unavoidable as a means of entirely revolutionising the mode of production.

I strongly agree with that assessment. Foster, in my view, has made an important contribution to the struggle against climate change by bringing Hansen's proposal to the attention of the left, and it will hopefully be taken a lot more seriously as the discussion develops. It is not the finished product as far as an exit strategy is concerned, but it is a much-needed big idea with a potentially big impact on the debate, and is a good start that should be built on. If the left is going to play a role in that, it has to be able to shake off some of the misconceptions of the past.

A major problem with other forms of carbon taxes mentioned earlier is the difficulty of winning broad consent for the scale of measures that would be needed in the time scale available. So, measures with no mobilising dynamic that would rely on government authority (or coercion) for implementation are not helpful.

An interesting article appeared recently in the 2018 summer issue of *Jacobin* by Anders Fremstad and Mark Paul, entitled *With a carbon tax and dividend, we can fight climate change — and reduce inequality*: it gave strong support to a version of a fee and dividend scheme proposed by the People's Policy Project.[157]

12 Economic growth and productivism

Our assaults on the ecosystem are so powerful, so numerous, so finely interconnected, that although the damage they do is clear, it is very difficult to discover how it was done. By which weapon? In who's hand? Are we driving the ecosphere to destruction simply by our growing numbers? By our greedy accumulation of wealth? Or are the machines which we have built to gain this wealth – the magnificent technology that now feeds us out of neat packages, that clothes us in man-made fibers, that surrounds us with new chemical creations – at fault?

Barry Commoner.[158]

The matter of economic growth and productivism have long been a problem on the British left: though it is better understood today than in the past. The socialist left in Britain supported economic growth for most of the 20th century, in both the Labour Party and the trade unions. In the 1980s, for example, the strategic bible of the Bennite left (inside and outside of the Labour Party) was a 150 page document entitled *The Alternative Economic Strategy*.[159] A key chapter entitled 'A Policy for Expansion' starts with the following: "The essential basis for any alternative economic strategy must be a policy for planned economic expansion".[160] The ecology of the planet is not mentioned anywhere in its pages. Today, the left has a stronger critique of growth than in the past, although it is far from universal, and it remains a particular problem in the unions.

The greens had far less baggage in this regard, although even there the discussion was underdeveloped. Derek Wall makes the following point in his book *Earth First! – and the anti-roads movement*:

By 1991 I had been active in the green movement for over a decade and had become increasingly interested in political strategy. Greens seemed to me to have a devastating critique of social and ecological ills, showing how a society based on ever-increasing economic growth is unsustainable and fundamentally unjust; they also had an attractive vision of an alternative society. Yet the movement in its very diverse manifestations seemed strategically naïve, having a limited conception of how fundamental economic and political forces that thrive on continuous productivist growth might be challenged.[161]

Growth is, however, a pivotal issue. Nicholas Stern, in *The Stern Review*, having pointed to the disastrous implications of the ecological crisis, not only insists that it can be resolved by market mechanisms, but that it can be done without interrupting economic growth in either the rich countries or the poor (as mentioned above in chapter 8). He puts it this way:

> The evidence shows that ignoring climate change will eventually damage economic growth. Our actions over the coming few decades could create risks of major disruption to economic and social activity, later in this century and in the next, on a scale similar to those associated with the great wars and the economic depression of the first half of the 20th century. And it will be difficult or impossible to reverse these changes. Tackling climate change is the pro-growth strategy for the longer term, and it can be done in a way that does not cap the aspirations for growth of rich or poor countries. [162]

This was, no doubt, exactly what Gordon Brown wanted to hear when he commissioned the *Report*. It is the standard establishment position. Or as Naomi Klein puts it in *This Changes Everything*: 'steady exponential material growth with no limits on resource consumption and population is the dominant conceptual model used by today's decision makers.'[163]

It is, however, total nonsense. Economic growth, along with population growth, is one of the main drivers of global warming and environmental destruction, and it cannot continue at its current rate without disastrous results. As the global economy grows, so does environmental pollution and global warming. Natural resources become over-exploited to the point of exhaustion. More waste is dumped into the global ecosystem than it can safely absorb, leading to dysfunction and collapse. The process and the consequences could hardly be clearer. Such a view was endorsed by the IPCC (no less) in its *Assessment of Measures to Mitigate Climate Change Report* published in April 2014. It puts it this way:

Globally, economic and population growth continue to be the most important drivers of increases in CO_2 emissions from fossil fuel combustion. The contribution of population growth between 2000 and 2010 remained roughly identical to the previous three decades, while the contribution of economic growth has risen sharply.[164]

Kate Raworth, in her 2017 book *Doughnut Economics – Seven Ways to Think Like a 21st Century Economist*,[165] does an important demolition job on mainstream economic theory that fails to integrate the environmental crisis into its analysis, but she does not oppose economic growth as such. We need economies, she argues, that take the ecological crisis into account whether or not they are based on growth.

The Limits to Growth Report

The problem of growth was clearly recognised in the 1972 book *The Limits to Growth Report* that had been commissioned by the Club of Rome and published by Universal Books NY.[166] [167] The *Report* sold 12 million copies, was translated into 37 languages, and remains the top-selling environmental title ever published. It was influential – along with Rachel Carson's *Silent Spring* 10 years earlier – in stimulating the emergence of the modern environmental movement that was taking place at the time.

The message of the *Report* was that it is impossible to have exponential growth in a finite system like the Earth without its systems sooner or later collapsing. It was attacked by the establishment, whilst the left was divided. The Austrian Frankfurt School philosopher and ecologist André Gorz defended the *Report* in his 1980 book *Ecology as Politics*. He said the following in response to critics.

> Even if the figures in the Meadows Report (*The Limits to Growth Report*) are unreliable, the fundamental truth of its thesis remains unchanged. Physical growth has physical limits, and any attempt to push them back (by recycling and purification) only pushes the problem around…[168]

The *Report* was strongly defended by Tim Jackson[169] in his 2009 book *Prosperity Without Growth*.[170] *The Limits to Growth*, he says, 'with the advantage of hindsight', has turned out to be a 'remarkably accurate' analysis.[171] Today, he says:

> Questioning growth is deemed to be the act of lunatics, idealists, and revolutionaries...
> But question it we must. The idea of a non-growing economy may be an anathema
> to an economist. But the idea of a continually growing economy is anathema to an
> ecologist. No subsystem of a finite system can grow indefinitely, in physical terms.
> Economists have to be able to answer the question of how a continually growing
> economic system can fit within a finite ecological system.

On population growth he says the following:

> A world in which things simply go on as usual is already inconceivable. But what
> about a world in which it an estimated 9 billion people all achieve the level of
> affluence expected in the OECD nations? Such an economy would need to be 15
> times the size of today's economy (75 times what it was in 1950) by 2050, and
> 40 times bigger than today's economy (200 times bigger than 1950) by the end of
> the century. What on earth does such an economy look like? What does it run on?
> Does it really offer a credible vision for a shared and lasting prosperity? ...[172]

In December 2012, Christian Parenti reviewed the *Report* on its fortieth
birthday in an article in *The Nation*. He says the following:

> In the spring of 1972, a slim book called *The Limits to Growth* dropped like
> an intellectual bomb on the developed world's most optimistic assumptions
> about itself. Peppered with computer-generated graphs and written in clear,
> dispassionate language by a team of MIT [Massachusetts Institute of Technology]
> graduate students led by two young scholars, Dennis and Donella Meadows, the
> book delivered a seemingly extreme argument, which ran as follows: if 1970
> rates of economic growth, resource use and pollution continued unchanged, then
> modern civilisation would face environmental and economic collapse sometime
> in the mid-twenty-first century. Yes, collapse – as in massive human die-offs.

A report published in 2006 by the left-of-centre New Economics Foundation,
entitled *Growth Isn't Working: Why We Need a New Economic Direction,* makes
the following observations:

Globally we are consuming the nations' services – using resources and creating carbon emissions – 44 per cent faster than nature can regenerate and reabsorb what we consume and the waste we produce. In other words, it takes the Earth almost 18 months to produce the ecological services that humanity uses in one year. The UK's footprint has grown such that if the whole world wished to consume at the same rate it would require 3.4 planets like the Earth.

Even Al Gore in his 2013 book *The Future* points out that:

The rapid growth of human civilisation – in the number of people, the power of technology, the size of the global economy – is colliding with approaching limits to the supply of key natural resources on which millions of lives depend, including topsoil and freshwater. It is also seriously damaging to the integrity of crucial planetary ecological systems. Yet 'growth' in the peculiar and self-defeating way we define it, continues to be the principal and overriding objective of almost all the global economic policies and the business plans of almost all corporations.[173]

Gore quotes the World Bank to the effect that the per capita production of garbage from urban residents in the world is now 2.6 pounds per person per day, and is projected to increase rapidly, with most of the increase in the developing countries. When you add to this the waste produced by energy production, the making of chemicals, manufacturing, paper production and agricultural waste the volume is enormous. In fact, the volume of waste created every day weighs more than the combined weight of the 7 billion inhabitants of the planet![174]

John Bellamy Foster spelled out the problems of economic growth very clearly when he spoke in London in July 2016.[175] He pointed out that a rate of growth of 3 per cent per year (that has been the average for the past 60 years) would grow the world economy by a factor of sixteen in the course of a century and by a factor of 250 over the course of this century and the next. Such growth rates, he said, are completely unsustainable.

Growth and campaigning

The establishment mantra has long been that green growth, which would be benign, will resolve the problem. That was the theme at the 2012 United

Nations Conference on Sustainable Development in Rio de Janeiro. Today, it is a core plank of the UN Sustainable Development Targets. But green growth turns out to have been based more on wishful thinking than evidence. In the years since Rio three major studies have arrived at the same conclusion: that even under the best conditions, the decoupling of GDP from resource application is not possible on a global scale.

The Marxist economist Özlem Onaran raised the issue of growth in her 2009 review, entitled *Climate Jobs and the Limits of Growth,* of the pamphlet *One Million Climate Jobs,*[176] published by the Campaign against Climate Change Trade Union Group in Britain.[177]

Her contention was that the CACCTUG pamphlet – which rightly (and importantly) campaigned for a million climate jobs as a central part of the struggle against climate change – had, in effect, a pro-growth position. She puts it this way:

> First, if the campaign achieves its aim of increased efficiency in renewable energy, this may radically reduce the share of expenditures on energy in the household budget. This is the rebound effect, which has been ignored in the pamphlet. This works as an increase in the real income of the households, and triggers additional expenditure in non-energy consumption, which again increases greenhouse gas emissions.

Secondly, we cannot seriously solve the problem of climate change unless we face the limits to global growth: if the use of environmental resources is to maintain a certain 'sustainable' level, global economic growth in the long term has to be zero or low, *i.e.* equal to the growth rate of 'environmental productivity'. Furthermore, advanced capitalist countries like Britain need to de-grow (slow down) to create space for development in the Global South as part of a broader strategy of climate justice. This type of zero-growth or even de-growth, however, has nothing to do with the disastrous recession caused by the crisis. This is a managed zero-growth path in the long run that redistributes existing wealth in accordance with the needs of the majority.

The ecological crisis we face is a result of an economic model based on growth. Excessive consumption of natural resources, especially of fossil fuels, in the West (and by rich sections of the population in developing countries) now poses grave threats to survival of life on our planet; and these threats are immediate rather than distant. In order to avoid the irreversible damage to our ecology that threatens life on Earth, we need to make a transition towards an ecological society that keeps economic growth under check, a society that breaks from the productivism of both capitalism and the previous so-called 'socialist' countries.

The radical left

Stalinism played a significant role in promoting economic growth and productivism in the post-war period, not least in the unions. The whole world – on both sides of the iron curtain – emerged from World War II thoroughly productivist. In the Stalinist states, Stakhanovism was dominant, despite the environmental measures taken by the Bolsheviks in the early years of the October Revolution.[178] Western Marxism – mainstream Marxism in the Global North, mainly but not only of the Communist parties (CPs) – was now devoid of any detectable ecological legacy from classical Marxism. As John Bellamy Foster put it recently, Marxism at that time was 'in denial of the dialectic of nature'.[179] The CPs were dominated by Stalinism and productivism, which was the orthodoxy of the whole of the left – both Marxist and socialist. Ecological issues were either ignored or denounced as a middleclass diversion from the 'real' struggles of the workers' movement around wages, working conditions, and the standard of living.

Even Trotskyists, the arch opponents of Stalinism, were not much better when it came to the environment. None of the Trotskyist groupings established in Britain in the post-war period displayed any interest in it. It is true that they were small beleaguered organisations taking on the Stalinist monolith and persecuted at every turn, but this is not an adequate explanation. It was a serious weakness, with consequences for the struggle to defend both the planet and the role of Marxism in the second half of the twentieth century.

Derek Wall points out in his 2010 book *The Rise of the Green Left* that Trotsky himself falls into the same trap.[180] Trotsky may have been a changer of history, a central leader of the Russian revolution, the creator of the Red Army, and the principal opponent of Stalin and Stalinisation; but he was not an environmentalist.[181] He was not only an advocate of productivism, but his views on the relationship between human beings and nature were no better. In *Literature and Revolution* (published in 1923) he said the following:

> ... nature will become more 'artificial'. The present distribution of the mountains and rivers, of fields, of meadows, of steppes, of forests, and of seashores, cannot be considered final. Man has already made changes in the map of nature that are few and insignificant. But they are mere pupil's practice in comparison to what is coming... Man will occupy himself re-registering mountains and rivers, and will earnestly and repeatedly make improvements in nature. In the end, he will have rebuilt the Earth, if not in his own image, at least according to his own taste. We have not the slightest fear that this will be bad.[182]

Wall adds, with justification, that Trotsky should not be singled out on this. What he reflected was the dominant view on the left at this time, including Marxists. The radical left shared these ideas with both the Stalinised USSR and Maoist China. As Derek Wall says, with this as the dominant position of the left at that time, it was unsurprising that many contemporary ecologists and greens came to see Marxism and socialism as anti-environmental traditions.

13 The Stalinist legacy

He who does not cry out the truth when he knows the truth becomes the accomplice of the liars and falsifiers.

Victor Serge[183]

Capitalism had ceased to exist, for most of the twentieth century, in over a third of the world, replaced by the 'planned economies' of the Stalinist states, in the shape of the Soviet Union, Eastern Europe and China. Yet environmental destruction in these countries was on a par with capitalism itself, and in many cases worse.[184] The ecological record of the Soviet Union, for example, was a disaster. It became notorious for polluted landscapes and rivers, deforestation, dustbowls (created by the virgin lands project), brown coal smokestack emissions, chemical lakes, and Chernobyl.

The Stalinist states were environmental disaster zones, worse than the capitalist states themselves. All the main currents – the Stalinists and the Maoists, who carried Marxism as a banner of convenience, and the Trotskyists who opposed them, turned their back on environmental issues – aided and abetted by social democracy. It is, therefore, entirely unsurprising that the fragile ecological conceptions established by classical Marxism was unable to withstand such an onslaught.

The USSR and the Eastern Bloc countries were amongst the biggest users of brown coal (lignite) in the world, which has a low heat capacity and high GHG emissions. The USSR produced poisoned rivers, polluted landscapes, chemical lakes, massive deforestation, soil degradation and then Chernobyl.[185] Maoist China followed the Stalinist model. Both the Great Leap Forward and the Cultural Revolution in China were environmentally disastrous as well as productivist. Production targets were set with no regard to environmental destruction: forests and pastures were destroyed, rivers diverted, lakes filled in and vast plains created to grow grain.

The environmental record of Maoist China was at least as destructive as both Imperial China that preceded it and the rabid form of capitalism that has followed it. The continuity of Stalinism was clear as well. Both the ecologically disastrous Three Gorges Dam project on the Yellow River, and the equally destructive Yangtze River dam project, were overseen by Soviet engineers.

In 1953, Khrushchev launched the Virgin Lands project. Thirteen million hectares of previously uncultivated land in the northern Caucasus, western Siberia, and northern Kazakhstan were ploughed and planted with wheat, where the climate was unfavourable to its cultivation. The result was a series of disastrous dust bowls and devastating impacts on water sources – such as the disastrous depletion of the Aral Sea, one of the biggest freshwater lakes in the region. Between 1960 and 1987 its level dropped 13 metres and its area shrank by 40 per cent.

The Bolsheviks

Yet it did not start this way. After the 1917 revolution, there was a strong ecological current in the Bolshevik Party, to which Lenin was sympathetic. In the early years, the Bolsheviks established a remarkably good environmental record. A Commission for Nature Protection was established under Nikolai Bukharin – a leading Bolshevik with strong ecological convictions.

Although he wanted to maximise Soviet Russia's industrial production, Lenin argued that nature had to be respected. Decrees were adopted to protect the forests from development. Protected zones were established to control erosion and protect watercourses. Hunting for fur (as distinct from meat) was restricted. In 1921, a number of nature reserves were established, and areas excluded from industrial development: the Astrakhansky Zapovenik reserve in the Volga delta, for example, and a similar reserve in the Urals, dedicated to the study of nature. Stalin reversed all this, with the consequences outlined above.

By the end of the 1930s, the Soviet environmentalists who had led these developments had disappeared into the gulag, or had faced the firing squad along with some of the more ecologically minded Bolshevik leaders, including Bukharin, Uranovsky and Vavilov, for 'counterrevolutionary activity'.

The loss of the ecological conceptions of classical Marxism, that took place in the first half of the twentieth century, had a damaging effect on the role the Marxist tradition was able to play for the rest of the century – in the Global North in particular. It denied the movement the theoretical anchorage it needed to cope with the massive challenges that were in store – including World War II and the onset of the Cold War.

Post revolution

Douglas R Weiner, however, a professor of history at the University of Arizona, specializing in Russian and Soviet history, in his monumental 1999 study of environmentalism in the USSR, *A Little Corner of Freedom: Russian Nature Protection from Stalin to Gorbachev*, argues that in fact the obliteration of the environmental movement by Stalin was not as complete as many have thought. He discovered through his researches in Soviet archives in the 1990s that, implausible as it might appear, an independent and critically minded movement for nature protection continued to exist throughout the Stalin years.[186]

A Little Corner of Freedom was an update of a previous 1988 work by Weiner entitled *Models of Nature: Ecology, Conservation and Cultural Revolution in Soviet Russia*, which detailed the environmental record of the Bolsheviks in the Soviet Union in the 1920s.[187] Weiner was not a Bolshevik, but his researches are nonetheless valuable.

Weiner discovered that a number of institutions established by the Bolsheviks in the 1920s, pre-eminently the All-Russian Society for the Protection of Nature (VOOP), the Moscow Society of Naturalists (MOIP), the Moscow branch of the Geographical Society of the USSR (MOG), and the All-Union Botanical Society, had survived the purges at least for a while. These societies, he argues, continued to function in sharp contrast to the general situation in Soviet society.

One of the products of this was the work of Vladimir Ivanovich Vernadsky, president of the Lenin Agricultural Academy. Vernadsky was a Ukrainian, a Soviet mineralogist and geochemist who is considered one of the founders of geochemistry, biogeochemistry, and radiogeology. He was also a founder of the Ukrainian Academy of Sciences.

He achieved international acclaim both for his analysis of the biosphere and as the founder of the science of geochemistry. He called for a scientific or dialectical stance in relation to the conservation of nature. His remarkable book *The Biosphere* was published in 1926 and argued with great clarity that the biosphere was a self-contained entity:[188]

> Living matter may be envisaged as an indivisible whole in the mechanism of the biosphere, but it is only a part of organic life which immediately utilises the rays of the sun, namely green vegetation, the carrier of chlorophyll. Under the influence of these light-rays, vegetable organisms produce chemical compounds which would be unstable in any other environment but that of the interior of a plant.
>
> The whole living world is connected with this green mass by a direct and indissoluble bond. Animal matter and other organisms are further developments of these compounds. One may therefore consider all this section of living nature as the ulterior development of the same process of transformation of the sun's light into active planetary force. Animals, for example, accumulate bodies rich in nitrogen. At the death of the organism, these compounds are released, performing work in the biosphere.
>
> We may, then, regard living matter in its entirety as the peculiar and unique domain for the accumulation and transformation of the luminous energy of the sun.[189]

Weiner also discovered that in June 1937 the leadership of VOOP drafted a letter to the Central Committee of the Communist Party, seeking a meeting to upgrade the party's commitment to nature protection. This was the very week that the high command of the Red Army had been arrested and accused of working for a foreign power. He discovered another VOOP document, written in July 1948, to the state security services questioning why secret police detachments were chopping down all the cypress trees in the Crimea.

How this could have taken place in the face of the Stalinist juggernaut is hard to credit. Weiner argues that the environment gave Soviet scientists an opportunity to push back against the clamp-down, at least to some extent, although they all eventually succumbed. Whether any of it had the slightest effect on anything that actually happened during this period, given the scale of environmental destruction that was by then taking place, was another matter altogether.

The All-Russian Conservation Congress was held in 1929. Present were 124 delegates with voting rights, 64 coming from the provinces and the rest from Moscow and Leningrad. The congress saw some real debates, of the kind which were being closed down across the USSR. Some of the delegates warned that the Five-Year Plan had set targets that seriously threatened the ecology of the country, with seals, sea otters and whales being threatened. Another debate was over logging and the clearing up of the steppes. It was revealed that the forest of an entire province was being 'planned into abolition'. By the time of the All-Union Conservation conference in 1933, the atmosphere had changed and the delegates were struggling against an increasing clamp-down.

Kunal Chattopadhyay, professor of comparative literature in Jadavpur University in West Bengal, in his paper *Early Soviet Commitment to Environment Protection and its Decline*, argues that Lenin as head of government was sympathetic to conservation.[190] Chattopadhyay puts it this way:

> Lenin's view that Communism is Soviet power plus the electrification of the whole country has been often quoted, but this is a simplification... He saw socialism and the overcoming of class antagonisms as a rational process, once the working class held power, where planning and a scientific approach were vital. At the same time, he stressed that it was necessary to understand the forces and laws of nature, because any desire for the increase of productive forces and the growth of socialism had to take place by obeying those laws and acting in tune with them. He was therefore fully interested in cooperating with scientists as scientists, regardless of their political positions.

Conservationists also had the support of Anatoly Vasilyevich Lunacharsky, people's commissar for education.

14 Population: an eco-feminist issue

Demographically, the challenges are clear. Countless women and men lack the power to make real choices about childbearing because of crushing poverty or persistent gender discrimination.

Laurie Mazur [191]

A sobering estimate of the total physical or material impact of human beings on the planet is contained in a research paper entitled *Scale and Diversity of the Physical Technosphere: A Geological Perspective*, published in the *Anthropogenic Review* of autumn of 2016. It was the work of a panel of 25 scientists, including Jan Zalasiewicz from Leicester University, who was its corresponding author.

It shows that what it calls the total physical technosphere – the sum of the material output/physical infrastructure/waste (landfill for example) of contemporary human society, including power stations, roads, buildings, vehicles, plastics etc., weighs in at 30 trillion tonnes – or 4,000 tonnes for every living person.

This technosphere, the report argues, is what gives modern humans the ability to populate the planet in numbers 1,000 times those attained by hunter gatherers, and 10 times those of pre-industrial society.

The rising population of the planet

It draws our attention to the issue of the rising global population of the planet. Of all the issues I have addressed in this book, the one I have found most perplexing has been the refusal of the radical left – or the vast majority of it – to accept that the rising global human population of the planet presents any kind of problem for its ecology.

It is a patently irrational proposition. How can 70 million additional human beings, added to the planet every year, not exert increased pressure on its ecosystems and its resources? Not every new person has the same impact, of course, the rich greater than the poor, but every new person needs basic resources – water, food, space, clothing – and every poor person, quite rightly, aspires to a better standard of life.

This is a debate that has been going on for over 200 years and therefore deserves to be dealt with in some detail. It has long been distorted by charges of neo-Malthusianism, or populationism against those who see rising population as a problem. For many years, just to raise the issue of population on the left has been to face charges of Malthusianism, or allegations that you are constructing a slippery slope to population control, forced sterilisations, and even eugenics. A kind of project fear. Even those who are longstanding and outspoken opponents of all such things face these allegations. For many years, what has passed for a debate on population has meant dragging out the same old Malthusianism allegations and giving them yet another relaunch.

In 1960, for example, Joseph Hansen, a leading member of the American Socialist Workers Party, published a booklet entitled: *Too Many Babies: The Myth of the Population Explosion*.[192] This booklet not only denounced those concerned about the rising population as Malthusians, but argued that a bigger human population is a good thing rather a liability. It would be entirely possible, Hansen insisted, to feed a global population of 28 billion people![193]

It remains an issue, however, that cannot be avoided. Any assessment of the ecological crisis today, or indeed any proposition as to what to do about it, that fails to take into account the rising human population, is in my view deeply flawed.

It is also a debate that raises centrally the issue of eco-feminism – an issue that cannot be properly discussed without going back to the debates between feminists (mainly but not only between North and South) before and after the 1994 UN Conference on Population and Development, held in Cairo. As a result of this dispute that conference was not only a major lost opportunity in terms of women's empowerment and women's rights – particularly for women in the impoverished parts of the Global South – but it compounded the problem of an objective discussion on the rising human population.

Exponential growth

The human population of the planet is growing by over 70 million people a year – almost the population of Germany. It has done so for the past 50 years, and shows little sign of slowing down. Yet most on the left see no problem in this, ecologically or otherwise.

The UN predicts that today's population of 7.6 billion will rise to 8.5 billion by 2030, by 9.7 billion by 2050 and to 11.2 billion by 2100.[194] It is difficult to claim that such a rate of increase is ecologically sustainable. While the global environmental crisis cannot and should not be reduced to the rising human population, it is hard to see how it can be tackled successfully with the human population increasing at its current rate.

For most of the 200,000 - 300,000 years that modern humans have been on the planet, our numbers, after a spurt following the emergence of agriculture, were stable at about 1 billion. This changed dramatically with the onset of the industrial revolution at the end of the 17th century. The population then rose to 2 billion by 1930, to 3 billion by 1960, to 4 billion by 1974, to 5 billion by 1987, to 6 billion by 1999, and to 7 billion by 2012. In other words it tripled in just 60 years – from 2.5 billion in 1952 when I started school – to 7.6 billion today.[195] Over the same period the number of wild animals on the planet declined in similar proportion.

We are told by the political and religious establishments, as well as by many on the left, not to worry about the rising population because we will be saved by what is called the 'demographic transition'. This is the notion that as people get richer the birth rate will fall and the population will stabilise naturally towards the end of the century to about 10 billion.

This has the ring of wishful thinking about it. Firstly, nearly half of the current global population is under 25, which is a huge potential for further growth. Secondly the per capita consumption of food, water and manufactured goods is already increasing at a higher rate than the population itself and will continue to do so. To assume that the planet can absorb a population increase of this scale under such conditions is reckless in the extreme.

Thirdly, capitalism's project to enrich its small coterie of the very wealthy and the very powerful shows little sign of encouraging a 'demographic transition'.

As Fred Magdoff and John Bellamy Foster point out in *What Every Environmentalist Needs to Know About Capitalism*, there are sound scientific reasons to be concerned:

> What makes the modern era stand out in this respect, however, is that there are many more of us inhabiting more of the earth; we have technologies that can do much greater damage and do it more quickly; and we have an economic system that knows no bounds. The damage being done today is so widespread that it not only degrades local and regional ecologies, as in earlier civilisations, but also affects the planetary environment, threatening the existence of a majority of species on the planet, including our own. There are therefore sound, scientific reasons to be concerned about the current rapid degradation of the earth's environment. [196]

The global birth rate

It is true that the global birth rate is falling, but so is the death rate – the other side of the equation – particularly infant mortality. Life expectancy is also increasing, mainly, but not only, in the Global North. These are major gains for humanity, of course, but they do not make today's population increase any more sustainable, or addressing it (or at least discussing it) any less urgent.

While a demographic transition might ease the problem, it also might not. Population predictions are notoriously unreliable, given that the economic and social conditions on which they are based can change dramatically. At the same time, because exponential growth is so powerful, even if only a small part of the global population continues to reproduce exponentially, this could nevertheless seriously affect the overall rate of growth.

Even if the global population stabilises as predicted, this still implies a population of 10 or 11 billion people by the end of the century – which remains unsustainable in terms of the ecosystems of the planet. There is also the precautionary principle. Why would we gamble on any of these figures? Surely, safety first is the best policy, and none of these calculations should be relied upon until they have been fully tested.

Statistical devices

Rising population numbers are highly popular with ruling elites, of course, who see in it expanding markets, higher profits, workers for the factories and services, and soldiers for the battlefields. Rising population also allows governments to boast of 'record numbers' of this and that (GDP, employment and spending for example) when per-capita figures would show a very different picture.

An important source of confusion is the way population figures are usually calculated: *i.e.* the difference between the rate of increase and the absolute increase. Although the *rate of increase* is falling the population is still increasing *in absolute terms* (*i.e.* actually increasing) by 70 million a year. This is because the rate of increase is calculated against a rising total. The absolute growth figure is rarely mentioned by those who want to minimise the impact of rising population, because it illustrates (rather than obscures) the reality of the situation. They stress instead the falling *rate of increase* which paints a more convenient picture.

The *absolute* increases, by decade, in the global population, since 1950 are as follows: 1950-60: 48,345,097; 1960-70: 66,716,714; 1970-80: 74,781,358; 1980-90: 82,480, 804; 1990-2000: 80,423,664; 2000-2010: 76,595,750; 2010-2020: 73,588,822 (projected). This is an average of just under 70 million a year.

Al Gore makes the same point in his 2013 book *The Future*:

> Although population growth has slowed in most of the world over the past several decades, the overall size of the population is now so large that even a slower rate of growth will add billions more people before our numbers stabilize, near the end of the century, at a total that is now difficult to predict but is estimated between 10 and 25 billion.[197]

An annual increase of 70 million people a year is, I would argue, ecologically unsustainable by any rational criteria. The planet is already stretched to its limits, and cannot absorb this rate of increase without serious damage to its biosphere. In fact such damage is already happening. Population pressure translates readily not only into ecological destruction but also into social conflict – usually over issues such as access to fresh water and land for living space, grazing animals, and growing food.

Today, half of the world's population growth is expected to be accounted for by nine countries: India, Nigeria, Pakistan, Democratic Republic of the Congo, Ethiopia, United Republic of Tanzania, the USA, Indonesia and Uganda, listed according to the size of their contribution to the total growth. By 2050, six countries are expected to exceed 300 million in population: China, India, Indonesia, Nigeria, Pakistan, and the USA. China and India remain the two most populated countries in the world, both with more than 1 billion people, representing 19 per cent and 18 per cent of the world's population, respectively. The population of India is expected to surpass that of China by 2022.[198]

At the same time, in many wealthy countries that are facing below-replacement fertility levels, the governments are urging people to have more children to maintain population levels.

Africa faces the most dangerous situation. Nigeria, for example, Africa's most populous country – and also its most ethnically diverse nation – has seen a remarkable ten-fold growth in population, from 37 million in 1950 to 194 million today. It is now expected to reach 278 million by 2050, and to surpass that of the USA by 2060 – at which point it would become the third most populous country in the world. Islam promotes large families, with the encouragement of early marriage and a polygamous family system, whilst the Christian religion prohibits the most effective forms of contraception, and most religious leaders are anti-abortionists.

At the same time the Sahara Desert is encroaching ever deeper into Nigeria from the north. This threat is driven by climate change, a factor which has long been fuelling ethnic conflict over resources and usable land: violent struggles over land have become increasingly prevalent. Chidi Oguamanam, a professor of law from the University of Ottawa, published his article 'How Climate Change is Driving Nigeria's Herdsmen Conflict' in the June 2016 Newsweek, spelling out the problem in terms of the conflict generated between Nigerian herdsmen: [199]

In the past several months tensions have escalated between nomadic cattle herders and traditional crop-farming communities. Some traditional and farming communities in central and southern Nigeria have been overrun by herders who are accused of grazing their cattle on crop fields.

The country's media is dominated by reports of maiming, killings, rape and other forms of banditry associated with highly armed nomadic herders. Unofficial figures put the death toll from one such incident in Enugu State, in the South-Eastern region, at about 100.

In the absence of state protection, these events have fuelled affected communities' support for ethnic or regional militias as a civic defence strategy. The clashes between herdsmen and farmers strike at the core of Nigeria's vulnerable ethno-political fault lines. They also have ramifications for climate change and food security.

Thomas Malthus

Today the population debate continues to be conducted (remarkably) in the framework set by Thomas Malthus in the 18th century – despite his theory having been obsolete, even in its own terms, by the middle of the 19th century, overtaken by developments in agricultural production and soil fertility.

Malthus was the eighteenth-century clergyman and classical economist who famously predicted that the growth of the human population would always outstrip that of the food supply, that the human population would always increase exponentially whilst the food supply would increase arithmetically, making 'natural' disasters like famines unavoidable. He set out these views in his 1798 book *An Essay on the Principles of Population*.[200]

His practical conclusion was that all efforts to relieve the sufferings of the poor were futile. Charity would only encourage more births, leading to yet more famine and starvation. He opposed the English Poor Laws, which offered a meagre existence to the destitute through the workhouse system. He argued that they encouraged large families through 'dependent poverty', and should therefore be closed down.

Marx famously attacked Malthus's writings – posthumously, since Marx was only 16 when Malthus died in 1843. In fact, Marx regarded Malthus as 'a professional sycophant of the landed aristocracy', a 'slavish plagiarist' who stole his population theory from his predecessors, and an 'utterly base' apologist who only 'draws such conclusions from the given scientific premises ... as will be agreeable (useful) to the aristocracy against the bourgeoisie and to both against the proletariat'.[201] What Marx and Engels railed against, however, was not whether or not there were natural limits to the size of the human population, but the social consequences of the 'solutions' Malthus was advocating.

In fact Engels, in his 1881 letter to Karl Kautsky on the Malthus debate, made it clear that in his view, population size might become a problem that would have to be dealt with, and a communist society might have to limit it. He argues it thus:

> There is of course the abstract possibility that the human population will become so numerous that its further increase will have to be checked. If it should become necessary for communist society to regulate the production of men, just as it will have already regulated the production of things, then it, and it alone, will be able to do this without difficulties. It seems to me that it should not be too difficult for such a society to achieve in a planned way what has already come about naturally, without planning, in France and Lower Austria. In any case it will be for those people to decide if, when and what they want to do about it, and what means to employ. I don't feel qualified to offer them any advice or counsel in this matter. They will presumably be at least as clever as we are.[202]

A good Marxist analysis of both Malthusianism and Marx's polemic against it can be found, I suggest, in John Bellamy Foster's 2002 book *Ecology Against Capitalism*.[203] Foster concludes that none of this was to deny 'that population growth is one of the most serious problems of the contemporary age. But demographic change cannot be treated in natural law terms but only in relation to changing historical conditions'.[204]

The problem we face today is not the production of enough food – which might well be possible for several billion more people. It is whether the planet can sustain the current population increase, including the food to feed it, without destroying its environment: this is an issue Malthus did not address.

The wider movement

In the wider movement, discussion on population has been more open. The 1972 *Limits to Growth* report, for example, starts from the assertion that the rising human population is a threat to the planet. The first point in its conclusion, for example, says the following:

> If the present growth trends on world population, industrialisation, pollution, food production, and resource depletion continue unchanged, the limits to growth on this planet will be reached sometime in the next one hundred years. The most probable result will be a rather sudden and uncontrollable decline in both population and industrial capacity.[205]

Edward O. Wilson in *The Diversity of Life*, puts it this way:

> Human demographic success has brought the world to this crisis of biodiversity. Human beings – mammals of the 50-kilogramme weight class and members of a group, the primates, otherwise noted for scarcity – have become a hundred times more numerous than any other land animal of comparable size in the history of life. By every conceivable measure, humanity is ecologically abnormal. Our species appropriates between 20 and 40 percent of all the solar energy captured in organic material and land plants. There is no way that we can draw upon the resources of the planet to such a degree without drastically reducing the state of all other species.[206]

Paul Ehrlich

Whilst it is not Malthusian to see the rising human population as a problem, it is Malthusian to see famine as inevitable and starving the poor as a solution to it.

The Population Bomb by Paul Ehrlich published in 1968, with its exaggerated analysis, populist style, and authoritarian conclusions is indeed classically Malthusian, and Malthus does feature explicitly in the book. And like its original, all Ehrlich's main predictions were soon proved wrong.

Ehrlich was Professor of Population Studies in the Department of Biology at Stanford University, and president of its Centre for Conservation Biology. The work was published by Ballantine Books, with the support of the Sierra Club and Friends of the Earth — though the extent to which they supported his detailed conclusions is unclear. In the first paragraph of the prologue Ehrlich states:

The battle to feed all of humanity is over. In the 1970s and 1980s hundreds of millions of people will starve to death in spite of any crash programs embarked upon now. At this late date nothing can prevent a substantial increase in the world death rate, although many lives could be saved through dramatic programs to 'stretch' the carrying capacity of the earth by increasing food production and providing for more equitable distribution of whatever food is available. But these programs will only provide a stay of execution unless they are accompanied by determined and successful efforts at population control. Population control is the conscious regulation of the numbers of human beings to meet the needs not just of individual families, but of society as a whole... Our position requires that we take immediate action at home (in the USA) and promote effective action worldwide. We must have population control at home, hopefully through changes in our value system, but by compulsion if voluntary methods fail. [207]

Ehrlich did not openly oppose women's right to choose, but made the deeply sexist argument that he didn't think it would work because women would make the wrong choices. He was also in favour of using US foreign aid to bludgeon its recipients into the introduction of various methods of compulsory birth control, including sterilisation. (Ehrlich has since disavowed some of his more extreme proposals and conclusions.)

The book, which became a bestseller, not only distorted the debate on population, but muddied the debate on the left – since anyone arguing that rising population was a problem for the planet could easily be associated (guilt by association) with Ehrlich's conclusions and discredited as a Malthusian reactionary.

Murray Bookchin, for example, in his hectoring and sectarian 1994 pamphlet *Which Way for the Ecology Movement* (which reflected his political evolution), constructs a direct linkage between Malthusianism, neo-Malthusianism and 'populationism' (*i.e.* 'populationist lite'), Hitler's racial purity programme, and extermination camps of World War II. He put it this way:

Barely a generation later [after social-Darwinism], Malthusianism acquired an explicitly racist character. During the early twenties, when 'Anglo-Saxon' racism peaked in the US against 'darker' peoples like Italians, Jews, and Eastern Europeans, the notion of 'biological inferiority' led to explicitly exclusionist immigration laws that favored Northern Europeans over other presumably 'subhuman' peoples...

Nazism [therefore] did not have to invent its racial imagery of sturdy 'Aryans' beleaguered by 'sub-human' dark people, particularly Jews... From Hitler's 'Northern European' viewpoint, Europe was 'overpopulated' in the 1930s, and the continent's ethnic groups had to be sifted out according to their racial background. Hence the gas chambers and crematoriums of Auschwitz, the execution squads that followed the German army into Russia in the summer of 1941, and the systematic and mechanised slaughter of millions in a span of three or four years.[208]

I can see why Joel Kovel describes Bookchin in his book *The Enemy of Nature* as 'charismatic as well as brilliant, but also unrelentingly dogmatic and vituperatively sectarian.'[209]

Fred Pearce

Although Fred Pearce's book *Peoplequake* was published 40 years after Ehrlich's *The Population Bomb* – in 2011 – it was a direct and detailed critique of *The Population Bomb*. Ehrlich he says: 'offered several scenarios. At worst, a billion people (almost a quarter of the world's population at the time) would starve to death by 1983'.[210] Indeed he did. In fact he took the completely opposite point of view to Ehrlich – and in my opinion equally wrong – that the rising human population offered no threat to the ecology of the planet. No wonder the debate became so confused.

He argued not only that Ehrlich's *The Population Bomb* – which he described not unreasonably as a 'potboiler for population control' – grossly exaggerated the dangers of population increase, but that the problem did not really exist at all, and the planet will be able to cope with whatever population numbers are thrown at it – partly via the demographic transition. How he reconciled this with the picture he painted in his book *When the Rivers Run Dry*, published five years earlier, is hard to see.

He also stoked up the Malthusian dimension, insisting, like Bookchin, that any attempt to reduce the birth rate, even on the basis of consent, would lead to Malthusianism, eugenics or even Nazism.

Peoplequake, which was highly influential on the radical left, has in recent years done more than any other book to instill complacency on the issue of human population growth. It also managed to encourage the use of Malthusianism in the debate on the left.

Daniel Tanuro in his 2009 book, published in English as *Green Capitalism: Why It Can't Work,* accuses those who raise what he calls 'so-called overpopulation' of attempting to put a green spin on Malthusianism, even of finding it 'easier to challenge the right of a part of humanity to exist than to challenge capitalism':

> Gurus spread panic in the hope of putting a green spin on the theory of population growth developed by Malthus, and to do so without anyone noticing. They are only too happy to attribute global warming to so-called over population; a worrying number of them seem to find it easier to challenge the right of a part of humanity to exist, than to challenge capitalism. They should not be underestimated with their reactionary rantings: they are beating a path to the highest levels of the ruling class.[211]

Martin Empson makes a similar point in *Land and Labour: Marxism, Ecology and Human History:* 'even if the world's population does not level off or decline in the next century, there is still the potential to feed increasing numbers of people.'[212] He goes on: 'While the modern neo-Malthusians do not yet call for the withdrawal of charity from the poor and the hungry, it is a small step from their current ideas.'

Jonathan Neale, in his book *Stop Global Warming: Change the World,* does not raise Malthus (much to his credit, I feel) but argues that rising population is not a problem:

> We can halt global warming with (CO_2 emission) cuts of 60 to 70 per cent now. We can also make room for both population growth and a richer world for everyone with bigger cuts of 82 to 87 per cent over the next 25 years.[213]

Challenging the taboo

The Malthusian taboo was challenged as long ago as 1983 by the Canadian Marxist Wally Seccombe, in an article entitled *'Marxism and Demography'.*[214] He argued that constant references to Malthus had 'placed the debate on population beyond the pale of legitimate scrutiny and investigation', and that in doing so, Marxists had abandoned the terrain to our enemies. He puts it this way:

> Marxism's traditional primary address to demography, dating back to Marx himself, has been through a virulent denunciation of its Malthusian versions. These polemics, however programmatically justified in countering largely reactionary Malthusian population policies, nevertheless have had an anaesthetic effect upon historical materialism – placing the demographic realm itself beyond the scope of legitimate scrutiny and investigation. In the process of dismissing Malthus and his successors, Marxists have abandoned the terrain to our enemies. And with the notable exception of some analysts of the Third World like Claude Meillassoux, this abdication has been perpetuated within contemporary Marxism. Indeed, there has been an unfortunate counterposition of the socio-economic to the demographic, as if these two dimensions of social relations were materially separable under capitalism or elsewhere, and as if the lines of causality ran, undialectically, only one way from the socio-economic and political to the demographic.[215]

Seccombe was also critical of the disjuncture between feminist theory and the population debate. He puts it this way:

> The feminist challenge to Marxism – with which my own work is concerned – also demands that this great evasion be squarely faced. A central demand of the women's liberation movement is for women themselves to gain full control over their reproductive capacities, and intense political struggles continue to rage over this issue. As the slogan 'control of our bodies, control of our lives' suggests, women can never control their lives in a full sense until they gain control of their own biological capacities. We can state this proposition obversely: the social control of women is *centered* upon the control of their reproductive capacities in a vast range of societies. If this generalisation is valid, then the conclusion seems to me inescapable: there are compelling feminist reasons for paying close attention to the demographic regulators of women's fertility and to their change over time. And yet, there has been surprisingly little attention paid by feminists to the field of demography.[216]

A Pivotal Moment

An important advance on this issue, in my view, came in 2010 with the publication of *A Pivotal Moment: Population, Justice and the Environmental Challenge* by Laurie Mazur. Mazur was the principal of the American organisation Population Justice Project, founded in 2007.[217] She saw the rising human population as a problem for the planet and argued for the empowerment of women to control their own fertility as the best approach to stabilise it.[218] I agreed with the book's overall framework.

Mazur strongly, and I think rightly, defended the decisions of the 1994 Cairo UN Conference on Population and Development, which had seen rising population as a problem and which had adopted a detailed *Programme of Action*, based on the empowerment of women and which governments were required to implement within a fifteen-year period.[219] She saw it as a major lost opportunity for women, brought about by a division amongst feminists at the conference and after it.

Previous such conferences, in Mexico in 1975 and Nairobi in 1985, had been derailed by big pro-life interventions and had got nowhere. In Cairo, however, the progressive side, including the feminists – or more precisely those feminists advocating an empowerment approach – were more numerous and better organised.

The *Programme of Action* (in paragraphs 4.4) included the following provisions:

Countries should act to empower women and should take steps to eliminate inequalities between men and women as soon as possible by:
- Establishing mechanisms for women's equal participation and equitable representation at all levels of the political process and public life in each community and society and enabling women to articulate their concerns and needs;
- Promoting the fulfilment of women's potential through education, skill development and employment, giving paramount importance to the elimination of poverty, illiteracy and ill health among women;
- Eliminating all practices that discriminate against women; assisting women to establish and realise their rights, including those that relate to reproductive and sexual health;

• Adopting appropriate measures to improve women's ability to earn income beyond
traditional occupations, achieve economic self-reliance, and ensure women's equal
access to the labour market and social security systems;

• Eliminating violence against women;

• Eliminating discriminatory practices by employers against women, such as those
based on proof of contraceptive use or pregnancy status;

• Making it possible, through laws, regulations and other appropriate measures, for
women to combine the roles of child-bearing, breast-feeding and child-rearing with
participation in the workforce.[220]

Mazur argued that the conference had offered a unique breakthrough – a
win-win situation that gave women the ability to improve their own lives
and help the planet at the same time.

By the empowerment of women, she meant making reproductive services
available to all women globally, giving them access to education and
employment, and lifting them out of poverty.

Today, for example, Nigeria has one of the highest population growth rates
in the world, and is at the same time the worst country in Africa in terms of the
education of girls. It means challenging the influence of conservative forces,
such as religion, patriarchal or communal pressure, that deny women the
right to choose. These are important objectives in and of themselves, whether
or not they exert a downward pressure on the birthrate. Rising population
levels give them an added (or additional) urgency. It is an approach that is
good for women and it is good for the planet.

Mazur made her position clear just prior to the publication of her book in
the *Bulletin of the Atomic Scientists* of October 2009, after she had been accused
of advocating population 'control':

'Population growth' isn't synonymous with 'population control' – the top-down
programs that have trampled human rights and health in pursuit of lower birth
rates, notably in India and China. Today, there is a broad global consensus that
the best way to slow growth is by ensuring that all people are able to make real
choices about childbearing. That means access to voluntary family planning and
other reproductive-health information and services. It also means empowering girls
and women through education and employment opportunities.[221]

This means supporting women in their struggle for contraception and abortion facilities. It means supporting their fight to break free of poverty, and ensuring that they get access to education and jobs – issues that have long been the demands of the feminist movement and of the left. Policies that involve lifting women out of poverty in the poorest parts of the globe, and enabling them to control their own fertility through the provision of contraception and abortion services, need to be supported; so too do challenges to religion and other conservative influences such as patriarchal pressure; and so does enabling access of women in impoverished communities to education and employment.

Eco-feminism

Laurie Mazur defends the position (rightly in my view) that population is first and foremost a feminist (or eco-feminist) issue. Women physically create each generation. They produce the children and take the main responsibility for nurturing them. Global fertility rates are ultimately determined by the size of the families they have – which in turn is related to whether they have access to contraception and abortion services, as well as education and jobs, and to the extent they are exposed to conservative ideologies that oppose such access.

This approach had support in the wider movement. Natalie Bennett, the former leader of the Green Party in England and Wales, and Caroline Lucas, one of its current leaders and its only MP, also defend such a position. Even Population Matters[222] (previously the Optimum Population Trust), which is headed by naturalists David Attenborough and Chris Packham, now presents its position in the framework of a woman's right to choose – despite a somewhat controversial past on the issue – whilst urging women to think carefully about the choices they make. They present it this way on their website:

> Your choice about how many children you have is one of the most important you can make. Even children raised in the most environmentally conscious ways still have an impact on the environment and end up consuming more of the Earth's resources. Each additional person – especially in the developed world – places a burden on the Earth, and makes it more difficult to ensure its finite resources can

be used sustainably and fairly by everyone. We should think very carefully about how many children to have.

Women have historically demanded and fought for the right to control their own fertility, and continue to do so today – including in those parts of the world with the highest birthrates. Women are the active agency in this field, including in the struggle against enforced control. Reproductive rights were the lynchpin of the feminist movement of the 1970s and 1980s; and by struggling for their own specific interests, women often become also the agents of wider change.

Al Gore in *The Future* also takes a similar view in terms of the empowerment of women. He identifies four relevant factors concerning the empowerment of women, all necessary but none by itself sufficient, which are:

- First the education of girls – the single most important factor. The education of boys is also important, but population statistics show clearly that the ability of girls to become literate and obtain a good education is crucial.
- The empowerment of women in society, to the point where their opinions are heard and respected, and they have the ability to participate in making decisions, with their husbands or partners, about family size and other issues important to their families.
- Third is ubiquitous availability of fertility management knowledge and technology, so that women can effectively choose how many children they wish to have, and the spacing of their children.
- Fourth is the mortality rate. As the African leader Julius Nyerere said midway through the twentieth century, the most powerful contraceptive is the confidence by parents that their child will live.[223]

More recently such a position is taken in *Why Women Will Save the Planet*, by Jenny Hawley, first published in 2015, with a second edition in 2018, and with the endorsement of Friends of the Earth.[224] The chapter by Carina Hirsch entitled *'Family Planning: A Win-win for Women and Sustainability'* says the following in its first paragraph:

Advancing and improving access to voluntary and rights based family planning is a win-win for both women and sustainability. Fulfilling and respecting women's and girls' rights to family planning is not only fundamental to ensuring human rights to health, well-being and empowerment (all critical ends in themselves), but also contributes to furthering sustainability goals. In this chapter, we explain the links between family planning, global population and environmental sustainability, and the ways in which family planning, when integrated with other development actions, can achieve greater development and sustainability than single sector programmes.[225]

Those of us fortunate enough to live in developed countries, it goes on, generally speaking have the rights and facilities to manage our own fertility. In many other parts of the world, however, things are very different:

> ... an estimated 214 million women and girls in developing countries have an unmet need for modern contraception. The WHO defines the 'unmet need' as those women and girls of reproductive age who either do not want children or want to delay their next child, but are not able to access any method of contraception.
>
> In sub-Saharan Africa 21 per cent of women and girls have an unmet need for contraception, while Southern Asia is home to the largest absolute number of women and girls who lack access – 70 million. The UN Population Fund estimates that 24 per cent of women and girls in Uganda, and 14 per cent in Niger, have an unmet need for family planning.

In answer to the question, 'With global fertility on the decline, hasn't the problem been solved?', Hirsch gives the following response:

> It's not quite that simple: global fertility levels may be declining but fertility is not declining in all areas of the world. Forty-six per cent of the world's population live in countries with below-replacement fertility (where women have on average fewer than 2.1 children over their lifetimes). But the population in some of the developing countries is still growing rapidly, and even when fertility does drop to replacement level, the population will continue to grow for several decades, as the youngest generations reach reproductive age. Between now and 2050, world population is projected to increase from today's 7.3 billion to 9.7 billion. More than half of this growth is projected to take place in Africa, where the population will double between now and 2050, and quadruple by the end of the century to reach over

4 billion. These levels of growth in the world's poorest countries will inevitably exacerbate the challenges already faced in alleviating poverty, ensuring food and water security, and providing access to health and education services for all.

Cairo consensus challenged

No sooner was the Cairo conference over than its *Programme of Action* faced a backlash from pro-life forces led by the Vatican and other churches and religious orders. Many of the governments that had initially supported the *Programme* in Cairo backed off, and eventually its provisions were largely side-lined.

Some on the left – scandalously in my view – also opposed the *Programme of Action*, denouncing it as a 'transmission belt to population control'. One of those was Vandana Shiva. Shiva has a long and distinguished record as an ecological theoretician and campaigner that can only be admired – as fully recognised in other parts of this book. But on this issue she is, in my view, wrong.

Shiva was heavily critical of Western feminists, and Western women's organizations, that supported the *Programme of Action*, regarding them as having been duped by the UN. The result was a (very unfortunate) division between feminists North and South at and after the conference, and her views on population have had a negative influence on the debate which remains unresolved.

She objected in particular to the way the *Programme of Action* linked the issue of rising population and the provision to women of reproductive rights. She argued that any programme designed to give women in the Global South access to reproductive services would inevitably end up introducing coercive population control. But how can rising population and women's reproduction be separated? One determines the other. It is the rate of reproduction – determined largely by the availability or lack of reproductive services – that determine both the rate of increase and therefore the size of the global population.

Any provision of reproductive services, however motivated, has two effects: one is to provide women with the basic human right to control their own bodies, and the other is to reduce the global reproduction rate. Reproduction is inseparable from population.

In fact Vandana Shiva was already an opponent of empowerment prior to the Cairo conference. In the report she wrote jointly with Mira Shiva (no relation),[226] immediately after the conference (in March 1995), she attacked the *Programme of Action* for reducing everything to reproductive rights, which she calls 'biological reductionism':

> At Cairo, women's multiple rights as full human beings in society were reduced to 'reproductive rights' alone. The Western women's movement contributed to this biological reductionism in Cairo by failing to focus on women's productive roles and by focusing exclusively on their reproductive roles, by failing to draw attention to denial of women's economic rights through structural adjustment and GATT, and allowing 'unmet needs' to be redefined as needs for contraceptives alone, and not needs for food, water and livelihoods. Further, by reducing women to their biology alone, and divorcing them from the economy and society, the western feminists have created a discourse which strengthens the hands of patriarchy based on religious fundamentalists. Western feminists thus strengthen religious fundamentalism in the Third World.
>
> The real gain of the women's movement over the past three decades has been the rejection of the view of women as only sexual objects or as reproductive machinery. Cairo reversed this gain by equating 'population' to 'women's rights' and 'women's rights' to 'reproductive rights'. The use of words such as 'rights' and 'choice' in this paradigm obscured the fact that demographic trends, whether they are positive or negative, are not merely reflections of the availability or absence of contraceptive technologies. They are reflections of the socio-economic patterns of society, which determine people's options in terms of family size.

Vandana Shiva claimed in the report that the Cairo conference 'was dominated by Northern women obsessed with individual sexual freedom and indifferent to society and to other freedoms.'

This was not only a caricature of the role that Northern women played at the conference, it was also a caricature of the *Programme of Action*. She was right, of course, to point to the inadequacies of the UN in terms of the role of GATT and its structural adjustment programmes. She was also right to point to the weakness of the UN in acting on its decisions. But she was wrong, in my view, to oppose the *Programme of Action*. The programme doesn't only talk about reproductive rights – it makes proposals concerning development, education, women's incomes, access to credit, and much more. If there are examples of the UN breaching the principles of the *Programme of Action* in the way that it was carried out, then the agencies concerned should have been (and indeed should be) exposed and closed down. To denounce in advance what was potentially the most important programme for many years, in terms of the provision of the very rights women themselves have been fighting for decades, is not advancing the struggle for women's liberation.

In fact the *Programme of Action* stresses throughout that it is crucial that the provision of reproductive rights do not stand alone but that they go alongside all the other stated objectives: lifting women out of poverty and giving them access to education, health care and employment. The section on objectives in the *Programme of Action* puts it this way:

> The objective is to raise the quality of life for all people through appropriate population and development policies and programmes aimed at achieving poverty eradication, sustained economic growth in the context of sustainable development and sustainable patterns of consumption and production, human resource development and the guarantee of all human rights, including the right to development as a universal and inalienable right and an integral part of fundamental human rights. Particular attention is to be given to the socio-economic improvement of poor women in developed and developing countries. As women are generally the poorest of the poor and at the same time key actors in the development process, eliminating social, cultural, political and economic discrimination against women is a prerequisite of eradicating poverty, promoting sustained economic growth in the context of sustainable development, ensuring quality family planning and reproductive health services, and achieving balance between population and available resources and sustainable patterns of consumption and production.[227]

It goes on:

> Widespread poverty remains the major challenge to development efforts. Poverty is often accompanied by unemployment, malnutrition, illiteracy, low status of women, exposure to environmental risks and limited access to social and health services, including reproductive health services which, in turn, include family planning. All

these factors contribute to high levels of fertility, morbidity, and mortality, as well as to low economic productivity.[228]

The *Programme of Action* also emphasises the issue of free choice:

> The principle of informed free choice is essential to the long-term success of family-planning programmes. Any form of coercion has no part to play. In every society, there are many social and economic incentives and disincentives that affect individual decisions about childbearing and family size. Over the past century, many governments have experimented with such schemes, including specific incentives and disincentives, in order to lower or raise fertility. Most such schemes have had only marginal impact on fertility and in some cases have been counterproductive. Governmental goals for family planning should be defined in terms of unmet needs for information and services. Demographic goals, while legitimately the subject of government development strategies, should not be imposed on family-planning providers in the form of targets or quotas for the recruitment of clients.[229]

Shiva and others argue that any UN programme designed to provide reproductive services organised by national governments, private charities, or anyone else, will become corrupted and will resort to coercive methods. Maybe there is such a danger: programmes should be monitored and if they deviate from their mandate they should be closed down. The problem with Shiva's approach is that it leads its advocates to find objections to family planning programmes in order to make their case, and even to opposing reproductive services per se, under conditions where there is a desperate need to be met.

Others had opposed the conference from its inception and continued to do so after it was over. Its decisions were backed by many feminists around the world as well as by the Clinton administration in the USA.

Too Many People?

The challenge to Laurie Mazur's *A Pivotal Moment*, with its empowerment message and positive take on the Cairo conference, came in 2011 with the publication of *Too Many People?* by Ian Angus and Simon Butler – which was strongly influenced by Vandana Shiva.

Angus and Butler are both well-known Marxist ecologists with long environmental records. I have worked with Ian Angus, in particular, for many years around promoting ecosocialist ideas. (My review of their book at the time of publication is carried as a debate with the authors in part four of this book.)

They argued that the rising human population is not a problem for the planet but a scare story by neo Malthusians or populationists who have to be slapped down – a task they undertake with some gusto. They then reduce the ecological crisis to global warming in order to argue that since the highest population growth is in the Global South where the carbon footprint is lowest population growth does not significantly affect global warming.

There are several problems with this. Firstly, the key measurement involved in such an assessment (as argued above) is not the carbon footprint of those populations but their ecological footprint – which measures their total impact on the ecology of the planet. It includes for example, deforestation in order to find food, to cook it, and to keep warm. Secondly, it is the ambition of these populations, and one we fully and actively support, to free themselves from poverty and raise their standard of living towards Western levels, with clear implications for their carbon footprint. This is already taking place in some countries.

The second objective of *Too Many People?* was to discredit both the Cairo conference and its *Programme of Action,* and in this regard they supported the Vandana Shiva thesis. One of the harshest critics of the Cairo conference and its outcome was the American academic and feminist Betsy Hartmann, who wrote a foreword for the book.

Like Hartmann in her book 1987 book *Reproductive Rights and Wrongs,*[230] they argue that any attempt to reduce the global birth rate – even on the basis of freedom of choice, human rights and social justice – where one of the objectives is to reduce the birth rate to take the pressure off the planet, would be population control by the back door, since reactionary forces would seize the agenda and push it in a right-wing direction.

The practical upshot of this is that the provision itself does not then take place. In fact, in the end it is an argument against any provision of reproductive services, since such provision (and reduction in the birth rate) will always help the planet as well as women themselves (though they need a planet too) since the two aspects are indivisible. In the end, it is the outcome that is decisive not the motivation.

In any case reactionary forces will call for reactionary solutions. They will oppose progressive solutions and programmes, because that is what reactionary forces do. The reality is in my view the opposite: the existence of a progressive solution makes it easier, not harder, to fend off reactionary forces. It would, as Laurie Mazur argues, be a win-win situation, benefitting both women's rights and basic needs, and the future of the planet. Part five of this book carries a debate between Betsy Hartmann and Laurie Mazur on these issues.

In any case, why should we allow reactionary forces to determine the approach of the left? We don't do it in other areas of politics. It is the absence of democratically based provision that will open the door to the right, not its existence.

Not that *Too Many People?* is consistent as to whether rising population is a problem for the planet. In the first paragraph of Chapter 1, for example It says:

> Other things being equal, a larger population will eat more food, wear more clothes, occupy more shelter, and generate more excrement than a smaller one. That is an indisputable biological fact.

It reinforces this by saying:

> No one doubts that the world population has soared since the industrial revolution began in the late 1700s. After millennia in which the numbers of people grew very slowly, our numbers increased sevenfold in two hundred years, and the growth hasn't stopped. For almost all of human history there were fewer than one billion human beings living on earth: by 2050 there will likely be over nine billion.[231]

It then goes on, throughout the book, to brand those who make exactly the same points as 'populationist' – a term which the authors say they prefer to the 'more traditional' Malthusianism. It defines 'populationists' as 'those who attribute social and ecological ills to human numbers'. It puts it this way:

> Populationists isolate one number – population size or growth – and claim that it is the underlying cause for all the rest. The population has increased; economic

activity expanded and environmental degradation has increased; so population must have caused the expansion and degradation. [But] that only shows *correlation* not *degradation*.[232] (stress in original)

Paul Ehrlich does this, as I argue above. But the bulk of those, myself included, who see the rising human population as a serious problem to be addressed, do not promote it as the root of all problems of the planet; and moreover, are opposed to authoritarian solutions of any kind. Such people are classified in the book as 'populationist-lite'.[233]

The book also – wilfully, I maintain – promotes confusion over the different meanings of 'control' in the context of a women's reproductive rights. In other words, it makes no distinction between the external 'control' of a woman's body, for example by the state, and the 'control' exercised by a woman herself, over her own body and her own fertility, in order to determine whether or not to have children. This 'confusion' allows the book consistently to lump people together as 'the populationists' or even as 'the populationist establishment'.

I would certainly qualify for this, yet I am strongly opposed to any kind of coercive 'control', and only support policies based on the empowerment of women – that is, a woman's right to control her reproductivity – the right to have more children as well as less – combined with greater access by women to political power and crucially to education.

Too Many People? is right to say that stabilising the population would not in itself resolve the crisis. It is right to say that we have to have an alternative economic and social model to capitalism's unlimited growth. All of this is clear. What is wrong is to dismiss rising human population as more or less irrelevant. The current rate of increase is unsustainable; and whether it will continue, or for how long, no one actually knows.

It is argued that enough food can be produced today to feed 8, 9 or 10 billion people – if it was efficiently produced and distributed: *i.e.* not subject to the ravages of the market, with its hugely wasteful distribution systems. True or not, the question is not whether enough food can be produced, using more and more intensified agriculture, with ever more chemical fertilisers, insecticides, and herbicides, and mono-cropping techniques, but whether enough food can be produced and distributed to an ever-increasing population, without destroying the ecology of the planet in the process. To conclude that this would be possible would be rash indeed.

A false debate

Too Many People? conflates the issues of population and immigration by inferring that to be in favour of limiting population growth is to be in favour of limiting immigration! But why? They are separate issues and attitudes depend mainly on where people stand in the political spectrum – right or left. Racism and xenophobia have existed historically, whatever the size of the global population, driven by a range of social and political factors; so too has opposition to racism and xenophobia, and support for migrants and asylum seekers. The struggle against racism also goes on irrespective of the trends in global population. There are many, like myself, who see the rising global human population as a problem for the planet, yet are completely opposed to immigration controls, and do not see a smaller global population as a solution to racism.

The book also resorts to what may be called extreme-exampleism: taking the most extreme example available from the other side of the debate and then infer that everyone on that side agrees with it. Paul Ehrlich's 1968 book *The Population Bomb* is a good example. Because Ehrlich argues that population is the root of all the problems of the planet, and that therefore an authoritarian solution is acceptable or even unavoidable, it implies that anyone who sees population as any kind of problem draws the same conclusions.[234]

Most, like myself, who see the need to limit the human population to a sustainable level, find Ehrlich's views repugnant. He advocated, for example, the use of punitive economic measures by the USA against any developing country that refused to implement population control, even by means based on free choice.

Angus and Butler enlist Barry Commoner in support of the thesis they advance in *Too Many People?* – that it is 'populationist' to suggest that the rising human population of the planet is an ecological problem that needs to be addressed. They do this on the basis of Commoner's long public battle with Paul Ehrlich. This is not, however, a fair representation of Commoner's views on the matter.

What Commoner objected to, as is clear in his most important book, *The Closing Circle: Nature, Man, and Technology,* was not the idea that the rising human population is a problem that needs to be addressed, but the catastrophist framework in which Ehrlich presented it in *The Population Bomb,* and the authoritarian solutions that Ehrlich proposed.

In fact, Commoner presents a remarkably nuanced view of the population issue in *The Closing Circle: Nature, Man, and Technology* (written in 1972, when the global population was half of what it is today). He recognises the problems of population growth and was not opposed to taking measures to reduce it, providing it was achieved by methods based on social justice and freedom of choice. He recognised what he called an 'intrinsic limit' to the size of the human population of the planet. He was hopeful that rising living standards would lead to a natural levelling off population growth by means of the demographic transition. He accepted, however, that population pressures are heavy on the developing nations of the Global South:

> The developing nations are poor: their rising populations press heavily on their scant resources; hunger is widespread and economic development difficult. In the poor nations, in contrast with a country like the United States, there does seem to be an immediate relation between the rate of population growth and the wellbeing of their peoples.[235]

After arguing strongly against Ehrlich's proposals (*The Closing Circle*) for coercive population controls in developing countries, he goes on to say that if it is necessary to reduce the birth rate, it should be done via the empowerment of women:

> On the other hand, if one's moral convictions and political views regard the previous course [Ehrlich's proposals] as dictatorial and corrosive of human values, then one can adopt the view that population growth in the developing nations of the world ought to be brought into balance by the same means that have already succeeded elsewhere – improvement of living conditions, urgent efforts to reduce infant mortality, social security measures, and the resultant effects on desired family size, together with personal, voluntary contraceptive practice. It is this view with which I wish to associate myself.[236]

He argued that rising population is the outcome of the abuse of poor nations by rich ones, and that the answer is to return to the poor countries 'enough of the wealth taken from them to give their peoples both the reason and the resources voluntarily to limit their own fertility'.

The authors of *Too Many People?*, although opposed to the Cairo conference because it recognised that rising population was a problem for the planet, felt obliged to give a gesture of recognition to its outcome – which they call the 'Cairo Consensus'. However, they then go on to 'explain' that in fact the decisions it had taken would in the end make matters worse:

> The Cairo Consensus was a significant defeat for 'right to life' forces. Although little of the promised funding for women's health programs actually materialised, the meeting gave women's rights activists in the third world a strong and credible programme that conservative governments could not easily dismiss. In particular, Cairo's resolutions have aided the fight against anti-abortion laws and for sexual rights.[237]

Yes, indeed it was! They then go on to qualify this by saying:

> But the meeting (*i.e.* the Cairo Conference) also strengthened the populationists, who came out of it with new credibility and a new way of arguing their case. In Cairo, populationists learned to say 'population stabilisation' or demographic transition' instead of 'population control', and to always include a sentence opposing coercive programs – but none of those purely verbal shifts changed their underlying assumption that the world's major problems were caused by poor women having too many babies.[238]

The book goes on effectively to junk the whole Cairo process, claiming that it is in any case impossible for Cairo to achieve its objectives on the basis of human rights and social justice, because any attempt to tackle the issue of the rising human population of the planet by providing, amongst other things, contraceptive services, might start with the principle of freedom of choice but, in the end, will inevitably slide into coercive methods:

> Many contemporary populationists (*i.e.* Malthusians) argue that population growth can be slowed or stopped in ways that respect the human rights of women and the poor...

But that's easier said than done. The idea that population control can be merged with a social justice agenda assumes that populationist policies don't contradict the goal of fundamental social change. In reality, far from making sustainable social change easier, populationist policies add divisive tensions and problems to environmental campaigns. In practice, it is just about impossible to 'do both'.

Support for Cairo

A positive assessment of Cairo was made, in 2003, by two Indian academics – Ashok Kumar of the Institute of Population Sciences in Mumbai and Dibya Lochan Mohanta of the Department of Anthropology, Utkal University, Bhubaneswar, India – in a paper entitled *'Population, Environment and Development in India'*.

They strongly supported both the Cairo conference and the *Programme of Action*, arguing that in India – the second most populous nation on Earth – the issues of population, environment and development remain a chronic problem, with the process of development unable to keep pace with the growth of population. India, they argue, has long faced degradation of the environment in the form of drought, floods, rainfall, ill health and pollution. Slow development processes, and the rapid growth of population, have forced the population to exploit the environment to an unsustainable degree:

> Thus, the environmental degradation of India can be attributed to the process of rapid population growth. Here [in Cairo] one attempt has been made to see the relationship between population, environment and development in India. Here one attempt has been made to see the complex relationship of different demographic and development indicators, viz: population growth, deforestation, urbanisation, industrialisation, health, land use pattern and globalisation with the environment in the Indian context.

Vandana Shiva and Maria Mies oppose a woman's right to choose

In fact, Vandana Shiva's stance on the Cairo conference directly reflects the position she defended in *Ecofeminism*, a book she published jointly with the German feminist Maria Mies, a year before the Cairo conference. This book has lots of positive material about the struggles of women in the Indian subcontinent, as noted earlier in relation to the struggles of the Chipko women; but when it comes to its approach to reproductive rights, and to women's right to control their own bodies, it is seriously problematic.

Maria Mies in particular launches an extraordinary attack on reproductive technology – for example, IV treatment – which she compares to genetic engineering and equates with fascism. Reproductive technologies, she argues, 'have been developed not because *women* need them, but because *capital* and science need women for the continuation of their model of growth and progress' (emphasis original). She goes on:

> Women's emancipation had for a long time been identified by many with women's control over their own fertility. The invention of various contraceptives, particularly the pill, was hailed by many as the decisive technological innovation that would eventually liberate women from their unruly fertility. Yet by looking at fertility as a disease, as a purely biological affair, women handed the responsibility for their generative powers to medical experts and scientists.[239]

One has to conclude from this that the only methods of contraception she would support are abstinence or the so-called rhythm method.

Like Shiva, she makes a sharp and valid critique of 'development', but then draws conclusions that pit the interests of women in different parts of the globe against each other. It is appropriate to point out the way that, like men, women in the Global North benefit in the short term from the impoverishment of women in the Global South, as they sew cheap clothes for the Global North. But to conclude for example as she does that 'there is no material basis for international women's solidarity'[240] is profoundly defeatist. She does say earlier in the same formulation, 'with such a structure', but then fails to suggest how such a 'structure' can be challenged, let alone replaced.

Vandana Shiva, in an article entitled *'Woman's Rights Reduced to Reproduction Issue'*,[241] written just before the Cairo conference, argues that the prevailing 'pro-choice' language 'reduces the issue of the well-being of women to reproduction, and then it reduces reproduction to abortion.' She has nothing positive to say about reproductive rights, either contraception or abortion. She argues that the promotion of reproductive rights is being used as an alternative to economic and social emancipation of women, that it should stop, and that the *Programme of Action* was (and is) a transmission belt to coercive methods – even if such programmes started on the basis of free choice.

To oppose all reproductive rights programmes on the basis that some might go off the rails, makes no sense. The upshot would be to deny large numbers of women, including impoverished women, the reproductive services that they desperately need.

The Global South

The fact that both the highest birth rates and lowest carbon footprints are to be found in the impoverished countries of the Global South, has led to the charge, in *Too Many People?* and elsewhere, that the empowerment approach leads to the targeting of the women of the Global South, or to blaming them for climate change.

This makes no sense. What empowerment actually targets is the appalling conditions the women of the Global South face, and the unmet need for reproductive services that they are forced to suffer. According to the UN, the full range of modern family-planning methods still remains unavailable to at least 350 million couples world-wide, many of whom say they want to prevent another pregnancy or to create more space between them.

More than 220 million women are denied basic reproductive services. These can be (and often are) the difference between life and death. There are 80 million unintended pregnancies a year – which equals the global population increase. Some 74,000 women die every year as a result of failed back-street abortions, with a disproportionate number of these from the Global South. Every year, around 288,000 women die from preventable causes related to pregnancy and childbirth, 99 per cent of them occurring in developing countries. The provision of reproductive services is a policy that helps the women of the Global South and helps the planet at the same time – as described above, a win-win situation.

In any case the proposition that most women in the Global South, given genuine choice, would choose to have the large families that many have today (or allow their husbands to insist on or determine such families) is unconvincing. Some would, but most would not, I suspect. Multiple pregnancies, with little space between them, wreak havoc in terms of the health and life expectancy of the mothers concerned.

But genuine choice is hard to come by. Most religious leaders oppose the empowerment of women to control their own fertility as interfering with divine purpose. Women are under pressure from state, from religion, from cultural factors, and from patriarchal pressures to have more children – or they are denied the means by which to avoid having more children.

It is not, however, just a matter of contraceptive services – important as these are. Empowerment means the whole package, if it is to be successful: contraception and abortion services, lifting women out of poverty, giving them access to education and jobs, and protection from patriarchal and conservative pressures, including those exercised by religious authorities. It is this combination of services and opportunities which can make a change to both the birth rate (in terms of the planet) and to the lives of the women involved.

There is a caveat. While lifting women out of poverty will, in most cases, lead to women having fewer children, this is not inevitably the case: they may still face countervailing pressures from conservative forces such as religion, patriarchy, and cultural factors, all opposing the use of reproductive services. In Catholic Italy, for example, religious strictures and laws are often outweighed by other factors, but in Saudi Arabia they are dominant.

Women still perform at least 80 per cent of domestic labour. More than a third of households in the Global South are female headed, and where they are not, women remain the primary providers of support.

Ecological footprints

It is true that the carbon footprint of the Global South is smaller than that of the North (around one metric tonne a year), as mentioned above. The first priority, therefore, is to reduce the carbon footprint of the high polluting populations of the Global North. The idea, however, that population growth in the Global South does not therefore matter is, in my view, mistaken. Every person on the planet has an ecological impact, grotesquely diverse as they might be. This is why we cannot just talk about *carbon* footprints. We have to talk about an even more important form of measurement: the *ecological* footprint – *i.e.* the total per capita impact on the environment, including soil erosion and depletion, deforestation, and the human impact on biodiversity.

There is another important reason as well. Populations trapped in poverty today rightly aspire to change their situation as soon as possible, and we are partisan with them in that. Some of the countries with the lowest carbon footprint today already have the highest economic growth rates, and therefore a big potential for such change. China's carbon footprint is already approaching 7 metric tonnes, after just two decades of capitalist growth. There is little point in assessing the impact of carbon footprints over the next 50 years on the basis of a snapshot of the situation as it is today.

It is argued that women have large families in impoverished societies because they are needed to provide labour, and to help their parents in old age. Impoverished women do indeed come under such pressures, but it does not necessarily ease the burdens they face. Every new pair of new hands is also another mouth to feed. Women's health is also undermined by repeated, often annual, pregnancies; smaller families would improve both their health and their quality of life. It would also give them a far better chance of reaching old age.

Expanding families are forced to degrade their own environment in order to get food, water, and fuel on which to survive. In the slums of today's megacities, entire families, including young children, are often forced to scavenge, often on the highly toxic waste tips.

Time for change

It would be a big mistake to continue to allow allegations of populationism or Malthusianism to skew or restrict debate and discussions on the population issue. We have to get beyond the nineteenth and early twentieth-century debates and name-calling, to a new dialogue which is taking place today.

The issue of population, we have to insist, is an important and wholly legitimate issue for the left to discuss. Human beings are a part of nature and have an obligation to live in harmony with it, rather than becoming the destroyers of biodiversity. This means recognising that the current rate of population increase is unsustainable. It means looking towards a society in which humankind can exist alongside other species without setting itself against their very existence. Such an approach is not anti-people but entirely pro-people. It is not a reactionary objective but a wholly progressive one. It is good for the planet and good for its biodiversity.

It is time that the left recognised that population is a serious problem and started to discuss the issue. A reduction in the rate of growth of the population, however, or even its stabilisation, is not a panacea. It would not resolve the ecological crisis or guarantee sustainability. Nor would it eradicate poverty or prevent hunger. A wide range of other ecological, economic and social measures, on a much shorter time scale, would be needed in order to achieve these things. But the chances of success would clearly be better.

I don't offer here a figure in terms of the 'carrying capacity' of the planet, the maximum human population it can sustain without irreparable damage – another taboo subject on the environmental left. But there clearly is one, and if it has not yet been reached, it is not far away. It is hard to reconcile the world, and the relationship of humans with nature that William Morris paints in his writings, with the population levels we are seeing today, and are expecting in the future.[242]

The left needs to get beyond the old debates and recognise that there is a serious problem to address as far as rising population is concerned, and that the way forward is through the empowerment of women to control their own lives. This would repair a gaping hole in our analysis of the climate crisis.

This is why we have to make the ecological struggle an integral part of the struggle against capitalism today. I am not arguing that rising population is the root cause of the ecological crisis and global warming. That is the fault of the capitalist system of production and the commodification of the planet – although pre-capitalist systems of agriculture were already degrading the ecology and the biodiversity before capitalism arrived. What I am arguing is that rising population is a major contributory factor.

I am not arguing that the stabilisation of the global population, would, in itself, resolve the ecological crisis. It would not eradicate poverty or prevent hunger. Continued reliance on fossil fuels could easily overwhelm any carbon emission reductions from slower population growth. A wide range of other ecological, economic and social measures, in a much shorter time scale, would be needed in order to do these things. But the stabilisation of the global human population would create a better basis on which to tackle the ecological crisis. It would be easier to provide food, fresh water, energy, and waste disposal, and protect the bio-diversity of the planet at less environmental cost, for a population of 8 billion rather than 11 billion or more.

15 The age of the Anthropocene

At every step, we are reminded that we by no means rule over nature like a conqueror over a foreign people, like someone standing outside nature – but that we, with flesh, blood and brain, belong to nature, and exist in its midst, and that all our mastery of it consists in the fact that we have the advantage over all other creatures of being able to learn its laws and apply them correctly.

Frederic Engels.[243]

The idea of the Anthropocene is that the impact of modern humans on the planet is now so great that it defines the current geological epoch: that is, whether the current epoch (the Holocene or interglacial period) should be superseded by the Anthropocene, or the 'age of modern humans'. This proposition was first advanced in 2000 by the Dutch atmospheric chemist Paul J. Crutzen (winner of a Nobel Prize in 1995 for his pioneering research on stratospheric ozone depletion, which led to international action to restore it) and by Eugene F Stoermer, a biologist from the University of Michigan.

This is a subject with challenging terminology for those of us who are not scientists or geologists, but there is no alternative. The adoption of the Anthropocene would involve a change to the International Chronostratigraphic Chart – the geological time chart that divides the Earth's 4.5 billion-year history into eons, eras, periods, epochs and ages.

The Holocene began with the end of the last ice age 11,700 years ago. It had a global average land surface temperature that remained broadly constant until anthropogenic global warming arrived and changed everything with the industrial revolution in the latter part of the eighteenth century.

We are currently in the Phanerozoic eon of the Cenozoic era and the quaternary period, which is further divided into two epochs: the Pleistocene and Holocene. The Pleistocene was characterised by climatic fluctuations and periodic ice ages in the Northern Hemisphere, the last of which was 11,700 years ago, leaving us in the current epoch of the Holocene.

A step towards the change

A landmark decision was taken in August 2016 that makes a definition change to the Anthropocene highly likely within the next few years. It was taken by a little-known but highly significant scientific body known as the Anthropocene Working Group (AWG) of the Geological Society, London. The AWG is a subcommittee of another scientific body, called the Sub-commission on Quaternary Stratigraphy (SQS) – also little-known outside of scientific circles. The AWG is comprised of 38 Earth systems scientists, and is convened by Jan Zalasiewicz, a geologist from Leicester University in Britain.

In 2009, the AWG (of which Paul Crutzen is a member) was asked to undertake a study of this proposition and make a recommendation in regard to it. Seven years later, in August 2016, the AWG agreed by a majority of 35 to 1 that the Anthropocene is indeed a 'scientifically and stratigraphically' sound proposition, and that such a change should be therefore be made.

The AWG's recommendation was first published at a plenary of the International Geological Congress, which took place in Cape Town in August 2016. Afterwards Chris Rapley, a climate scientist at University College London, stressed the importance of the decision this way in an interview with the *Guardian*:

> Since the planet is our life support system – we are essentially the crew of a largish spaceship – interference with its functioning at this level and on this scale is highly significant. If you or I were crew on a smaller spacecraft, it would be unthinkable to interfere with the systems that provide us with air, water, fodder and climate control. But the shift into the Anthropocene tells us that we are playing with fire, a potentially reckless mode of behaviour which we are likely to come to regret unless we get a grip on the situation.[244]

Such a momentous proposition, if finally endorsed, would mean that for the first time a geological epoch had been determined by the impact of a single species rather than by the planet's main flora and fauna composition or by geophysical events. It would (rightly) imply that humanity itself has now become a geophysical force equal to some of the great forces of nature such as meteorite impacts, volcanic eruptions and chemical changes that have previously brought about such changes.

The AWG proposition now forms the basis of a recommendation to the Sub-commission on Quaternary Stratigraphy, its parent body. If supported there, it will go to the SQS's parent body – the International Commission on Stratigraphy. After that, it will still need to be ratified by the Executive Committee of the International Union of Geological Sciences – and by a 60 per cent majority. If all of this is successfully completed, the new geological epoch of the Anthropocene will then be officially added to the Geological Time Scale.

According to those in a position to judge, the AWG recommendation is likely to prove decisive, and there could be an official adoption of the Anthropocene within two or three years.

The implications of the Anthropocene

The persistence of Crutzen and Stoermer paid off. And the result, if the AWG recommendation is accepted, will be a crucial addition to the armoury of those who are struggling to save the planet from ecological destruction. It will be a warning sign to all those who doubt the depth and scope of the ecological crisis and how close we are to the point of no return.

It sounds the alarm, in a clear and unavoidable way, as to the full depth and character of the ecological crisis and the anthropological driving force behind it. Any tendency to dismiss the Anthropocene as an obscure geological debate amongst the scientific community should be firmly rejected. The scientific community has, not for the first time, made a very important contribution to the defence of the planet.

A number of books have been published, in the course of the AWG deliberations, backing the approach it has been developing. These include *The Anthropocene: The Human Era and How It Shapes the Planet* by Christian Schwagerl (2014). In his foreword, Paul Crutzen describes the book as a 'navigation system for the new world of the Anthropocene that lies before us'.

The Geological Society's AWG published its own book, *A Stratigraphical Basis for the Anthropocene* (Waters *et al.*, 2014), which sets out the evidential basis of their thinking. *The Anthropocene and the Global Environmental Crisis* (2015), edited by Clive Hamilton, Christophe Bonneuil and François Gemenne, is an excellent introduction to a complex subject.

The best book, from a Marxist point of view, I have read on the Anthropocene is *Facing the Anthropocene: Fossil Capitalism and the Crisis of the Earth System* (2016) by Ian Angus. Although it was written before the AWG made its recommendation, it was coincidentally published just after. It combines a clear warning of the scale of the crisis we face, with a well-informed exposition of what the Anthropocene is and why we need to take it seriously. It is an unequivocal declaration that the Anthropocene is here; that its implications in terms of life on this planet, including our own, are dangerous in the extreme; and that it determines the framework in which the struggle now takes place to save the biosphere of the planet as a habitable space.

The concept of the Anthropocene goes to the heart of the debate on the ecological crisis today. It has implications for the kind of eco-socialism that is crucial for a successful ecological struggle in the twenty-first century.

The date of the Anthropocene

One of the more controversial questions the AWG had to deal with was the precise date from which the Anthropocene epoch should be deemed to have started. They discussed a range of proposals in this regard: from the time modern humans entered the scene 160,000 years ago; the beginning of agriculture; the onset of industrialisation; the date of the invention of the steam engine; and various dates in the mid-20th century. Crutzen and Stoermer had proposed the onset of the industrial revolution as the starting date.

This reflected the need of geologists to identify the Anthropocene in changes in the fossil record – in rock sediment or glacier ice for example – which mark the point at which the transition took place. Other suggestions ranged from the plutonium fallout from nuclear weapons testing in the early 1950s; plastic pollution; soot from power stations; concrete particles; and even the bones left by the global proliferation and consumption of the domestic chicken.

The date they eventually agreed on was mid-twentieth century, around 1950, which coincides with what has become known as the 'great acceleration' in terms of the human impact on the planet. This is the time when chemical pollution and carbon emissions, in particular, went into overdrive. This was not a problem for Crutzen and Stoermer since they had always made clear that their proposal for the industrial revolution was just a suggestion and that they expected there would be further debate on the issue.

I find the need for a precise date unconvincing, however. I see the Anthropocene as much more of a process, and one that took place over a much longer period of time and culminated in a qualitative change in the middle of the twentieth century.

There has long been a debate around the destruction of the megafauna as to whether the main cause was modern humans or naturally occurring climate change – for example Paul Hunter of the University of Arizona and his 'overkill' thesis in 1972.

While ecological destruction increased dramatically with the industrial revolution, the destructive impact of modern humans on the planet long preceded the arrival of both industrialisation and capitalism. It is what George Monbiot in his (2017) book *How Did We Get into This Mess?* calls 'trophic cascade' – or the collapse of ecosystems from the top when major components such as megafauna are removed.[245]

A study in 2014 entitled '*Global Late Quaternary Megafauna Extinctions Linked to Humans, Not Climate Change*' found that the culprit was overwhelmingly modern humans.

This is supported by Simon L. Lewis and Mark A. Maslin in their 2018 book, *The Human Planet and How We Created the Anthropocene*, which deals at some detail with the issue. They argue that the main culprit was the second wave of *Homo sapiens* that emerged out of Africa around 50,000 years ago, bringing with it an unprecedented ability to affect the environment of the planet. With this migration, they argue:

> We truly became the world's apex predator by working in very large groups and planning, coordinating and adapting strategies depending on the prey we were after. As soon as early second-wave *Homo sapiens* migrated into a new region, they

started systematically to hunt populations of larger animals – defined as over 40 kg in weight – called megafauna. At the same time, about half of all large-bodied mammals world-wide were lost: 4 per cent of all mammal species. The losses were not evenly distributed: Africa lost 18 per cent, Eurasia 36 per cent, North America 72 per cent, South America 83 per cent and Australia 88 per cent of their large bodied mammals. The greatest losses were on continents that did not have ancestral hominin species present. The culprit, it appears, was us.

Since Paul Martin at the University of Arizona put forward his 'Pleistocene overkill' hypothesis in 1972, academics have debated whether all these extinctions were caused by changes in climate, particularly at the end of the last glaciation, or by the pressure of human hunting. There is very strong evidence that it was mostly down to us. Megafauna had been continuously abundant both on land and in the seas for hundreds of millions of years and have survived the fifty or so glaciations-interglacial cycles of the Quaternary Period over the past 2.6 million years. It is only in the last 50,000 years, coinciding with our ancestors' spread, that megafauna species started to go extinct in large numbers. There is even evidence of earlier hominin-caused extinctions in Africa beginning about 1 million years ago with the loss of 'proboscidean' elephant-like species and sabre-toothed cats, which continue to flourish in regions uninhabited by our ancestors.

Almost all of the documented megafauna losses coincide closely with the expansions of *Homo sapiens*. For example megafauna losses occurred in Australia about 45,000 years ago, Europe between 50,000 and 7,000 years ago, Japan about 30,000 years ago, North America between 15,000 and 10,000 years ago, South America 13,000 to 7,000 years ago, the Caribbean about 6,0000 years ago, the Pacific Islands between 3,000 and 1,000 years ago, Madagascar about 2,000 years ago and New Zealand about 700 years ago. Considering all of these cases together, the climate change thesis does not fit well; the strongest correlation is with the arrival of humans.

… Using approximations of the numbers of animals that lived in each of these habitats, we can estimate that the few million people that lived at the end of the Pleistocene killed a staggering one billion very large animals.[246]

Lewis and Maslin note that: 'even after *Homo sapiens* had spread across every continent except Antarctica, we totalled between 1 and 10 million people world-wide, less than the present-day population of just one of today's big cities'.[247]

In Europe, deforestation and the onset of farming methods transformed the medieval landscape beyond recognition.

Whilst this activity did not define the geological epoch (*i.e.* challenge the Holocene), it is clear that modern humans have always had a unique ability to change the environment at the expense of other species.

It is true that this destructive capacity increased dramatically with the industrial revolution, and the capitalist mode of production, in the latter part of the eighteenth century; but that does not mean we can ignore the rest of human history in this regard.

In my view, species extinction as a result of human activity is the single most significant factor in the case for the Anthropocene. Today, we are facing the biggest extinction of species – the 'sixth extinction' – since the demise of the dinosaurs 65 million years ago. Today 40 per cent of all mammal species face a short to medium term threat of extinction, against a background rate of one every 700 years. Amphibians are disappearing at a staggering 45,000 times the background rate. This is a rate of extinction that ultimately puts at risk all species on the planet, including, eventually, our own. Species extinction on this scale is not only at the heart of the ecological crisis today, but is the single most compelling factor in the case for the Anthropocene.

Don't mention the species

Although the Anthropocene thesis is increasingly accepted amongst Marxist environmentalists during the short time it has been discussed, this is by no means universally the case. There are those in the wider movement, such as Naomi Klein, who oppose the concept, as do some Marxist ecologists.

In my view, the most coherent case against the Anthropocene is made by the Marxist ecologist (and FI comrade) Andreas Malm, of Lund University in Sweden. In his (otherwise excellent) book *Fossil Capital: The Rise of Steam Power and the Roots of Global Warming*, he brands it as both a 'myth' and a form of 'species thinking'.

It is not human beings as such, he argues, that are driving the ecological crisis, but the capitalist mode of production and individual industrialists. He therefore proposes instead the concept of the 'Capitalocene' – in other words, the idea that it is capitalism and not human activity in general that is driving this change – and driving indeed the ecological crisis.

The Capitalocene, he argues, is based on 'the geology not of mankind, but of capital accumulation.'[248] Steam engines, he says, 'were not adopted by some natural-born deputies of the human species. By the nature of the social order of things, they could only be installed *by the owners of the means of production.*' [emphasis original] 'Is there any reason to consider it any more truly representative of 'the human enterprise' than the Luddites or the plug drawers or the preachers of steam demonology? We should 'not mistake capitalists for human beings' he argues.[249] The Anthropocene, Malm insists,

> might be a useful concept and narrative for polar bears and amphibians and birds who want to know what species is wreaking such terrible havoc on their habitats, but, alas, they lack the capacity to scrutinise and stand up to the human actions; for those who may do so – other human beings – species thinking on climate change conduces to paralysis.[250]

Malm appears to suggest that any notion of assessing the environmental impact of modern humans as a species, runs counter to a class based (or Marxist) analysis of society. But why? The idea of the Anthropocene does not imply that human beings are equally responsible for their collective impact on the planet. The scientists who proposed it don't think so. Nor do those Marxists advocating the Anthropocene, such as John Bellamy Foster, think so.

Malm seems to suggest we have no responsibility for the collective impact of our own species on the planet whist capitalism exists, and will only assume this after capitalism has been removed.

The problem with the Capitalocene proposition is that it could be applied equally to climate change as to the Anthropocene. In *Green Capitalism*, in fact, Daniel Tanuro does exactly that. Global warming is not, he argues, a product of human activity as such but of capitalism as a system. It is caused, he argues by:

> over-production which leads to over-consumption on the one hand and growing poverty and under-consumption on the other. In the final analysis, therefore, it is a social crisis and it would be infinitely more accurate to refer to capitalist climate change instead of anthropogenic climate change.[251]

The Capitalocene proposition also has nothing to say regarding the ecological record of the non-capitalist societies that existed for 70 years in the last century. Surely, if you want to argue that ecological destruction is only due to capitalism, then you should at least define it as something like 'Stalinist-Capitalocene'.

The Anthropocene concept – and indeed anthropogenic climate change as such – is in my view entirely consistent with the approach of classical Marxism (Marx, Engels and William Morris), in terms of human beings as a living part of nature and not in conflict with it. They talked repeatedly about the impact of 'human beings' on nature and not only of capitalists.

We not only need to deal with the impact of our own species on the planet: we have a duty to do so. This does not mean that we ignore the class divisions that exist in human society, or the fact that the rich, the powerful, the corporate interests, bear the main responsibility for the ecological crisis. While recognising all that, we cannot ignore the overall impact of our species on the planet, or the fact that we are a part of that species.

Andreas Malm is not alone on the left in proposing the notion of the Capitalocene. His views are strongly reflected in two books published in 2016: *Anthropocene or Capitalocene*, edited by Jason W. Moore and *The Shock of the Anthropocene* by Christophe Bonneuil and Jean-Baptiste Fressoz.

Jason W. Moore, it should be added, is a very sharp critic of John Bellamy Foster's views as contained in *Marx's Ecology: Materialism and Nature*. He elaborates this in *Capitalism in the Web of Life: Ecology and the Accumulation of Capital*, published in 2015, where he is sharply critical of Foster's notion of the ecological content of classical Marxism, and of a metabolic rift between nature and human society.[252] This has resulted in a sharp debate between Foster and Moore. Ian Angus interviewed Foster on this dispute on his *Climate and Capitalism* site in June 2016.[253]

Neither of these books, however, adds much of substance to the position originally set out by Malm: that it is the capitalist system, not modern humans as a species, that is responsible for what is happening to the planet. They both expand on the ecologically destructive nature of capitalism – with which I strongly agree. Capitalism is indeed the most environmentally destructive system of society that modern humans have produced – with the possible exception of Stalinism. I don't dispute that.

But it misses the point. The question is not simply whether capitalism is ecologically destructive, but whether the ecological crisis can be reduced to capitalism. To do so is, in my view, far too narrow a perspective from which to make a judgment on either the character of the epoch or the impact of modern humans on the planet. In any case, in the end capitalism is a human activity, a human construct. At the moment, it is the current expression of human activity – even if a temporary one. It is the way human beings have been organised for most of the past 300 years – which they can and hopefully will change in the not too distant future.

The industrial revolution

This raises the matter of the industrial revolution itself, which in my view cannot be simply conflated with capitalism either – despite the fact that capitalism was a product of the industrial revolution. The industrial revolution, the invention of the steam engine and then the internal combustion engine, alongside the massive expansion of production and population made possible by these inventions, continues to pose a huge challenge to the ecology of the planet, largely irrespective of the prevailing mode of production.

If the problem is simply capitalism, this implies (in reverse) that its removal would resolve – partially at least – the ecological crisis. But there is no evidence that this would be the case. In fact, major existential challenges would continue to exist, and the ecological struggle would have to continue long after capitalism had left the scene.

16 Food and agriculture

Walking through the English countryside on a glorious autumn morning, it is hard to imagine that a battle is raging over the future of our food and the countryside. Dappled shades of green and brown line my path; glistening grass, gently kissed by the weak morning sun; heavy spits from my boots with every step.

Philip Lymbery[254]

The impact of modern agriculture on the planet is gigantic. Agriculture uses 70 per cent of all available fresh water worldwide. Sixty per cent of global biodiversity loss is directly due to agriculture. The cattle sector of Brazilian Amazon agriculture, driven by the international beef and leather trades, has been responsible for about 80% of all deforestation in the region, or roughly 14% of the world's total annual deforestation. It is the world's largest single driver of deforestation.[255] Yet with a rising human population and rapidly changing diets in the emerging economies, the trend is towards much higher global meat consumption. In fact the demand for food could double by mid-century – and fresh water usage by a similar amount.

The poorest people on the planet have long been subjected to disastrous famines and food shortages. In 2007 and 2008, dramatic increases in world food prices created a global crisis, with economic instability and social unrest, particularly in the poorest regions of the world. Those who were 'normally' subjected to famine and starvation were joined by millions more. Seventy-five million people were officially classified as hungry, and 15 million were driven into extreme poverty.

It was the food crisis that triggered the Tunisian revolution in January 2011, and consequently the Arab Spring. A young Tunisian vegetable seller, the lone breadwinner of a family of seven, set himself on fire in front of a government building after police confiscated his unauthorised cartload of vegetables. It followed protests over food prices as well as corruption, social inequalities, unemployment and political repression.

If the developing countries of Asia, Africa, and Latin America are to avoid such disasters, they have to avoid the free-for-all model of globalised capitalism which is currently the norm. In the Global South, over 800 million people are malnourished, 40 million die every year from hunger or diseases caused by hunger. Almost 2 billion people do not have regular access to clean drinking water, and 25 million people die as a result every year. One in four of the world's children suffer stunted growth. In developing countries, the proportion can rise to one in three. Sixty-six million primary school-age children attend classes while hungry across the developing world – 23 million of them in Africa alone.

The situation of these countries is exacerbated by the domination of the WTO (World Trade Organisation), IMF (International Monetary Fund), World Bank and G8 (Group of Eight – the major economies of the Global North). These are the neoliberal gatekeepers of capitalism: they have saddled the developing countries with massive debt, and forced them to produce monoculture crops for the multi-nationals while bankrupting their farmers by subsidised competition from the Global North. This leaves developing countries unable to tackle the ecological threat; and compounds the dependency from which they suffer, destroys their economic and social conditions, and distorts the markets in which they operate.

Desertification, salinification and floods are making large areas of the planet unsuitable either for human habitation or for growing food. Climate chaos is creating extreme weather events, in which loss of life and destruction of dwellings and infrastructure have inflicted death, disease and further poverty on millions.

Remarkably, despite all this, some still argue that it is possible to feed not just todays 7.6 billion people, but even, if things were organised differently, the projected population of up to 11 billion people that could be here by the end of the century. One such is the biologist, writer (and GMO crops supporter), Colin Tudge, in the shape of his 2007 book *Feeding People Is Easy*. His argument is that this can be achieved, not just for 10 or 11 billion projected population, but for an unlimited population and for an unlimited period of time. He puts it this way:

> The message of this book, I modestly claim, is the most important that can be conceived: that we, human beings, can feed ourselves to the highest standards of both nutrition and gastronomy; that we can do so effectively for ever – for the next

10,000 years, or indeed the next million; that we can do this without cruelty to
livestock and without wrecking the rest of the world and driving other species to
extinction; and that if we can do the job properly, we will create human societies
that are truly agreeable, co-operative and at peace, in which all manner of people
with all kinds of beliefs and aspirations can be personally fulfilled.[256]

This is wishful and dangerous nonsense. The UN Food and Agriculture
Organisation (FAO) estimates that farmers would have to produce 70 per
cent more food by 2050 to meet the needs of the expected 9 billion global
population. That amounts to a billion tonnes more wheat, rice and other
cereals, and 200 million tonnes more beef and other livestock.

It is true that if food was produced and distributed rationally and efficiently,
the situation could be improved. Almost a half of all food produced is wasted
while a billion people go short every day. Corruption and speculation exist
on a grand scale, and vast quantities of food are wasted simply because it
becomes unprofitable.

It is also true that some famous past predictions that population
growth would inevitably outstrip food supply, have turned out to be
wrong – from Thomas Malthus in the late eighteenth century with *An
Essay on the Principle of Population*, to Paul Ehrlich in his *The Population
Bomb* published in 1968 by the Sierra Club (which became a best seller).
Despite valid criticisms of such arguments, however, it would be a big
mistake to conclude that there is no problem in feeding an ever-increasing
population, even if the distortions of the market were removed.

Malthus and Ehrlich failed to take into account the huge increase in
productivity that could be achieved through ever more intensified agriculture, by
the use of industrialised farming. Whilst traditional farming, with no pesticides
or artificial fertiliser, is more efficient in terms of calories of food produced for
every kcal of energy expended, when it comes to total output, industrialised
agriculture produces around ten times as much per hectare as traditional farming.

The big question

The big question posed therefore is not just whether enough food can be
produced and distributed to feed the existing human population of 7 billion,

or indeed the 9 or 10 billion people projected by mid-century – which might be possible if today's grotesque inequalities, corruption, and the market distortions were resolvable: the question posed is whether such numbers can be fed without destroying the biosphere of the planet in the process. In other words, can it be done without further extension of intensified agriculture (factory farming) and by the ever-increasing use of artificial fertilisers, pesticides, hormones, antibiotics, and mono-cropping techniques.

The environmental cost of the latter would be huge. Sixty per cent of global biodiversity loss is directly due to food production, and is responsible for the destruction of 91 per cent of Amazonian rain forest – the most environmentally diverse habitat on the planet. The distribution of vast quantities of food backwards and forwards across the globe – food miles – is also unsustainable.

In Britain, food miles have a huge impact on the environment. 95 per cent of our fruit comes from abroad, and half of our vegetables are also imported. Food imports increased from 13.5 million tonnes in 1992 to just over 16 million tonnes by 2002. Whilst only 1 per cent of food is transported by air, it accounts for 11 per cent of carbon emissions. Since 1992, the amount of food transported by air has risen by 140 per cent. Rainforest the size of ten football pitches is felled every second, much of it to make room for export based food crops.

Agriculture is a massive contributor to greenhouse gas emissions, including methane from livestock, nitrous oxide from the soil, GHG from fuel for machinery, the production of vast quantities of artificial fertiliser, and the transportation of food to the market place. It is also responsible for a massive runoff from the use of mineral fertilisers to produce arable crops, for both human consumption and animal feed, therefore increasing damage to the wider environment.

The most remarkable statistic concerning food production is that the greenhouse gas emissions (CO_2 equivalents) generated by meat production for human consumption are greater than the emissions generated by the entire world-wide transportation system combined: cars, trucks, trains, ships and aircraft! Yes, cars, trucks, trains, ships and aircraft!

The agricultural transition

During the twentieth century, agriculture underwent what is known as the agricultural transition – ushering in not just fertilisers and pesticides but mechanisation – bringing about the greatest change since agriculture was first developed by human beings some 13,000 years ago.

According to the John Hopkins Research Centre, most US farms in the early twentieth century were diversified, producing a variety of crops and animal species together on the same farm. Farmers were skilled in a wide range of trades, and had autonomy over how to manage their crops and animals. Animals were typically raised with access to the outdoors. Most of the work on the farm was done by human or animal labour.

Despite this, two-thirds of global food production is produced by the world's 570 million small and family-run units. Family farms cover about 75 per cent of the world's agricultural land. Over half of the world's small farms are in China and over 20 per cent in India. The trend, however, is sharply towards both bigger farm units and industrialised agriculture. The richer the country, the stronger this trend.

Although fewer and fewer people are farmers, agriculture employs 1.3 billion men and women: 40 per cent of the working population. Peasants are still the majority of working people in Africa and Asia. Over the past two decades, in Asia, Africa and Latin America, peasants have faced 'conservative modernisation' policies, posing deep challenges to peasant societies in the attempt to adapt them to capitalist globalisation. The peasantry faces many threats beyond the future of food systems and environmental balance, in particular the powerful rise of agribusiness, land grabbing, expansion of export-based monocultures at the expense of food-producing agriculture, and pressure on natural resources. Takeover of lands is a global phenomenon, undertaken by local, national and transnational elites as well as investors and speculators, with the complicity of government and local authorities. It leads to the concentration of landownership and natural resources in the hands of major investments funds, plantation owners and major firms involved in forestry, hydroelectric power stations, and mines. It is exacerbated by the tourism and real estate industries, and authorities managing port and industrial infrastructure.

Land grabbing goes hand in hand with increasing control by big business over agriculture and food, through greater control over land, water, seeds and other natural resources. In this race for profit, the private sector has strengthened its control over food production systems, monopolising resources and gaining a dominant position in decision-making processes.

Governments of countries in the South, often under the pressure of debt payments, have in recent years increased agricultural exports and extractivist policies. There again, peasant populations have borne the brunt of the consequences in environmental destruction and control over their lands by the big agribusiness corporations.

Food sovereignty

Big business dominates our global food system. A small handful of large corporations control much of the production, processing, distribution, marketing and retailing of food. This concentration of power enables big businesses to wipe out competition and dictate tough terms to their suppliers. It forces both farmers and consumers into poverty. Under this system, around a billion people are hungry and around 2 billion are obese or overweight.

Movements of people across the world are therefore fighting for 'food sovereignty' – a term coined in 1996 by *La Via Campesina*. Food sovereignty allows communities to maintain control over the way food is produced, traded and consumed. It seeks to create a food system that is designed to help people and the environment, rather than make profits for multinational corporations. The food sovereignty movement is a global alliance of farmers, growers, consumers and activists. It is counterposed to the demands of governments around the world for 'food security' – a concept that instead aims to ensure that the global demand for food is met by free market methods and ever more industrialised faming systems.

La Via Campesina is one of the biggest social movements in the world, bringing together more than 200 million small and medium-scale farmers, landless people, women farmers, indigenous peoples, migrants and agricultural workers from 70 countries. The Brazilian Landless Workers Movement (MST), with 1.5 million members, is one of the biggest components of *Via Campesina*. It campaigns for access to land by the poor and for land redistribution. It has led land occupations by the rural poor, forcing the Brazilian government to resettle hundreds of thousands of families.

One of the main reasons for hunger and malnutrition is the lack of access by small farmers to natural resources – in particular land, water and seeds –

since most of the best land is in the hands of the big transnational companies, which impose a model of agricultural production designed for export rather than for local consumption. They impose a commercialised, intensive agriculture, that puts economic interests before the needs of people.

In contrast, food sovereignty puts the local agricultural producers at the centre of the system, supporting the right of the people to produce their own food independent of the conditions established by the market. It is about prioritising local and national markets, and reinforcing agriculture by promoting food production, distribution and consumption on the basis of social, economic and environmental sustainability.

The industrial agriculture model threatens the existence of traditional farming and fishing and small-scale food production. Women have a central role to play: in the Global South they produce 80 per cent of food. At the same time women and children world-wide are the most affected by hunger and famine. In many parts of the Global South, the law denies women the right to own land, and even where they can legally own it, they are denied that right. As a result of this, many individual and groups of women are joining the farmers' movements to seek protection.

In many parts of the world, recent decades have also seen major population movements driven by climate change and other facets of environmental crisis. These movements will become increasingly important, involving people who are among the poorest on the planet. This new offensive against entire communities is fomenting movements of popular self-organisation and struggle against climate disasters and destructive projects. Many struggles by peasant communities have led to the founding of cooperatives that seek to control production and distribution themselves. These experiences, though limited, raise not only the question of control but of production linked to social needs.

Many local struggles have involved both peasant and indigenous movements in Africa, Latin America, Asia and Europe. The questions of land and of food sovereignty are at the heart of all these struggles. They have all been marked by a broad unity of struggles, anti-capitalist, environmentalist, feminist, and against discrimination and ethnic oppression. The question of democracy and sovereignty in the face of governments and multinationals is also at the heart of their demands. *La Via Campesina,* which federates more than 160 organisations in 70 countries, has succeeded, over twenty years, in bringing together millions of peasant men and women, small producers. And it has put feminist, indigenous and environmental issues at the heart of its concerns.

In Latin America those struggling for the rights of indigenous communities and the right to the land often face murderous repression, as in Brazil and Honduras. In Asia, in Africa – for example, in Mali – on all continents, peasant movements lead the mobilisations against land monopolisation.

Peasant women and men, landless people and indigenous peoples, and especially women and youths, precarious farm workers, are dispossessed of their means of subsistence by practices which also destroy the environment. Indigenous peoples and ethnic minorities are excluded from their lands, often by force, making their lives more precarious and in certain cases amounting to modern slavery. Although the concept of food sovereignty relates most strongly to the countries of the impoverished South, it also exists in the Global North. In fact the first European forum on food sovereignty was held in Krems in Austria in 2011.

La Via Campesina's seven principles of food sovereignty are as follows:

Food as a basic human right. Everyone must have access to safe, nutritious and culturally appropriate food in sufficient quantity and quality to sustain a healthy life with full human dignity. Each nation should declare that access to food is a constitutional right and guarantee the development of the primary sector to ensure the concrete realisation of this fundamental right.

Agrarian reform. A genuine agrarian reform is necessary which gives landless and farming people – especially women – ownership and control of the land they work and returns territories to indigenous peoples. The right to land must be free of discrimination on the basis of gender, religion, race, social class or ideology; the land belongs to those who work it.

Protecting natural resources. Food Sovereignty entails the sustainable care and use of natural resources, especially land, water, and seeds and livestock breeds. The people who work the land must have the right to practice sustainable management of natural resources, and to conserve biodiversity free of restrictive intellectual property rights. This can only be done from a sound economic basis with security of tenure, healthy soils and reduced use of agrochemicals.

Reorganising the trade in food. Food is first and foremost a source of nutrition and only secondarily an item of trade. National agricultural policies must prioritize production for domestic consumption and food self-sufficiency. Food imports must not displace local production nor depress prices.

Ending the globalisation of hunger. Food sovereignty is undermined by multilateral institutions and by speculative capital. The growing control of multinational corporations over agricultural policies has been facilitated by the economic policies of multilateral organisations such as the WTO, World Bank and IMF. Regulation and taxation of speculative capital, and a strictly enforced Code of Conduct for TNCs, is therefore needed.

Social peace. Everyone has the right to be free from violence. Food must not be used as a weapon. Increasing levels of poverty and marginalisation in the countryside, along with the growing oppression of ethnic minorities and indigenous populations, aggravate situations of injustice and hopelessness. The ongoing displacement, forced urbanisation, repression and increasing incidence of racism against smallholder farmers, cannot be tolerated.

Democratic control. Smallholder farmers must have direct input into formulating agricultural policy at all levels. The UN and its related organisations will have to become more open and democratic for this to become a reality. These principles form the basis of good governance, accountability and equal participation in economic, political and social life, free from all forms of discrimination. Rural women, in particular, must be granted direct and active decision making on food and rural issues.[257]

Meat

The biggest agricultural challenge by far, however, is the current global level of meat consumption – which is totally unsustainable. It is also unnecessary from a dietary point of view. Red meat, moreover, is recognised by the WHO as carcinogenic.

Today, 70 billion land animals (*i.e.* excluding fish) are slaughtered every year for human consumption. This sum has doubled in the last 50 years, and is set to double again by 2050. Two-thirds of these animals are reared by intensive methods – or concentrated animal feeding operations (CAFOs) as they are known in the trade. They consume vast quantities of corn, maize, and soy that could otherwise be eaten, far more effectively, by the human population including the planet's billions of hungry people. By far the biggest source of food waste today is not from domestic consumption or the restaurant industry, serious as that is, but from feeding human edible grain crops to industrially reared farm animals.

Feeding corn to livestock to produce meat for human consumption makes absolutely no sense, however it is looked at, since the calories conversion rate is so low. In *Dead Zones,* Lymbery quotes a study by the University of Minnesota which concludes that for every hundred calories fed to cattle (that have the worst conversion rate) in the form of grain, as little as 3 per cent are returned in the resulting meat. The picture in relation to protein is little better. The same study found that for every 100 grams fed to animals, we receive only about 43 grams of protein from milk, 35 from eggs, 40 from chicken, 10 from pork, or 5 from beef.

Lymbery goes on to quote the UN Food and Agriculture Organisation as saying:

> When livestock are raised in intensive systems, they convert carbohydrates and protein that might otherwise be eaten directly by humans, and use them to produce smaller quantities of energy for the protein.[258]

The US has led the world in large-scale farming, pioneering the use of intensive livestock rearing in pig farms, cattle sheds and sheep pens. There are now more than 50,000 facilities in the US classified as CAFOs, with another quarter of a million industrial-scale facilities below that threshold.

The issue of the vast quantities of greenhouse gas generated by meat production was raised in 2006 in the UN Food and Agriculture Organisation (FAO) report entitled *Livestock's Long Shadow: Environmental Issues and Options*. It concludes that global meat production is projected to more than double from 229 million tonnes in 1900 to 465 million tonnes in 2050; and that milk production will grow from 580 million tonnes to 1,043 million tonnes in the same period. The environmental impact of livestock production will have to be cut in half, it says, just to keep the damage at the present level.

Livestock production, it says, is responsible for 18 per cent of greenhouse gas emissions including the production of fertiliser, the cultivation of feed crops, the consequences of deforestation to provide the land, the transport of the feed crops, the emission of methane and nitrous oxide from the animals and animal manure, and the transportation of animal products for consumption. Some studies put this as high as 51 per cent.

In terms of land usage, the report concludes that livestock was the biggest single anthropogenic user of land, occupying 26 per cent of the ice-free surface of the planet. An additional 33 per cent of arable land is dedicated for feed stuff for the animals, totalling 70 per cent of all agricultural land and 30 per cent of the land surface of the planet.

Livestock production, it concluded, is also a key factor in deforestation, especially in Latin America, where the greatest amount of deforestation is occurring – 70 per cent of previously forested land in the Amazon is now pasture for grazing. Feed crops for the animals cover a large part of the remainder. Around 20 per cent of the world's pastures and rangelands – but 73 per cent in dry areas – have been degraded, mostly by overgrazing, compaction, and erosion. Between 1961 and 2009, global soy production expanded nearly ten-fold, and it has doubled since the mid-1990s. The USA used to produce the most soy, but large amounts of fertile land, water resources and low labour costs have fuelled explosive growth in South America, particularly in Brazil.

Approximately 75 per cent of soybean production is used for animal feed. China is by far the biggest importer of soybeans (at 55 million tonnes) and is expected to increase its soy imports annually by 5 per cent, reaching 50 per cent more by 2021. Soybean imports to Asia are expected to grow from approximately 75 million tonnes in 2009 to 130 million tonnes in 2019.

The livestock sector of the report notes that agriculture is the biggest source of water pollution, contributing to dead zones in coastal areas and damage to coral reefs. In the USA, with the world's fourth largest land area, livestock are responsible for an estimated 55 per cent of erosion, 37 per cent of pesticide use, 50 per cent of antibiotic use, and a third of the nitrogen and phosphorus deposits into fresh water courses. Since 1980, palm oil production on deforested land has increased tenfold, with estimates that production will increase 50 per cent by 2050. The global palm oil trade is worth $40 billion a year, accounting for over 30 per cent of the world's vegetable oil production.

Malaysia and Indonesia are now the two biggest palm oil producing countries and are rapidly replacing their abundant rainforests with oil palm plantations. These two countries account for 84 per cent of the worlds palm oil production. In South America palm oil production has recently increased in Colombia, Ecuador and Guatemala. The second largest global vegetable oil, soya, takes up 120 million hectares, producing 48 million tonnes of soya oil.

These developments in the Global South are a product of two separate phenomena. On the one hand, much of the livestock production in these countries is for export to the rich north. But on the other hand, an increase in local meat consumption, especially amongst the growing middle classes, is seen as a status symbol.

Agriculture and water

Fred Pearce, in *When the Rivers Run Dry*, provided some remarkable facts about the use of fresh water in food production. He points out, for example, that it takes between 2,000 and 5,000 litres of water to grow one kilo of rice. That is more water than most households use in a week. It takes 1,000 litres to grow a kilo of wheat and 500 for a kilo of potatoes. And when it comes to feeding grain to livestock to produce meat and milk, the numbers become even more startling. It takes 24,000 litres to grow the feed to produce a kilo of beef, and between 2,000 and 4,000 litres for a cow to produce a litre of milk. It takes 5,000 litres to produce a kilo of cheese and 3,000 litres to produce a kilo of sugar. It takes around 2,000 litres to produce a kilo jar of coffee, around 250 litres to produce a glass of wine or a pint of beer, and a staggering 2,000 litres to produce a glass of brandy.

Pearce argues that:

The water footprint of Western countries on the rest of the world deserves to become a serious issue. Whenever you buy a T-shirt made of Pakistani cotton, eat Thai rice, or drink coffee from Central America, you are influencing the hydrology of those regions – taking a share of the River Indus, the Mekong or the Costa Rican rains. You may be helping the rivers run dry.[259]

He introduces the concept of 'virtual water' – the water used in the production or manufacture of a product. Those countries exporting such products, he argues, are in fact exporting 'virtual water'. The USA, he says, is rapidly depleting crucial underground water reserves in order to export a staggering 100 cubic kilometres of virtual water in beef production alone. Other major exporters of virtual water include Canada (grain), Australia (cotton), Argentina (beef) and Thailand (rice).

Meat production

Of the 95 million tonnes of beef produced in the world in 2000, the vast majority came from cattle in Latin America, Europe and North America. All of sub-Saharan Africa – a region with nearly three times as many people as the entire USA – produced just 3 million tonnes of beef. Farm animals consume 1.3 billion tonnes of grain each year – and nearly all of it is fed to livestock, mostly pork and poultry, in the developed world and in China and Latin America.

In July 2014, a study by Prof Gidon Eshel, of Bard College in New York State, writing on the impact of beef production on the environment, demonstrated that red meat dwarfs all others meat products for environmental impact[260]:

The heavy impact on the environment of meat production was known; but the research shows a new scale and scope of damage, particularly for beef. The popular red meat requires 28 times more land to produce than pork or chicken, 11 times more water and results in five times more climate-warming emissions. When compared to staples like potatoes, wheat, and rice, the impact of beef per calorie is even more extreme, requiring 160 times more land and producing 11 times more greenhouse gases...

Agriculture is a significant driver of global warming and causes 15 per cent of all emissions, half of which are from livestock. Furthermore, the huge amounts of grain and water needed to raise cattle is of concern to experts worried about feeding an extra 2 billion people by 2050.

The 2015 Horizon TV programme *'Should I Eat Meat? How to Feed the Planet'*[261] pointed to the scale of the problem. Human beings consume a staggering 65 billion animals (meat and poultry) a year. A third of the entire global landmass is given over to producing and maintaining the animals we use for human consumption. In fact, 14.5 per cent of all greenhouse gas emissions worldwide come from meat production: the same as the entire emissions from all form of transport: cars, lorries, buses, ships and aircraft.

The average American (apparently) consumes 120 kg of meat a year, the average Britain 80 kg. Whilst these levels are stable at the moment in the USA and Britain, in the developing countries, where being lifted out of poverty often means eating a lot more meat, consumption is going up rapidly. Thirty years ago in China, for example, the average consumption was just 4.4 kg per year. It is now 55 kg and rising.

Each year the livestock sector globally produces 586 million tonnes of milk, 124 million tonnes of poultry, 91 million tonnes of pork, 59 million tonnes of cattle and buffalo meat, and 11 million tonnes of meat from sheep and goats. That's 285 million tonnes of meat altogether – or about 36 kg (80 lb) per person, if it were all divided evenly. It's not, of course – Americans eat 122 kg of meat a year on average, while Bangladeshis manage on 1.8 kg.

A quarter of all grain produced in the USA is used to feed cattle. Livestock consume 80 per cent of the world's annual soy crop, and most of this is grown on cleared lands that were once tropical rain forests. This involves the use of huge quantities of mineral fertiliser and pesticides, of antibiotics to control the infections that result from confining them in too small a space, and of hormones to fatten them more and faster. Overgrazing the less productive areas of land as they become needed, leads to degradation and desertification.

Today one third of the entire cereal harvest, and nearly all of the world's soya, is devoted to feeding industrially reared animals. Lymbery also notes that the increasing use of antibiotics in livestock farming is also a problem: the WHO identifies it as a major factor in the rise of superbugs and the increasing resistance of bacteria to the antibiotics available in our hospitals. All this is simply not sustainable, and cannot be made so by a few changes in the structure of farming and the methods used.

At the same time we face the growing impact of climate change on food production, as reflected in floods, fires, droughts and extreme weather events on a more frequent basis. This is depleting water supplies, expanding the desserts and disrupting agriculture.

The amount of methane produced by cattle is huge – putting the equivalent of 2.8 billion tonnes of carbon into the atmosphere. One cow produces 550 litres of methane a day – which is about the same CO_2 equivalent as the average family car. Globally cattle produce 150 billion gallons of methane every day from their digestive processes – and methane is 86 times more potent as a greenhouse gas than CO_2.

This grim picture was reinforced in the 2016 film and then the book *Cowspiracy*, by Kip Anderson and Keegan Kuhn. In his introduction to the book Chris Hedges, of Princetown, New Jersey, says that, depending on the precise study used, livestock along with their feed, their waste, and their flatulence account for up to 32 billion tonnes of CO_2 per year, or 51 per cent of all worldwide CO_2 equivalents. Livestock generate 53 per cent of all emissions of nitrous oxide (mostly from manure) which is a greenhouse gas with 298 times the warming potential of CO_2. Crops grown for livestock feed consume 56 per cent of all water used in the USA.

Philip Lymbery, in *Dead Zones: Where the Wild Things Were*, argues that food production has become just another industry churning out raw materials in a way that is grossly wasteful. With artificial fertilisers abundant during the great depression, corn production went into overdrive as cheaply produced grain was used as cattle feed.

The idea that under such conditions enough food can be produced for an additional 2 to 5 billion people by mid-century, seems optimistic in the extreme.

Chickenisation

If red meat is the most damaging kind of meat to the planet, that does not mean that mass produced chicken is a benign product. Lymbery calls this chickenisation, and points out that around 60 billion chickens a year are currently produced for meat – a tenfold increase on 50 years ago. It comes, he says, at a terrible cost to the farmed birds themselves, and is a serious human health and environmental concern.

Lymbery also points out that:

Poultry meat and eggs are a major source of infection from another serious food-poisoning bug: salmonella. Keeping chickens in large flocks or in cages can dramatically boost the risk: studies have shown that caged hens are up to ten times more at risk of salmonella than birds kept free-range... Farmers routinely attempt to safeguard their birds against such bugs by dosing them with antibiotics... Indeed, half of all the antibiotics produced in the world are fed to chickens, cows, pigs and other farmed animals.[262]

There are serious implications in this for human health in terms of antibiotic immunity.

Fish farming

A similar situation exists in terms of fish farming, which in recent years has also become big business. Close to 40 per cent of the seafood we eat nowadays comes from farmed sources, in what is now a $78 billion industry; and 62 per cent of the world's farmed fish is produced by China. The species used most commonly worldwide in fish farming are carp, tilapia, salmon, tuna, catfish and shrimp.

Fish farms are analogous to vast cattle ranches in terms of their impact on biodiversity. There are concerns about the impact that the concentrations of nitrates have on the surrounding areas beyond the farms themselves, particularly when they are situated in sheltered bays where tides have less chance to dilute these chemicals before they impact on other populations. The antibiotics used to keep the fish healthy also have a dangerous impact.

These problems are further compounded by the overfishing of wild fish in the oceans – in which 80 per cent of life on this planet lives. Unsustainable fishing methods are increasingly used. Giant nets, designed for unselective fishing, have a huge impact on the marine environment when the bycatch ends up being thrown back into the sea.

Crucial tipping-point

Lymbery argues that although the planet is remarkably resilient, we are now reaching a tipping point in its ability to take any more punishment; and that agriculture is playing a major role in this, feeding a global population that is now over 7 billion, but swallowing up nearly a half of the planet's useable land and two-thirds of its fresh water, and inflicting damage on the soil that is vital for the food we eat.

As the human population rises, Lymbery argues, 'so the quest intensifies for more land to cultivate'. Right now, we are in no danger of running out of food (distribution problems not withstanding), but the environmental damage attached to the way we are choosing to produce it may be irreversible.

An area of cereal cropland the size of France and Italy combined will be needed by 2050 to keep pace with the demand for food. Up to a fifth of the world's remaining forests, he argues, will be gone in the next three decades – much of it to grow crops for feeding animals for the meat trade:

> Great swathes of extra cropland look set to join the chemical-soaked arable monocultures of East Anglia in England. The seas of swaying corn in the Midwest of America and soya in Brazil are set fair to extend still further. There'll be more fields of maize like the ones I saw in rural Asia… The encroachment of agriculture into the remaining wildlands, together with the onward march of industrial farming, will almost certainly cause irreversible damage to biodiversity, forests soil and water.[263]

He is cautious about giving an opinion on the rising human population of the planet, but he is clearly concerned. 'To me', he says, 'the link is obvious. An extra billion people come with 10 billion extra farm animals, together with what that means in terms of land water and soil.'

Throughout human history, he goes on:

> for better or for worse, *Homo sapiens* have outdone all comers, from the magnificent mammals like the bison that roamed the American plains in vast numbers, to birds like the passenger pigeons that once flocked in great grey rivers through the sky, and to species of fellow humans like the Neanderthals. Whatever has stood in our way, and more often just in our reach, we have erased it. Now we have met our match. The great irony is that our most fearsome competitor for food – livestock – has been put there by us.[264]

The conclusion to all this is clear. Although a big proportion of food continues to be produced (globally) by small and medium sized producers, industrialised agriculture is now irreplaceable without major reorganisation, but is unavoidable in meeting the demands of rising population today, particularly in regard to the increasing demand for meat.

The radical left

Remarkably, the idea that enough food can be produced to feed today's rising numbers if things were organised better, is also present on the environmental radical left.

Ian Angus and Simon Butler, for example, argue in their 2011 book *Too Many People? Population, Immigration, and the Environmental Crisis*, that if food production and distribution were rationally organised, more than enough food could be produced and distributed to feed the rising population of the planet – even a population of 9 or 10 billion can be adequately fed.

Martin Empson, in *Land and Labour: Marxism, Ecology and Human History*, argues that, even if the current rising population does not level off, and population levels of 10 or 11 billion are reached, 'there is still the potential to feed increasing numbers of people'.[265] I think this approach is a mistake.

When it comes to meat consumption, Martin Empson disputes a pamphlet published by the British Vegetarian Society, *Why It Is Green to Go Vegetarian*, which claims that: 'Going vegetarian is an easy way to lower your own environmental impact and help ensure that worldwide food security.'[266]

In fact, the pamphlet makes a strong point. The dietary choices you make, particularly in relation to eating meat, have a big environmental impact. Not everyone is in a position to become a vegetarian or a vegan, but it is a serious issue. While some forms of meat and dairy products are more harmful to the environment than others, all are more harmful than a diet based on plant protein.

It is not, however, a binary choice. Any reduction in meat eating, particularly in red meat, is a positive contribution. Whether it is cutting your daily meat consumption or having meat free days every week, this can make a very big difference.

Empson accepts that some diets do have a large environmental impact:

> But the problem is not diet on its own, it is the way that agriculture and food production have become tied into a system based on profit. Rather than seeking to produce healthy sustainable food, the food industry is trying to maximise profits.

He goes on to say that:

> The modern meat industry designed around producing large volumes of cheap meat for the supermarkets is the problem, not the consumption of meat itself.[267]

Whilst there is some truth in this, since the profit motive clearly compounds the problem, it is in the end a rationalisation of meat-eating. It's true that cattle fed on grass in the summer months are less environmentally damaging than those fed on corn or soya all the year round: but it's only a matter of degree. Any production of beef and milk still requires large amounts of water, and cattle emit large amounts of methane from their digestion process, which is a particularly powerful greenhouse gas. There is also the question of whether there is enough land available for grazing on the scale that would be needed. Anderson and Kuhn make the point that:

> The average American eats at least 209 pounds of meat a year. The Markegard model[268] of raising animals requires 4,500 acres to produce 80,000 pounds of grass-fed meat. If all 209 pounds of meat were grass-fed, only 382 people could be fed by the Markegards' land. In terms of land use, taking the 4,500 acres that the Markegards graze, dividing it by the 382 people gives us 11.7 acres per person. So, it takes 11.7 acres of land to raise enough grass-fed meat for one American, and that comes out to 3.7 billion acres of grazing land to feed the United States their meat, if it were all grass-fed.[269]

Unfortunately, Anderson and Kuhn say, there are only 1.9 billion acres of land available, and much of this is unsuitable for grazing livestock anyway. Grass-fed animals are also leaner than corn-fed animals (that was the rationale for 'corn beef') so a lot more animals would be necessary to produce the same weight in beef.

17 Lifestyle and personal responsibility

'But man is a part of nature, and his war against nature is inevitably a war against himself.'

Rachel Carson

Most on the radical left, remarkably in my view, reject the idea of individual responsibility. This stance is strongly reflected in the writings of radical left ecologists – in fact it is the norm. Just two examples, though there are many.

The Australian ecosocialist Terry Townsend wrote in Ian Angus's *The Global Fight for Climate Justice* in 2009, challenging Al Gore's defence of individual action as expressed in his 2009 book *An Inconvenient Truth.* Townsend countered:

> However well-intentioned, appeals to people to change their individual habits – 'don't drive a car,' 'don't keep your appliances on standby',' stop being a consumer' – bring trivial results when measured against the problem. If there is no adequate public transportation, if there is no thoughtful city plan that lets workers live close to jobs, hospitals and recreation – how can they stop driving cars? If every appliance the big manufacturers churn out is designed to be on standby by default, it makes it bloody difficult.

He goes on:

> Such views amongst genuine environmental activists reflect a well-meaning but ultimately utopian belief: that it's only if enough of us decide to drastically reduce our demand on the world's resources – greatly reducing personal consumption, purchasing from firms with sustainable production techniques and non-polluting

technologies – that big business and governments will respond to 'market signals' and accept and adapt to a slow-growth or no-growth economy. ...

...Of course, we should not dismiss the importance of environmental consciousness and radicalisation, which is often expressed in an attempt to live in ways consistent with sustainability. It is a good thing if people try to organise their lives so that they can live more ecologically... But we have to be clear that that alone will not be enough to halt the crisis. It certainly cannot be the main strategy of the mass environmental movement, as it will let the real culprits off the hook and divert precious activist energy away from the underlying dynamic that is driving ecological degradation.[270]

I am with Al Gore on this. Why is it 'well-meaning' or 'moralistic' to have regard to your personal impact on the planet? Doesn't it make sense? Would it be better if people had no regard for their personal impact and just carried on eating more hamburgers, driving more miles, and taking more flights? Of course not. It would be even better if they follow the logical progression of their actions and go on to demand governmental and corporate action as well. How does switching off warning lights 'divert precious activist energy away from the underlying dynamic that is driving ecological degradation'? Where is the evidence? Surely those taking individual action are already more aware of environmental problems than those who see no reason to do so, and are more likely to demand collective action and to take part in it. How does this 'let the real culprits off the hook'?

The left doesn't take this approach in regard to any other arena of politics – women's liberation or antiracism, for example. In those areas of struggle, what you say is expected to be reflected in what you do and how you conduct yourself; it's not voluntarism, because anything less would be unacceptable. It's not regarded as 'moralism' to respect women's rights or LGBTQ rights, or to oppose racism. What is so different about the struggle to save the planet?

Joel Kovel takes the same approach as Terry Townsend in his book *The Enemy of Nature: The End of Capitalism or the End of the World*. He defines individual action as 'voluntarism'. He even argues that such things as using low energy light bulbs or turning down the thermostat works, in the end, to the advantage of capital and its drive for profit! He also targets Al Gore on the issue:

> … At the end of an *Inconvenient Truth* is an embarrassing recital of 'things you can do to save the planet,' vis: use compact fluorescent lightbulbs, set the thermostat down, etc. We can call these 'voluntarisms'. A voluntaristic act is one that arises from good intention and more or less stays there, without special connection to social movements consciously directed, in this case, towards the ecological crisis. Thus it is an action taken towards an individual magnification of the crisis, and carried out primarily on moral or psychological grounds.
>
> Such actions are understandably popular, as they comprise a risk-free way of feeling good about oneself in the face of overwhelming crisis. But they stand as much chance of overcoming the ecological crisis as handing out spare change on the subway does of overcoming poverty…

He concludes:

> Ultimately, the touchstone of voluntarism is this: that it is an ecopolitics without struggle, *struggle* against the inertia and fear within, and the great weight of capitalist rationalisation and repression without. It is an easy path at a time when sacrifice and heroism are called for.[271] (emphasis original)

No wonder there has been tension with environmental activists. To say that reducing your personal footprint is a voluntaristic way of avoiding real struggle, is deeply offensive to activists who whilst having regard for their personal ecological impact engage in collective, often direct, action. No wonder the radical left is even more marginal to the direct action campaigns than the wider climate movement. To argue that 'such voluntarism will stop at its own border' makes no sense either. A plastic bottle thrown into the sea from a British beach by someone who assumes no personal responsibility can end up killing wild life on the other side of the world.

In this, Kovel even distorts Al Gore, who says in the first paragraph of the section referred to: 'By educating ourselves and others, by doing our part to minimise our use and waste of resources, by becoming more politically active and demanding change—in these ways and many others, each of us can make a difference'.[272]

The tensions around lifestyle and personal impact were evident at the big climate camps, in 2007 and 2008, at Heathrow and Kingsnorth, where all organised food was vegan, all toilets composted, no litter tolerated, and a low-impact lifestyle on display. It was a form of prefiguration that had its roots in the feminist movement.

I don't accept, as Terry Townsend suggests, that those who take responsibility for their own actions have been duped into thinking that such actions are a solution in themselves to the ecological crisis. I doubt if many think that.

Having concern for your own impact is not voluntarism. Voluntarism is the substitution of individual action for collective action. In fact taking individual responsibility for your own impact is likely to lead to more effective collective action, not less. Put the other way around, it's difficult to see how someone with little or no regard to their individual impact on the planet, would be strongly motivated towards collective involvement in its defence. It is a contradiction in terms.

Opposition to individual action also seems to assume that domestic energy consumption – or that part of energy consumption which is dependent on individual choices – is a marginal part of overall energy consumption, when it is nothing of the sort. According to a report produced by the Cambridge MIT Institute (a partnership between the University of Cambridge and the Massachusetts Institute of Technology) entitled *Domestic Energy Use and Sustainability*, domestic energy in Britain amounts to 58 per cent of total usage. In the USA it is even more, at 65 per cent.

Not everyone can live up to the standards on display at the climate camps, of course (including me). But it is not a zero-sum game. There is a lot the individual person can do to reduce their impact on the planet short of becoming a vegan or even a vegetarian. If you can't stop eating meat you can eat less of it – limit it to once a day or once a week or have a meat free day each week. The issue is to be conscious of your own action and take the planet into account. Not everyone can stop using air travel, or even long-haul flights, but everyone can think carefully about if first.

Action on Energy, for example, estimates that every home in the UK could reduce the amount of energy it uses by 20 per cent with some simple measures. One of the most publicised energy-wasting habits is to leave electrical products on standby. Over £740 million pounds-worth of electricity is used every year in Britain by leaving power appliances on standby. This averages at around £30 per household.

In fact, using low-energy light bulbs, turning the thermostat down, and putting a lid on saucepans (most trivialised on the left) are important considerations that can save large amounts of energy. We can add to that the way we feed ourselves, the way we use cars, and use air travel – particularly short haul flights.

It is true, of course, that this saving is constrained by the actions (or inaction) of governments, which reject crucial measures such as free public transport; but this does not mean that the individual person has no responsibility under prevailing conditions.

Not all radical left environmentalists have taken this view, of course. The American pioneering socialist and environmentalist, Scott Nearing, published *Economics for the Power Age* as far back as 1952. In it he stressed the finite resources of the planet, and warned of the over-exploitation and degradation of nature, and the demands of the human population, at the same time pioneering a lifestyle that reflected personal responsibility. And there are comrades today who strive to match their way of life to the logic of the ecological crisis: we are unfortunately still in a minority.

Nearing recognised that tackling this crisis will have to involve radical lifestyle changes, and individuals have an important role to play in this. The scale of change we need will only come if these personal changes are accompanied and encouraged by government action, which has to provide the framework for such changes in life style to take place.

We have to insist that there is no contradiction between controlling your own carbon footprint and campaigning for government action and structural change. They are entirely complementary. How can there not be a responsibility to reduce your personal ecological footprint, or impact on the planet, where you are in a position to do so?

18 Cars and transportation

... whilst travelling in a narrow boat on the Pontcysyllte Aqueduct and along the Llangollen Canal I discovered the pleasures of slowness.

Winfried Wolf[273]

In 1997, before my involvement in ecological issues, Winfried Wolf, a German Marxist ecologist and a comrade, gave me a copy of his new book *Car Mania – A Critical History of Transport*. It was, as the title implies, a history of transport in the context of the rise of the car and its impact on the ecology of the planet. Winfried was an independent member of the German Parliament. He has written several books on transport, including *Berlin: a City for the People*.

I found his book interesting not least because it contains a very good history of the 17th / 18th century canal network in Britain. His principal message in terms of the impact of the motor car on the planet, however, passed me completely. It was not until I reread it ten years later, after I had begun to take ecological issues seriously, that I appreciated its importance.

At the time Winfried wrote his book – in the mid-1990s – there were 600 million cars on the world's roads. Today the statistics of car ownership and the implications of them are frightening. There are 1.3 billion cars on the world's roads, and this is set to rise to 2 billion by 2040 as global wealth grows – a figure that is completely unsustainable in terms of the ecology of the planet. Every gallon of petrol or diesel burned produces about 20 lb of CO_2 emissions.

In Britain, since 2011, the number has increased by about 1.6 million in England, 142,000 in Scotland and 69,000 in Wales. The largest rise has been in south-east England, with 373,200 more cars over five years. The passenger car fleet Europe-wide has also grown over the last five years. The highest numbers of cars per inhabitant were recorded in Luxembourg, followed by Malta, Italy and Finland.

Globally the number of motorised vehicles of all types – cars, trucks, buses, scooters and motor bikes – are set to increase by around 3 per cent a year and will reach 2 billion in a couple of years' time – by 2020. The highest growth rates are expected to be in China and India. Currently CO_2 emissions from vehicles amount to 8 per cent of global emissions.

Nor is it 'just' CO_2 emissions and global warming. Some air pollutants and particulate matter from cars can be deposited on soil and on surface waters, where they enter the food chain; these substances can affect the reproductive, respiratory, immune and neurological systems of animals. Nitrogen oxides and sulphur oxides are major contributors to acid rain, which changes the pH of waterways and soils, and can harm the organisms that rely on these resources.

Car culture

Car usage has been driven not only by transport needs and economic availability, but by a very powerful car culture that has made the car the ultimate status symbol.

According to an article in the *Washington Post* in July 2016, the car culture of the twentieth century, which has been so damaging to the environment, has peaked and is on the decline in the country that originally defined it. The article put it this way:

> Few technological breakthroughs have had the social and economic impact of the automobile. It changed America's geography, spawning suburbs, shopping malls and sprawl as far as the eye could see. It redefined how we work and play, from the daily commute to the weekend trek to the beach. It expanded the heavy industry – steel-making, car production – that made the Midwest the economy's epicentre for decades. And, finally but not least, the car became the quintessential symbol of American mobility, status and independence. Now there are signs that the car and its many offshoots (SUVs, pickup trucks) are losing their grip on the American psyche and pocketbook.[274]

An article in the *Chicago Tribune* in September 2015 put it this way:

> For nearly all of the first century of automobile travel, getting your license meant liberation from parental control, a passport to the open road. Today, only half of

millennials bother to get their driver's licenses by age 18. Car culture, the 20th-century engine of the American Dream, is an old guy's game.

Mike Berger, who studies the social effect of the car, argues that social media has had undermined the car culture of the 20th century. He told the *Tribune*: 'The automobile provided the means for teenagers to live their own lives. Social media blows any limits out of the water. You don't need the car to go find friends.' In fact, the miles Americans drive each year are down about 9 per cent over the past two decades. The article points out that the percentage of nineteen-year-olds with driver's licenses has dropped from 87 per cent two decades ago to 70 per cent last year. Most teens now do not get licensed within a year of becoming eligible, according to a study by the AAA Foundation for Traffic Safety.[275]

In Britain it is difficult to tell. Young people have been so impoverished in the past twenty years that things available to most of their parents, such as cars and mortgages, are well beyond their reach.

The problem is that, whilst car culture shows signs of receding in North America and Europe, it is rapidly increasing in the big emerging economies with the highest rates of growth. And the implications of rapidly rising vehicle ownership in China today are truly staggering. A 2012 article entitled 'Will China's Vehicle Population Grow Even Faster than Forecasted?' by Yunshi Wang, Jacob Teter and Daniel Sperling in *Access Magazine* pointed out:

In 2010, China surpassed the US and all other countries in vehicle sales, and will no doubt retain its number one ranking for decades. But how big will China's vehicle market become? The answer is of great importance for the entire world. Rapid Chinese motorisation has alarming implications for both the environment and global energy resources...

The majority of forecasts anticipate relatively slow growth in China's vehicle population. China's fast growth in motorisation may threaten global oil supplies and exacerbate climate change. Indeed, if China's vehicle ownership rate reaches 600 to 800 vehicles per 1,000 persons, equivalent to rates in Europe and the US respectively, then China's total vehicle population would approach one billion – more than four times the number of vehicles in the United States today. Even at a much lower level of 300 vehicles per 1,000 persons, the worldwide impact would be huge: Chinese vehicles alone would consume 12 to 18 per cent of the total oil produced today.[276]

China produced 29 million cars in 2017 and now has over 300 million motor vehicles, which almost equals America's total population. Today 10 of the 25 most car congested cities in the world are in China. There are now 40 Chinese cities that have car ownership of more than 1 million and in eleven cities including Beijing, Shanghai, Shenzhen and Tianjin, car ownership exceeds 2 million.

An article in the *Shanghai Daily* on 28 January 2018, entitled 'China's Maturing Auto Market Gives Rise to Car Culture and Individuality', states:

> In 40 years of reform and opening-up, China has transformed itself from a land of bicycles to a global automobile market, where a wide range of car brands and models can be seen on the road. It has become more and more common for Chinese families to purchase a second or a third car. Automobiles have greatly extended the sphere of Chinese people's lives. But more than that, they have become a symbol of individuality.

Electric vehicles

Today, with global car ownership still increasing, the task we face is the elimination of the internal combustion (most urgently diesel) within not much more than a decade, if the global temperature increase is to be kept within the 1.5°C – within the context of an overall reduction in individual car usage. It is one of the major structural changes that the IPCC is talking about. We also need a big reduction in air travel, the ending of short-haul flights (in favour of rail) and an end to airport expansion.

Major structural changes will be necessary in order to be able to travel without destroying the planet. The starting point in the here and now has to be a rapid and complete conversion of cars, vans, and buses to electric power. The electrification of cars is (bafflingly) opposed by some on the left, on the basis that they are 'opposed to all cars'.

In Britain the government has announced that no petrol or diesel cars will be allowed on the roads after 2040 – all cars will have to electric or hybrid. This is, of course, a ridiculously long time-scale; but it's an important landmark and is already forcing car manufacturers to reconsider future plans. There is already a demand to bring the date forward, and there is no doubt that will happen. London's black taxi cabs are already required to become electric by 2021. They will be partially hybrid, however, due to inadequate battery technology. The first 80 miles after each charge will be electrically (i.e. battery) powered with additional (rescue) miles covered by a small petrol engine.

This means a crash programme to build the infrastructure for electric cars, in particular charging points, that currently does not exist. It also means improving battery technology to extend the range of a single charge.

It requires extending the capacity of the national grid, which will experience a major additional demand as cars and vans go onto it. It will mean turning the grid over to renewable energy, and ending its current supply from fossil and nuclear fuel.

The grid will not have to take the full impact of electric vehicles, however. Electric vehicles can use the grid far more efficiently than most users, because electric cars can benefit, like storage heaters, from night time electricity, using power for which there isn't a demand and would otherwise be disposed of back into the ground. In fact cars can be charged in a non-emergency situation by smart chargers which will select the cheapest energy from the 24 hour period.

Free public transport

Today even China is being forced to change its ecological direction as people in big cities have difficulty seeing to the other side of the street. The associated health problems are mounting by the day.

A crucial element in changes of the magnitude needed is the idea of free public transport – the time for which has come with a vengeance. Nor is it a futuristic idea or some kind of pipedream. It is a practical solution to a major problem, and is increasingly being seen as such.

In fact the mayor of Paris, Anne Hidalgo, recently announced a feasibility study for free public transport in Paris to tackle pollution. We don't know if this will happen, but that it is actively under discussion is a sign of the times. She told the French daily newspaper *Los Echos*: 'To improve public transport we should not only make it more extensive, more regular and more comfortable, we must also rethink the fares system'.

The German government is considering plans to make public transport free in cities suffering from air quality problems. It wants to test the measure in five cities including Bonn and Essen.

The UK government report concludes that: 'Air pollution is a national health emergency, resulting in an estimated 40,000 early deaths each year and costing the UK £20 billion annually. It is unacceptable that successive governments have failed to protect the public from poisonous air.' It notes that: 'Despite a series of court cases, the government has still not produced a plan that adequately addresses the scale of the challenge. Nor has it demonstrated the national leadership needed to bring about a step change in how the problem of air quality is tackled.'

Its recommendations are a step forward but entirely inadequate. They include:

- Bringing forward the date by which manufacturers must end the sale of conventional petrol and diesel cars, in line with more ambitious commitments from around the world.
- Aligning climate change schemes, urban planning, public transport and fiscal incentives with air quality goals, to prevent Government policy from working at cross-purposes.
- Taking greater account of the costs of air pollution when establishing taxation and spending policy.

The report is right to demand the bringing forward of the date for the phasing out of conventional powered cars from the Tories' scandalous 2050 to a more useful 2020. There is no mention, however, of the key to this situation which, as shown above, is the introduction of free public transport.

Free public transport is not a futuristic demand under today's conditions. It works, and it is effective. While the revenue from fares would be 'lost', there are big savings to be made, not just in administration but in clearing up the damage made in the first place. It needs to be a part of an overall plan for a big reduction in individual car usage, and to get freight back on to an improved railway system.

Congestion charges

Another device that can both cut emissions caused by idling engines and reduce traffic pollution, particularly in the big cities, are congestion charges – that have also been controversial amongst many on the left.

Ken Livingstone, London's mayor from 2000 to 2008, introduced a congestion charge in central London of £5 a day in February 2003, with the aim of reducing traffic congestion and pollution in and around the charging zone. It was increased to £8 a day from July 2005 and to £10 from January 2011.

The charge is now widely supported in London due to the scale of the problem it addressed; and any proposal to abolish it now would be highly controversial. Livingstone introduced it as a directly elected mayor and was subsequently re-elected. The Tories waged a big campaign against the charge, pledging its instant abolition, but made no impact on Livingstone's vote. The Greens strongly supported it, of course, as did the Liberal Democrats. The radical left Respect Party, which existed at the time, supported the charge, but called for improvements in its structures and provisions: the introduction of various progressive elements (including exemptions from it) around both engine size and CO_2 emissions. The radical left as a whole, however, was divided on it.

There were always exemptions from the charge. Disabled people, and institutions supporting disabled people, were exempt, as were residents living inside the zone, zero-emission vehicles and motor bikes. Patients travelling to and from hospital and too unwell to use public transport are exempt. NHS staff and fire fighters can also claim exemption for work-related travel.

The London congestion charge worked, and still works, at the level of reducing traffic in the zone. There is less traffic, fewer traffic jams, and traffic moves faster than prior to its introduction. Transport for London (TfL) claimed the reduction was initially 30 per cent, dropping to 25 per cent a few weeks later. Various estimates now put it at between 20 and 25 per cent. Predictions that traffic would gradually build back up to something approaching original levels have not been borne out. TfL claims that road journey times in the zone have been cut by up to half.

The discussion on the left around the charge was that we should judge it, as with other things, on how it affects the working class. This is correct, of course; but in making such an assessment we have to break from any narrow view of the working class and its interests, both conceptually and geographically. We cannot assess the impact of the charge on the working class solely through the cost of car driving. We need to recognise that a reduction of CO_2 emissions is also a gain for the working class as a whole. This includes too those sections of the working class who live in impoverished parts of the world, where global warming is wreaking havoc as a result of emissions in rich Western countries. In the same way, cleaner air and a better environment are gains for the working class. Even the faster travel time through London resulting from the charge, is a gain for the working class, especially if it shortens the journey to and from work or the hospital when it's needed.

Airport expansion

As the British government was claiming to be well on its way to meeting its commitments to the Paris agreement, it was at the same time announcing its intention to build a third runway (and a sixth terminal) at Heathrow in London – to the north west of the existing runways. The aim is to make Heathrow into a major European hub, taking its passenger capacity to around 120 million a year.

It would further pollute what is already one of the most polluted parts of London, where air quality is already at illegal levels. Around 4,000 homes would be demolished, and hundreds of thousands of people exposed to additional aircraft noise. This will suck economic activity even more into London and the South East and the rest of Britain. It would further congest roads in West London that are already bursting at the seams.

It is not the first attempt to build such a runway. The last Labour government, under Gordon Brown, made the same proposal in 2007. It divided the unions. Brown was supported by the TUC and the main Heathrow unions: Amicus, the TGWU/Unite, the GMB and the pilot's union, BALPA. TUC general secretary Brendan Barber argued that the impact a third runway would have on CO_2 emissions, could be offset by carbon trading. He was opposed by Unison, Connect, the PCS, and the rail unions – the RMT, ASLEF and TSSA.

A broad-based campaign was mounted against expansion which brought these unions together with local people, direct action campaigns, environmental NGOs and the environmental left.

In August 2007, what was called a Camp for Climate Action took place about a mile from Heathrow itself. On its final day, 1500 people protested at Heathrow and 200 people blockaded the British Airports Authority (BAA) HQ. The protest was supported by a range of organisations including the Campaign against Climate Change, the Green Party, Greenpeace, Friends of the Earth, the RSPB, the Woodland Trust, the National Trust, Friends of the Earth, and many more.

John McDonnell, the local MP, and now Shadow Chancellor of the Exchequer, strongly supported the campaign. He spoke at its demonstrations and participated in many other actions against the expansion.

In February 2008, five members of the direct action group Plane Stupid, staged a two-hour protest on the roof of the Houses of Parliament in protest at the close links between BAA and the government. Banners were unfurled which read 'BAA HQ' and 'No third runway at Heathrow'. In March 2009, a Plane Stupid protester threw green custard over then Business Secretary Peter Mandelson, at a low carbon summit hosted by Gordon Brown.

The campaign resulted in a spectacular victory, in March 2010, when a High Court judge ruled that Heathrow expansion was 'untenable in law and common sense' and (ironically) that it was inconsistent with Labour's own Climate Change Act. When the incoming Tory/Liberal Democrat coalition in 2010 was forced to cancel Heathrow expansion as a result of this ruling, the TUC criticised the decision, arguing that it would cost large numbers of jobs. Today, the reasons for opposing Heathrow expansion are much the same as in 2007. The issue is not whether a new airport in the south of England should be in London or the Thames estuary.

The direct result of airport expansion is aviation expansion. Aviation is the fastest growing and most dangerous form of greenhouse gas emissions we face. The impact of CO_2 emissions at high altitude is around double of such emissions at surface level—a factor which is conveniently ignored by the international aviation industry and by the Tory government.

A new runway at Heathrow is incompatible with Britain's compliance with the Paris agreement. Fortunately, it will not be easy for the Tories to get this proposal through Parliament or to implement it even if it does, although the situations in the unions may well be no better today than it was in 2007.

Unfortunately the reaction of most of the unions is also the same today as it was then. The TUC General Secretary Frances O'Grady said: "The case for Heathrow expansion was proven long ago. It will create thousands of high-quality jobs and apprenticeships. And it has the backing of both trade unions and businesses. This needs to be a clear and final decision. Work must start as soon as possible, with the government doing all it can to keep progress in the fast lane". This was a disappointing statement, given that the TUC's overall position on climate change has strengthened since 2007.

The most important factor, however, will be the position taken by the Labour leadership under Jeremy Corbyn. Whilst there are signs that they are moving towards opposition to a third runway it is far from clear that this will be in the framework of opposition to airport expansion per se rather than just Heathrow.

19 The environmental struggle in Britain

A successful struggle against global warming and climate change will require the broadest possible coalition, involving the trade unions and the social movements that have strengthened and radicalised in recent years, as well as the many campaigns that have entered the struggle and are waging important battles against CO_2 emissions, such as Ende Gelände in Germany.

In Britain, longstanding organisations, such as Friends of the Earth, Greenpeace and the Green Parties have grown and radicalised in recent years, and new groupings such as Avaaz and 38 Degrees have come on the scene. These groups have also radicalised, particularly in the run up to Paris, and have an impressive mobilising ability. The same can be said of Global Justice Now (formerly the World Development Movement), War on Want, 350.org and even the World Wide Fund for Nature, Christian Aid, Islamic Aid, and Oxfam.

The Campaign against Climate Change (CACC) was established over twenty years ago and has played an important role in Britain and internationally. Its trade union group (CACCTUG) has the support of six national unions, and is also important. Its One Million Climate Jobs campaign has received wide support, including from the TUC in Britain and the ITUC internationally.

In Britain, other campaigns active around climate change include Stop Climate Chaos, Zero Carbon Britain, Greener Jobs Alliance, Biofuel Watch, Time to Act on Climate Change, The Climate Coalition, People and Planet, and the Climate Action Network. Direct action campaigns include Reclaim the Power, and recently, Extinction Rebellion; Plane Stupid, who have targeted power stations and airports; also campaigns such as Frack Free, Frack Off, the Extreme Energy Action Network, Frack Free Lancashire, Frack Free Somerset, and Artists Against Fracking.

The unions

The trade unions are an important arena of the ecological struggle, but also one of the most difficult. There has been an increasing awareness of the environmental issues in the unions – certainly if measured by the number of policy documents produced – and increased support for projects such as the campaign for one million climate jobs. There has also been an increase in workplace environmental reps, although this remains fragile and has no legal status. And there has been increased support for the idea of a 'just transition', the rights of workers to alternative employment as the changeover from fossil fuel takes place – particularly at the level of the International TUC (ITUC) and the TUC in Britain, though practical action in this regard is hard to find.

The TUC, on paper at least, has had a stronger position than most of the individual unions. The 1990 Congress discussed a resolution recognising 'the enormous threat to the people of the world from the effects of global warming'. It recognised that the newly established International Panel on Climate Change (IPCC) argued that climate change will have a profound effect on industry as a whole. This initially positive response, however, came to an end by 1992 with the return of the Tories to government.

At the 1994 Labour Party conference, a document on energy policy called *In Trust for Tomorrow* was defeated. It called, amongst other things, for a moratorium on road building,. The TGWU and the AEEU voted against, while the GMB abstained on the basis that it was a threat to jobs in the opencast mining, nuclear energy and road building industries.

The election of a Labour government in 1997 put the matter of climate change back on the political agenda, but also placed it firmly within New Labour's (Blairite) business orientated agenda.

The 2005 TUC Congress called on the Labour government 'to develop a green industrial strategy, embracing the employment, training and research aspects of a new energy policy'. In 2007, TUC general secretary Brendan Barber welcomed the Climate Change Bill as proposed by the Blair Government. In fact, when the Bill was discussed by the TUC's On Target conference in June 2007, the conference argued that a reduction of 60 per cent of CO_2 emissions against the 1990 baseline by 2050 was not enough, and that the figure should be 80 per cent. Eventually, after a lobbying campaign by the TUC and some affiliated unions, the Bill was amended so that the Act when adopted set the level at 80 per cent.

Six months after the Climate Change Bill became law, Labour lost the general election and the resulting Tory/Liberal Democrat coalition kicked the Act into the long grass and implemented the 'dash for gas'. Five years later in 2015, the Tory government, first under Cameron and then May, put government action on climate change even further on to the back burner.

Carbon capture and storage

Whilst it was good that the TUC had raised the profile of climate change to the extent that it had, it still gave strong support to a number of disastrous policies. One of these was the idea of 'clean coal' – carbon capture and storage (CCS) – long after it had become clear that this technology was going nowhere. The key technical problems involved – *i.e.* how to store vast quantities of carbon safely – remain entirely unresolved. In any case CCS could never eliminate CO_2 emissions from the burning of fossil fuel, only reduce it. The most optimistic estimates predicted an 80 per cent reduction, the more cautious around 50-60 per cent. It is a technical fix that simply will not work, at least for the foreseeable future.

The crunch for CCS came in 2008, with the proposal for a new coal-fired power station, to be built by E.ON UK at Kingsnorth, on the Medway Hoo peninsula, as part of a government sponsored competition for making CCS work.

The new plant was strongly opposed by a wide coalition of the environmental movement, and a 'camp for climate action' was set up close to the site in August of that year.[277] It was supported, however, by the TUC and the unions on the site – with the proviso that the plant would be 'carbon capture ready'. The police put a cordon round the climate action camp and intimidated anyone attempting to break through it. Fifty people were arrested trying to break into the plant itself.

After the camp came to an end, Greenpeace continued a high profile (and highly successful) campaign against the new plant. That October, Greenpeace activists occupied part of the plant, having accessed the site from the Medway using boats including the *Rainbow Warrior*. When Greenpeace projected campaign messages on the turbine building, management brought in a bulldozer to block the image until the following morning, when the protesters were served with a high court injunction. In November 2008, a protester entered the plant undetected and shut down one of the turbines leaving a message reading 'no new coal'. In June 2009, ten Greenpeace activists boarded a coal ship bound for Kingsnorth. Soon afterwards plans for the new plant, along with the CCS competition, were shelved.

Nuclear power

The TUC also supports nuclear power. Its report on energy policy *Powering Ahead*, published in 2016, has this to say about nuclear power:

> Support must continue for the development of Hinkley Point C, but the future of nuclear energy, including the commissioning of new nuclear reactors, cannot be pursued as Hinkley has been pursued. In future, the government should produce a comparative study of nuclear technologies, including small modular reactors, and make decisions according to viability and price.

Unfortunately some environmentalists, notably including George Monbiot, have also backed nuclear power, at least in short term, presumably on the basis that it is a lesser evil than the rising global temperature.

Although the TUC has been more willing to give support to some of the big mobilisations (in fact TUC general secretary Frances O'Grady spoke at the London demonstration in advance of the Paris COP), the support it gives remains limited and conservative. At the 2016 TUC Congress, for example, a radical motion on climate change from the TSSA entitled 'After Paris: climate change, just transition and green jobs' was rejected on the advice of the General Council, on the basis that it went too far. It did, however, win the votes of a third of the conference for the resolution. Both Unite and the GMB voted against it. The motion said the following:

> Congress welcomes the recognition in the COP22 Paris Agreement of 1.5 degrees rise as a safe limit and the role of fossil fuels in climate change, but regrets its failure to deliver the binding legal commitments necessary to achieve this or any safe containment, including any immediate action on fossil fuel and climate justice.

Congress condemns the government's dash for oil and gas, and welcomes, in contrast, Jeremy Corbyn's backing for one million climate jobs and a zero carbon Britain by 2050.

Congress welcomes the Paris-launched 'Break Free from Fossil Fuels', the global justice movement formed by frontline communities affected by fossil fuel extraction to accelerate a just transition to 100 per cent renewable energy.

Congress commits the TUC to an active energy and climate change strategy, and to work with other organisations to campaign for: energy democracy and a just transition from fossil fuel; a stop to airport expansion; promotion of alternatives to short-haul flights, including publicly owned rail in Britain and Europe; a genuine commitment to reducing lethal air pollutants; and a just transition employment strategy to climate jobs and well-paid, sustainable employment.

The 2017 TUC Congress passed a much stronger motion, moved by the Bakers' Union and strengthened by amendments from the CWU, FBU, ASLEF and TSSA. While the motion ducked the formula which was so contentious with the industrial unions the previous year ('to accelerate a just transition to 100 per cent renewable energy'), it was in other ways a stronger commitment than previously – in particular in engaging unions through their pension funds in the growing move to divest from funding fossil fuels.[278]

Paul Hampton argues, rightly, that the concept of a just transition is the most distinctive trade union framing of climate change policies to date. Although usually expressed in terms of ecological modernisation, it also has significant class undertones, and draws together a range of themes found in the climate literature from a trade union perspective. Hampton claims that:

The idea is usually attributed to Tony Mazzocchi, an official from the Oil, Chemical and Atomic Workers Union in the United States. According to his biographer, Mazzocchi developed the idea from the late 1960s, after he realised that 'there was no way to protect workers and society from toxic substances without banning them'. But banning these products would cause workers to lose their jobs. Mazzocchi's jarring solution was 'for society to pay workers not to make poisons' because conservation had its limits.[279]

The parallels today with workers currently employed in fossil or nuclear-powered power plants (or indeed with the production or operation of nuclear weapons systems) could hardly be clearer.

Individual unions

The situation in individual unions is even more uneven. The main industrial unions, Unite and the GMB, are heavily influenced by short-term job prospects in the main industries they represent: for example, the nuclear and car industries. Both these unions support airport expansion and nuclear power – and indeed nuclear weapons. In the summer of 2015, the GMB not only supported fracking but signed an agreement with several fracking companies.

Some of the smaller unions, however, the PCS and FBU in particular, along with the RMT, TSSA, UCU, NUT (now part of the NEU), Prospect, and the CWU, have much better environmental records. Tony Kearns, the senior deputy general secretary of the CWU, has a long record of involvement in climate change campaigning and has spoken at several climate change conferences, as has Graham Peterson of the UCU.

The PCS have a subcommittee of their executive working on climate change. Mark Serwotka, the general secretary, is strong on the issue. Chris Baugh, the assistant general secretary, also has a very strong record in terms of campaigning on climate change and promoting the issues in both his own union and the wider trade union movement. The PCS puts the idea of a 'just transition' to alternative employment into practice. The union is opposed to both nuclear power and nuclear weapons, despite having substantial membership in both industries. It has policies defending their members in these jobs on the basis of alternative jobs and alternative technologies.

The most important trade union action, from an environmental point of view, was the iconic occupation, by twenty workers for eighteen days in August 2009, of the Vestas wind turbine blade factory on the Isle of Wight, against the closure of the plant and the relocation of production to China and the USA. Vestas was at that time the biggest wind turbine manufacturer in the world. The dispute was boosted when many of the workers – there were 600 on the site – left Unite, the union they were in, when it failed to back them, and joined the RMT. The RMT and its then general secretary, Bob Crow, strongly backed the occupation, helping to build a national campaign around it and calling for the nationalisation of the site. Crow offered to hire a helicopter to take food into the site if this became necessary.

Although the dispute failed to stop the closure, it brought the issue to national prominence in a dramatic way that had an impact on the wider issue of climate change. Whilst the TUC did not play a prominent role in the dispute, it was given high profile at the TUC Congress that year, resulting in an emergency resolution being adopted on the Vestas dispute and the need for, and defence of, green jobs.

The Labour Party

The Labour Party (LP) has been better than the Tories on the environment in recent years. It was a Labour government that commissioned the Stern Review in 2006, and Labour (under Gordon Brown as prime minister with Ed Miliband as secretary of state for Energy and Climate Change) that put the Climate Change Bill through Parliament in 2008. This commits Britain to reduce net carbon emissions by at least 80 per cent by 2050 against 1990 levels to avoid dangerous climate change – which if implemented was potentially ground-breaking.

Labour, however, had been trapped in a neoliberal (Blairite) straightjacket for twenty years, and whether it would have implemented the Act in a serious way was never put to the test. When Labour lost the 2010 election the Act was handed over to the Tory/Lib Dem coalition. Far from implementing it, the Tories, both in coalition and as a majority Tory Government, took environmental policy sharply in the opposite direction. They went on to implement not only the dash for gas, but the introduction of extreme energy extraction such as fracking.

The Labour left was also historically weak on the environment. Its main theme was economic growth and then more economic growth, which would be made possible by the rapid expansion of North Sea oil.[280]

Despite this, however, Benn and others on the Labour and trade union left gave strong support to the Lucas Plan of 1976, which was drawn up by the Lucas Aerospace combine shop stewards committee, working with supporting academics, in response to the threat of 1,200 redundancies at the company's Burnley plant. In fact Benn, as secretary of state for industry under Harold Wilson, initiated the idea of the plan when a delegation of Lucas shop stewards met him to discuss the looming redundancies.

Although the main part of the Lucas plan dealt with a switch from weapons of war to 'socially useful production' across the combines 17 plants – such things as medical equipment and public transport vehicles – it also had a strongly ecological framework, since it defined 'socially useful production' in the following way:

> The product must not waste energy and raw materials, neither in its manufacture nor its use. The product must be capable of being produced in a labour-intensive manner so as not to give rise to structural unemployment. The product must lend itself to organisational forms within production which are non-alienating, and without authoritarian instructions. Instead the work should be organised so as to link practical and theoretical tasks and allow for human creativity and enthusiasm.[281]

The plan also had a section on alternative energy technologies, and directly referenced the problems of fossil fuel energy – which is remarkable for the mid-1960s. It says the following:

> The recent energy crisis has brought home to many people the political and economic insecurity of our advanced technological society, resting as it does on fossil fuel energy supplies, access to which is limited. And beyond this there is are absolute and finite limits to the resources that are available, and to the capacity of the ecosystem to absorb pollutants and environmental degradation without undergoing irreversible changes.

Unfortunately, however, there was no generalisation from the Lucas plan and its environmental dimension during the Bennite movement of the 1980s, despite the fact that the concomitant movement against the siting of American cruise missiles at Greenham Common itself had an environmental aspect. The Socialist Conferences organised by Benn had no significant discussion of the environment or climate change, for example.

Environmental policy under Corbyn

The election of Jeremy Corbyn to the leadership of the Labour Party in 2015, and then the spectacular gains made by Labour in the general election of May 2017, have not only stood politics in Britain on its head but have been a gamechanger for environmental policy. Corbyn is committed to defending the environment and has none of the constraints imposed by the austerity policies of the Blairites. He spoke – and brought the whole of his environmental team – at the London demonstration before the Paris COP. Shadow Chancellor John McDonnell has a long personal record in environmental campaigning – particularly against the third runway at Heathrow. Shadow environment secretary at the time, Barry Gardiner, declared at the Labour Party conference in 2016 that Labour in government would ban fracking and move forward from the previous mealy-mouthed approach of a 'moratorium pending further research on the environmental impact of this technique'. Such an approach ignores the extensive evidence from the USA of the actual impact of fracking itself – but equally importantly dismisses the impact of rising CO_2 emissions on climate change.

Before the election was announced, Corbyn had published a policy statement on the environment which included the following:

In 2015 the world came together to agree the landmark Paris Climate Agreement aimed at keeping global temperature rises to 1.5 degrees above pre-industrial levels. Instead of accelerating action to tackle climate change, the Conservative Government have introduced new tax breaks for oil and gas that will cost the UK taxpayer billions, cut support for renewables and for energy efficiency, and are going 'all out' for fracking. Yet we are facing a climate crisis. 2016 is set to be the hottest year on record and greenhouse gas emissions globally are still not falling. We are seeing the impacts of climate change much earlier than anyone predicted – around the world and at home. The Labour Party must stand for a different Britain – one that would play a leading role internationally and committed to cutting carbon emissions at home.

On the issue of renewable energy, the policy statement says the following:

> Our broken energy system is holding Britain back. Starved of investment by the big
> six energy companies, our electricity system is expensive, inefficient and polluting,
> and in urgent need of renewal to keep the lights on.

Yet we have enough wind, wave and sun potential not only to power our economy, but to export. Scotland recently met more than 100 per cent of its electricity needs with renewable energy alone.

A nation of draughty homes has left seven million households seriously struggling to pay their energy bills and yet we have the skills, technology and people needing quality jobs to fix them. 29,000 people die early every year from air pollution primarily caused by burning dirty fossil fuels. We will deliver clean energy, affordable heating and electricity - energy for the 60 million, not the big 6 energy companies.

The 2017 general election

Labour's 2017 election manifesto was not only the most radical it had ever produced: it was the strongest ecologically. It pledged full support for the Paris agreement, greater environmental protection, a new clean air act and a ban on all fracking.

This was continued at the 2018 Labour Party conference: Jeremy Corbyn not only put the environment right at the top – saying that it was the most important issue bar none – but pledged that Labour would 'kick-start a green jobs revolution that would tackle climate change, provide sustainable energy for the future, and create skilled jobs in every nation and region of the country'.

Both Jeremy Corbyn and Labour's shadow Secretary of State for Business, Energy and Industrial Strategy, Rebecca Long-Bailey, gave a strong commitment at the conference to climate jobs and to a steep reduction in emissions.

Labour is now pledged to bring Britain's energy system back into public ownership and provide the necessary investment to connect renewable energy sources to the grid. It is pledged to invest in wind, solar and other renewables, and to support the creation across the country of a viable renewables industry with good unionised jobs. It is also very good that Rebecca Long-

Bailey supported and attended the recent protest actions against the start of fracking at Preston New Road in the North West of England. She also raised the issue in the House of Commons.

There are weaknesses in Labour's positions as well, however. Ducking the issues of nuclear power, airport expansion and high-speed rail (HS2) remains a problem. The failure to develop a real discussion on economic growth and its contradictions is equally dangerous. These are unresolved problems that need to be discussed.

There remains, however, a big potential to strengthen Labour's position on the environment. The tens of thousands of young people who have joined the Labour Party since Corbyn became leader are a fertile constituency for environmental issues. Many of them were in any case a part of what became known as the 'green surge' into the Green Party a few years ago, and have now left to join Labour under Corbyn. Green Party membership rose from 30,000 to 60,000 in less than two years in the 'green surge'. Since then, around 10,000 of these have switched to the Corbyn movement that became a parallel development amongst young people. There is therefore now a very big constituency for green, red / green politics inside the party.

As mentioned above, Labour has had an affiliated environmental grouping, the Socialist Environment and Resources Association (SERA), since 1973. Its creation at that time was a radical response to the creation of the People Party – which later became the Ecology Party and then the Green Party of England and Wales. It seems to have been side-lined during the long years of Blairism but now has the potential to assume a new significance with the much-expanded membership and an influx of greens and also ecosocialists.

At the same time, Red Green Labour (RGL),[282] a loose network of ecosocialists that has developed recently inside the Labour Party, is promoting political discussion on environmental issues at all levels inside the party. It is also actively involved in a number of the key campaigns, such as those against fracking and Heathrow expansion. At the 2018 Labour Party conference, RGL organised a low key protest over the fact that there was a 'Heathrow lounge' stall at the conference, and that Heathrow expansion had a full-page advert in the official conference guide.[283]

20 Conclusion

The Campaign Against Climate Change, for its London demonstration on 1st December 2018, in advance the UN COP 24 in Poland, has adopted the slogan '1.5 to stay alive'. This was, as mentioned above, the campaigning slogan at the Paris COP in 2015 of those countries under imminent threat from the rising sea level, led by the Marshall Islands and known as the High Ambition Coalition that convinced the Paris summit to adopt a target of a 1.5°C maximum average global surface temperature in order to curb global warming.

The slogan is entirely appropriate, indeed crucial, for the struggle today. It reflects the fact that the IPCC '1.5°C' special report published in October (and referenced in earlier chapters) has already had a greater and more durable impact that any previous such scientific climate report. Even the media, with its highly dubious record on climate change (in Britain at least), finds itself running almost daily coverage on multiple aspects of the environmental crisis. In Britain the climate deniers have largely been silenced; even the most vocal and hardline of them, ex-Tory government Minister Nigel Lawson, failed to emerge following the publication of this report, as he has following countless previous such events.

Climate scientists, on the other hand, who have played such an irreplaceable role in raising awareness of global warming and climate change to its present level, but who have tended to be over-cautious when under attack from the deniers, are becoming emboldened and more definitive.

Many aspects of the wider environmental struggle are also receiving greater attention – from wars and conflicts over land and water, to the deteriorating situation of the climate refugee crisis, to the accelerating rate of species extinction. The 2018 WWF Report, with its demand for an international agreement for the protection of biodiversity, has been more widely covered and has had a greater impact than previous such reports.

At the same time there are huge setbacks.

We have Donald Trump as President of the USA, who thinks that global warming is a hoax, has withdrawn from the Paris agreement, has slashed federal spending on all aspects of climate related research accessible to him, and is vigorously promoting coal production – the most polluting form of fossil energy.

Now Brazil has elected as its president a neo-fascist Jair Bolsonaro who, not content with reversing the gains won since the end of the dictatorship in 1985, is threatening an environmental holocaust[284]. He plans to open up the Brazilian rainforest – the lungs of the world – to previously unheard-of levels of exploitation and land grabs, backed by militias who attack the communities that live in these areas, strip the ingenious peoples of all rights, and attack the very existence of the landless movement.

The clock, however, is not so easy to turn back. Whilst Trump rubbishes global warming from the White House, his strictures are widely ignored at other levels of American society – including at state level. Even the fossil fuel corporations have caught on that history is against them, and are reluctant to reinvest in deep coal mining, even when under pressure from Trump.

In fact, as I write this conclusion in mid-November 2018, a US federal judge has just blocked the construction of the planned 1,179-mile Keystone XL pipeline, designed to take 830,000 barrels a day of crude oil from Canada's Alberta tar sands to US refineries on the Texas Gulf Coast. Trump authorised the construction by executive order just two days after taking office, reversing a decision of the Obama administration to block the project. The pipe-line is seen by the American ultra-right as critical infrastructure to provide ongoing fossil-based energy security for the United States economy.

Opposition to the XL pipeline has been led by an unprecedented coalition of indigenous and First Nation peoples from both the USA and Canada, on the basis that it violates their ancestral lands and crosses the most important fresh water source in the world. They argued that the pipeline would support the extraction of crude oil from tar sands, a process that pumps even more greenhouse gases into the atmosphere than standard crude oil extraction.

The decision does not permanently block the pipeline, but requires the administration to conduct a more complete review of potential adverse impacts related to climate change, cultural resources and endangered species.

It reflects a form of guerrilla warfare that is being conducted against Trump as the implications of what he is doing in terms of the future of the planet become starker.

Two weeks ago, in London we saw the emergence of a new environmental campaign called Extinction Rebellion.[285] It is a dynamic action-based movement with a strong emphasis on wildlife protection a bio-diversity. In fact as I write these lines on November 17 2018,five London Thames bridges are blocked by Extinction Rebellion protesters, cutting London in half, bring traffic to a standstill and calling for actions to protect the environment. Many have been arrested.

At the same time California is facing the worst outbreak of wild fires in its wildfire-prone history. The town of Paradise in Butte County, with 30,000 inhabitants, has been wiped out by a fireball in just a few hours, with an initial death toll of 80 and with hundreds unaccounted for. The driving force behind these fires is not difficult to identify. It is human induced global warming, which intensifies year on year. More heat means more fires: there is no mystery about it.

These fires tell us once again that a major reduction in CO_2 emissions is now critical – but it will not be easy to achieve in the 12 years science is giving us. It will require the broadest possible coalition of forces. It will need to embrace the unity of red and green environmentalists, alongside established organisations such as Friends of the Earth and Greenpeace which have grown and radicalised in recent years, and with new groupings that have come on the scene such as Avaaz and 38 Degrees. These have radicalised, particularly in the run up to Paris, and have an impressive mobilising ability – sometimes known as big organisation. Such a movement has to look wider, to embrace the trade union movement, and also the indigenous peoples around the world along with major social movements, such as La Via Campesina and the Brazilian Landless Workers Movement (MST),

It will also need a sharp strategic focus, with high impact campaigns and demands that can bring about big change in a short period of time. One approach to this, as argued in chapter 9, is via carbon pricing; and the best proposal currently on the table in this regard, is in my view James Hansen's fee and dividend proposition. This offers an effective framework for a very big reduction in CO2 emissions, here and now whilst capitalism still exists, in the time scale that science is giving us, and on a basis of measures that are politically progressive, economically redistributive, and socially acceptable.

The Paris COP 21, with all its weaknesses (and there are many), must also be defended and reinforced. It was an important gain for the movement (imagine if it had been defeated) in that it recognised for the first time the anthropogenic nature of the climate crisis (in sharp contrast to Copenhagen) and set a target containing the increase in the average surface temperature of the planet below 1.5°C – which is a target with transitional implications. The task now is to build on the gains – i.e. the new targets and objectives established in Paris – whilst fighting to ensure that the individual countries meet the commitments to which they have agreed in terms of carbon reduction.

The involvement of the trade unions in the climate struggle is crucial, though it remains difficult in such a defensive period. Progress has nevertheless been made via initiatives such as the campaign for a million green jobs in Britain, which has the support of most major trade unions and the TUC, and the 'just transition' campaign (i.e. a socially just transition from fossil fuel to green jobs) which has the support of the ITUC at the international level, and addresses the issue of job protection in the course of the changeover to renewable energy. In this way it opens the door for a deeper involvement of the trade unions in the ecological struggle.

It will also need a strong radical left component if the struggle to save the planet is to be conducted within the framework of an ecosocialist world view, and lead towards a post-capitalist society that is socially just and ecologically sustainable.

As I argue in chapter 5, classic Marxism had many vital insights into the relationship between our species, *homo sapiens*, and the rest of the natural world. These insights, however, were lost during the second half of the 20th century to the growth and productivist onslaught, backed by the counterrevolution in the Stalinist states. They were only rescued for the many socialist ecologists who refused to bow to this situation – to whom I have dedicated this book – and on whose shoulders we stand today.

The left can only play a central in the environmental struggle, however, if it breaks with the leftist notion that socialist overthrow of global capitalism within the next 12 years, at a time when global politics is moving to the right, is the answer to global warming, climate change and other aspects of the ecological crisis. In other words, the intervention of the radical left in defending the ecology of the planet cannot be reduced to propaganda for socialism, or to lists of demands that are important and necessary components in the longer run, but will not stop global warming and climate change in the time available to us. The need to understand the importance of a transitional approach to politics is nowhere so important as in the environmental struggle, where the race against the clock is what faces us today.

Some the left argue that capitalism is incapable of resolving the issue of global warming and climate change, and even that it is prepared to see the planet destroyed in order to oppose measures to resolve global warming. But it depends what we mean by 'resolve'.

In the end, if capitalism is faced with the destruction the planet's capacity to sustain human life, and with increasing environmental disasters in rich parts of the world, they will finally act to resolve it. The problem is that they will leave it until it is too late to avoid massive destruction; and they will carry it out by dictatorial means and at the expense of the most impoverished people on the planet. The struggle to save the planet, therefore, can be defined more precisely as a struggle to save the planet in a way that is democratic, socially progressive, and ecologically sustainable.

This book is, therefore, as argued in its introduction, an appeal to the left, in the light of this advanced stage of the crisis, to become far more engaged with the environmental struggle. No struggle could be more important or urgent.

PART IV

IMPORTANT DEBATES

This section carries some important debates pertinent to some of the key themes in this book. These include: a piece by myself specifically for this book, on the long running and complex debate as to whether (or not) Marx was a productivist; a debate between Betsy Hartmann and Laurie Mazur on population; a debate between myself and Ian Angus and Simon Butler on their 2011 book *Too Many People?*; and a debate between myself and Derek Wall on population, originally published in the *Morning Star*.

Alan Thornett:
Was Marx a productivist?

The conclusions reached by John Bellamy Foster and Paul Burkett, in regard to the strong ecological content of classical Marxism, are not uncontroversial, particularly their defence of Marx against charges of productivism – or Prometheanism as it is often called.[286] As long ago as 1962 the German Marxist philosopher Alfred Schmidt, a member of the Frankfurt school of critical Marxism – in his book *The Concept of Nature in Marx* – not only questions the idea of metabolism but argues that Marx was essentially productivist, or Promethean – a critique that has persisted as a strain of thought since then. [287]

Foster and Burkett along with Brett Clark – an ecologist and professor of sustainability at the University of Utah – made a very effective rebuttal of Schmidt's position on this in the June 2016 *Monthly Review* in an article entitled Marx's Ecology and the Left.[288]

The most persistent challenge to Marx in this regard more recently has involved the laws of thermodynamics – in particular the second law of entropy.[289] This was raised, for example, by the Spanish economist and socialist Joan Martinez Alier, author of the much-respected *Ecological Economics: Energy, Environment and Society* published in 1990.[290] Martinez Alier accuses Marx of ignoring the second law of thermodynamics and Engels of rejecting it.[291]

Podolinsky

Martinez Alier claims that Marx and Engels had rejected the pioneering work of the nineteenth-century Ukrainian socialist Sergei Podolinsky – one of the founders of energetics and a pioneer of ecological economics – despite the fact that both Marx and Engels corresponded with Podolinsky at the time. This rejection Alier claims is at the root of 'the Marxist neglect of ecology'.[292]

Someone who supported Alier in this dispute was the American Marxist economist and sociologist James O'Connor, the co-founding editor of the journal *Capitalism, Nature, Socialism*.[293] He accused Marx of turning a 'deaf ear' to Podolinsky. (O'Connor introduced the idea of a 'second contradiction of capitalism', the first being between capital and labour and the second between capital and nature.)[294] [295]

The French Marxist Daniel Bensaïd also argues in his 2002 book *Marx for Our Times*, that Engels, in particular, had failed to incorporate the second law of thermodynamics – and its ecological implications – into his analysis.[296] Bensaïd also claimed that Engels rejected the concept.

Foster and Burkett responded vigorously to all this in an article entitled *'Classical Marxism and the Second Law of Thermodynamics: Marx/Engels, the Heat Death of the Universe Hypothesis and the Origins of Ecological Economics'*, published in *Organisation and Environment* in March 2008.[297] The abstract at the beginning of the article outlines the issue this way:

Today's understanding of the significance of Karl Marx and Frederick Engels's work for the development of both ecological economics in particular and ecology in general has been hindered by persistent claims that Engels (and by imputation Marx) rejected the second law of thermodynamics. It is demonstrated here through textual analysis that Engels criticised not the entropy law itself but the extrapolation of this into the 'heat death theory of the universe' hypothesis. The historical debate surrounding this hypothesis is examined, showing that Engels and Marx remained consistent with the natural science of their day. This opens the way to the recognition that Marx's political economy was unique in the 19th century in incorporating thermodynamics into the core of its analysis, thus providing the foundations for an ecological economics.

This article was republished in Foster and Burkett's book *Marx and the Earth: An Anti-critique*, published in 2016 specifically to engage this debate.[298]

In chapter two of that book, Foster and Burkett go back to original texts to establish exactly what Podolinsky had said. What they discovered was that the positions of Marx and Engels on his work had been distorted by confusions in chronology and translation. Podolinsky's work had been published in four different languages between1880 and 1883, and there were significant differences between the four versions. The first appeared in Russian in *Slovo* in 1880; the second in French in *La Revue Socialiste* in June 1880; the third in Italian in *La Plebe* in 1881; and the final version in German, in *Die Neue Zeit* in 1883 – after the death of Marx.

Paul Hampton, who reviewed this debate in May 2010, summarised it thus:

> Burkett and Foster argue that the text of the *Revue Socialiste* article, as far as we can deduce from Marx's extracts from the draft version sent by Podolinsky, contains significant additions to the earlier draft. Among these additions are the main reference to Marx's concept of surplus labour, the calculation of energy equivalents for agricultural labour and its output, and the attempt to analyse the energy efficiency of labour utilisation under the feudal, slave, capitalist and socialist modes of production. Burkett and Foster arranged for a full translation of the Italian version published in La Plebe. Their conclusion was that 'Podolinsky had not even come close to establishing a plausible thermodynamics basis for the labour theory of value that could have been adopted by Marx and Engels.[299]

Foster and Burkett themselves put it this way in *Marx and the Earth*:

> Podolinsky did not establish a plausible thermodynamic basis for the labour theory of value that could have been adopted by Marx and Engels. Moreover, Marx and Engels did not neglect nor abruptly reject Podolinsky's work as is commonly supposed, but took it seriously enough to scrutinise deeply in the spirit of critique. Although verifying Podolinsky's rightful place as a forerunner of ecological energetics, our analysis highlights the severe limitations imposed by his tendencies towards energy reductionism and closed system thinking, as compared to Marx and Engels's metabolic and open-system approach to nature and to human production.[300]

Read both ways

Daniel Bensaïd, in *Marx for Our Times* argues that Marx can be read either way on Prometheanism.[301] He argues thus:

> Productivist evil genius or ecological guardian angel? Whether we blame him [Marx] for bureaucratic productivism and its catastrophes, or conveniently claim him as

a green, dicta to support the verdict can easily be found in Marx. From the early works to the *Marginal Notes on Wagner*, his oeuvre is certainly not homogeneous. But faced with the test of the present, some trails long obstructed by the dead weight of didactic vulgarisation are once again open.[302]

He answered his own question as follows:

Obviously, it would be anachronistic to exonerate Marx of the Promethean illusions of his age. But it would be just as inaccurate to make him a heedless eulogist of extreme industrialisation and unidirectional progress. We must not confuse the questions he posed with the answers subsequently given by social democrats or Stalinist epigones. On this point as on others, the bureaucratic counter-revolution in the USSR marked a rupture.[303]

Ted Benton, the veteran socialist and environmentalist (and professor of sociology at Essex University) sums this up very well in his review of John Bellamy Foster's 2009 book *The Ecological Revolution: Making Peace with the Planet*, published in March 2010, [304] where he makes the following observation:

The thesis here [*i.e.* of J.B. Foster] is that Marx and Engels had an ecological vision at the core of their analysis, and had already developed the concept of sustainable development as key to their conception of the socialist future. One difficulty for this is that the historically dominant readings of Marx and Engels – by sympathisers and opponents alike – have been 'Promethean', in the sense that they have been held to premise future human liberation on the ever-advancing human mastery of the forces of nature. The environmental record of the state-centralist regimes that legitimated themselves by reference to the Marxian heritage was dire, but the European socialist and social democratic parties that originally grounded their political projects in Marxism also fought centrally for higher material living standards for organised labour on the basis of state support for economic growth – often at great environmental cost.

Another challenge has been to the notion of the metabolic rift. Joel Kovel in his 2002 book *The Enemy of Nature: The End of Capitalism or the End of the*

World,[305] calls into question Foster's conception of the metabolic rift, as set out both in *Marx's Ecology* and then in *The Ecological Rift.* Kovel puts it this way:

> Life is best defined as self-replicating form, and while metabolic processes are necessary for comprehending life they are not sufficient. Terms like metabolism are not more than anatomical metaphors, in my view, for the Heraclitean belief that change and transformation is the most fundamental feature of reality, whether in nature or society. Marx saw things this way, as should we all, but his theory of alienation went further, to demonstrate which kind of transformation conduce to the flourishing evolution of society and nature, and which spell doom.[306]

Foster replied to this in a keynote article entitled *'Marxism and the Rift in the Universal Metabolism of Nature'* in *Monthly Review* in December 2013.[307]

> The main reason, no doubt, that a handful of left critics, struggling with this conceptual framework, have characterised the metabolic-rift theory as a form of Cartesian dualism is due to a failure to perceive that within a materialist-dialectical perspective it is impossible to analyse the world in a meaningful way except through the use of abstraction which temporarily isolates, for purposes of analysis, one 'moment' (or mediation) within a totality. This means employing conceptions that at first sight – when separated out from the overall dynamics – may appear one-sided, mechanical, dualistic, or reductionist. In referring, as Marx does, to 'the metabolic interaction between nature and man' it should never be supposed that 'man' (humanity) actually exists completely independently of or outside of 'nature' – or even that nature today exists completely independent of (or unaffected by) humanity. The object of such an exercise in abstraction is merely to comprehend the larger concrete totality through the scrutiny of those specific mediations that can be rationally said to constitute it within a developing historical context. Our very knowledge of nature, in Marx's view, is a product of our human-social metabolism, *i.e.,* our productive relation to the natural world.

Energy: 'A Trojan horse in Marx's Ecology'

The Belgian Marxist ecologist Daniel Tanuro, in his 2010 book *Green Capitalism: Why It Can't Work,*[308] argues that, whilst the work of Foster and Burkett is valuable in locating the ecological strengths of classical Marxism, when it comes to the idea of the metabolic rift they bend the stick too far and exaggerate their case. (My review of *Green Capitalism* can be found on the Socialist Resistance website.)[309]

Tanuro argues that both Marx and Engels failed to recognise the significance of burning fossil fuel, and that Foster and Burkett are remiss in failing to point this out. He does not argue that they (Marx and Engels) should have predicted global warming, but that they should have recognised the significance of the changeover from bio-fuel (*i.e.* wood), which fuelled the first hundred years of the industrial revolution, to coal and steam: *i.e.* from renewable to non-renewable. In fact, he goes on to say that 'the energy question represents a veritable Trojan horse in [Foster's] *Marx's Ecology*.[310] He puts it this way:

> In fact, Marx is much more of an 'ecologist' than many of his successors realise. The exceptions to this are John Bellamy Foster and Paul Burkett; for them, ecology is 'at the heart of Marxism'. These two writers have the credit for rehabilitating 'Marx's ecology' but they tend to go too far in the other direction... I feel that it is pointless to exaggerate: the concept of 'rational regulation of exchange between humanity and nature' is authentically ecological, but a global vision of the ecological dimension of a socialist is only briefly apparent in Marx's thought. Furthermore, in my opinion this vision is undermined by a serious error in the field of energy resources.
>
> It is striking that in their analysis of the industrial revolution, Marx and Engels have simply failed to grasp the enormous ecological and economic potential of the transition from a renewable source of energy, produced by photosynthesis of solar radiation – wood – to a fossil fuel source, produced by the fossilisation of solar radiation and thus exhaustible in a historical time period – coal. Let us make no mistake: in the eyes of Marx, technology is not neutral. He makes a clear distinction between pre-industrial and industrial technologies, 'specifically capitalist' according to his definition. But this distinction is absent in the field of energy sources, as if these could be neutral.[311]

He then adds the following:

> However negligible it may be, an error at this level cannot but acquire a systematic character. This is why we may say that the energy question represents a veritable Trojan horse in Marx's ecology and in Marxism in general, in all its various tendencies.[312]

A robust response

Foster and Burkett's response to Tanuro, Bensaïd and Kovel (and others that have written on similar lines) was extremely robust. In fact, they published a new 300-page book specifically for the purpose – *Marx and the Earth: An Anti-critique* (2017).[313] Their strongest reaction is to Danial Tanuro's remarks – which they refer to as the 'Tanuro Thesis'. In fact, they take a 20-page section of *Marx and the Earth* to reply to him.

> In claiming that one cannot speak without substantial reservations of Marx's ecology, Tanuro insists that Marx fell prey to what he variously calls: 'a major ecological flaw'; 'a serious error'; 'a defect'; 'a failure'; 'a blind spot'; 'a shadow zone'; 'a lack of understanding'; 'an ambiguity'; 'a confusion'; 'an inconsistency'; 'a contradiction'; an unacceptable flaw'; an inner antagonism'; 'a slippage'; and a Trojan Horse. All of this is meant to describe a single contradiction that Tanuro purports to have discovered: namely, Marx and Engels' alleged failure to distinguish between renewable and non-renewable (fossil fuel) energy. More specifically, Tanuro claims that Marx and Engels fell prey to the fallacy of energy neutrality – *i.e.* 'the implicit conclusion that energy sources are natural' – ignoring altogether the *forms* of energy.'[314] (emphasis original)

They go on to point out that:

> Drawing on a metaphor taken from a quote by Leon Trotsky, Tanuro contends that the 'major ecological flaw' in Marx's analysis was left largely unattended in subsequent Marxist thought, and thus went 'from a scratch to the danger of gangrene'. The infection that set in was of such a 'systemic nature', so we are to believe, that the body of Marxist thought became gangrenous, seriously undermining its organic integrity and even the longevity as a system of thought...

They conclude that:

> Classical Marxism is thus presented by Tanuro as in effect a 'degenerative' methodological research programme in Imre Lakatos's sense, rather than a 'progressive' research programme, in that it is seen as having a shrinking rather than a widening empirical content, and is no longer able to generate novel facts.[315]

Whether Marx and Engels got everything right is another matter. It would have been remarkable if they had done so. It is true that the scientific basis of global warming – *i.e.* the greenhouse effect – was discovered in 1861 by the Irish physicist John Tyndall (after whom the much-respected Tyndall Centre for Climate Change Research in Manchester is named). Marx took great interest in the scientific developments of the day. In fact he attended some of Tyndall's lectures and was especially intrigued by his experiments on solar radiation.[316] It is a big step from this, however, to an understanding of the full significance of the greenhouse effect, or indeed of climate change: it was a science still in its early stages.

I share the more nuanced view of Michael Löwy in *Ecosocialism: A Radical Alternative to Capitalist Catastrophe*,[317] where he says the following on the matter of productivism:

> Ecosocialists accuse Marx and Engels of productivism. Is this justified? Yes and no. No, to the extent that no one has denounced the capitalist logic of production for production's sake – as well as the accumulation of capital, wealth, and commodities as a goal in themselves – as vehemently as Marx did. The very idea of socialism – contrary to its miserable bureaucratic deformations – is that of production for use values, goods necessary for the satisfaction of human needs. For Marx, the supreme goal of technical progress is not the infinite accumulation of goods ('having') but the reduction of the working day and the accumulation of free time ('being').
>
> Yes, to the extent that one often sees in Marx and Engels (and all the more in later Marxism) a tendency to make the development of the productive forces the principal vector of progress, along with an insufficiently critical attitude towards industrial civilisation, notably in its destructive relationship to the environment.[318]

In the end, however, the question is not whether Marx and Engels were clear on everything in relation to the ecology of the planet. It is how advanced they were on these issues for the period in which they lived and the strong direction of travel they took on the ecological issues. It is also about the extent to which their method provides the basis for us to develop an ecosocialism for the twenty-first century.

Daniel Tanuro, in *The Impossibility of Green Capitalism*, argues that if ecology really were at the heart of classical Marxism, as Foster and Burkett contend, then 'we would need to explain why all currents of Marxist thought missed the opportunity to engage with the ecological questions during the 1960s and the 1970s'.[319] This is a dangerous conclusion: it implies that the fatal flaw in terms of the twentieth century was located in classical Marxism itself!

It was the bureaucratic counterrevolution in the USSR in the form of Stalinism – the 'actually existing socialism' of the Stalinist states, viz the USSR, China and Eastern Europe – that were responsible for this. Tanuro partly recognises this in other parts of his book, but then says it was not entirely responsible – which suggests that the fatal flaw was in classical Marxism itself.

Betsy Hartmann and Laurie Mazur debate population

This debate between Betsy Hartmann and Laurie Mazur was first published in the magazine *On the Issues: A Magazine of Feminist Progressive Politics*, in the autumn of 2009.

Betsy Hartmann is the author of *Reproductive Rights and Wrongs: The Global Politics of Population Control* published in 1987, and *The 'New' Population Control Craze: Retro, Racist, Wrong Way to Go*, published in 2009. She is also director of the Population and Development Program at Hampshire College in Amherst, Massachusetts.

Laurie Mazur is the director of the_Population Justice Project. She is also the editor of *A Pivotal Moment: Population, Justice and the Environmental Challenge*, published in 2009.

Betsy Hartmann

It's back to the bad old days of the population bomb. That was the title of an alarmist book by Stanford biologist Paul Ehrlich that appeared in 1968. He suggested that world catastrophe would ensue unless women in poor parts of the world were prevented from having too many children.

This fall's junk mail carried an alarmist appeal from Population Connection, using its former name of Zero Population Growth (ZPG). According to ZPG, you can blame just about everything on population growth, from traffic congestion, overcrowded schools and childhood asthma to poverty, famine and global warming.

Retro racism and sexism are back in vogue, but now with a bit of a faux feminist twist. Along with the bad news that women's fertility is destroying the planet comes the good news that family planning is the solution. In other words, you don't have to feel guilty about blaming poor women for the world's problems because you can help them improve their lives by having fewer babies.

Don't get me wrong. I support the provision of contraception and abortion as a fundamental reproductive right and as part of comprehensive health services. What I'm against is turning family planning into a tool of top-down social engineering. There's a long and sordid history of population control programs violating women's rights and harming their health. That's why feminist reformers in the international family planning field have fought hard to make programs responsive to women's – and men's – real reproductive and sexual health needs. A world of difference exists between services that treat women as population targets, and those based on a feminist model of respectful, holistic, high-quality care.

Contrary to received wisdom, population control programs remain alive and well. India and China have especially coercive ones, but in many places in the world, from sub-Saharan Africa to public clinics in the US, poor women of colour are denied real contraceptive choice and targeted with long-acting contraceptives like Depo Provera, despite their substantial health risks, in order to keep birth rates down.

Reality vs. hype, overconsumption vs. numbers

The recent resurgence in overpopulation rhetoric flies in the face of demographic realities. In the last few decades population growth rates have come down all over the world so that the average number of children per woman in the Global South is now 2.75 and predicted to drop to 2.05 by 2050. The so-called population 'explosion' is over, though the momentum built into our present numbers means that world population will grow to about nine billion in 2050, after which point it will start to stabilise. The real challenge is to plan for the addition of that three billion people in ways that minimise negative environmental impact. For example, investments in public transport rather than private cars, in cluster housing rather than suburbia, in green energy rather than fossil fuels and nuclear, would do a lot to help a more populated planet.

Dollars, not sense, are driving the population bandwagon. Ironically, the main reason for the resurgence is that we have a new Democratic administration in Washington.

After eight years of George W. Bush's assault on reproductive and sexual health funding, population agencies see a welcome opportunity to expand international family planning assistance. The trouble is that some, like the influential Population Action International, are strategically deploying fears of overpopulation to win broader support inside and outside Congress. Their main tactic is to blame climate change on population growth so they can promote family planning as the magic bullet.

This kind of messaging is intensifying in advance of the upcoming world climate conference in Copenhagen in December.

These arguments threaten not only to distort family planning, but to derail climate negotiations by weakening US commitment to curbing carbon emissions and inciting the anger of nations in the Global South. Industrialised countries, with only 20 per cent of the world's population, are responsible for 80 per cent of the accumulated carbon dioxide in the atmosphere. The US is the worst offender.

Overconsumption by the rich has far more to do with global warming than population growth of the poor. The few countries in the world where population growth rates remain high, such as those in sub-Saharan Africa, have among the lowest carbon emissions per capita on the planet.

Serious environmental scholars have taken the population and climate change connection to task, but unfortunately a misogynist pseudo-science has been developed to bolster overpopulation claims. Widely cited in the press, a study by two researchers at Oregon State University blames women's childbearing for creating a long-term 'carbon legacy.' Not only is the individual woman responsible for her own children's emissions, but for her genetic offspring's emissions far into the future. Missing from the equation is any notion that people are capable of effecting positive social and environmental change, and that the next generation could make the transition out of fossil fuels.

A second study to hit the press is by a population control outfit in the UK, Optimum Population Trust (OPT), whose agenda includes immigration restriction. OPT sponsored a graduate student at the London School of Economics to undertake a simplistic cost/benefit analysis that purports to show that it's cheaper to reduce carbon emissions by investing in family planning than in alternative technologies. Although the student's summer project was not supervised by an official faculty member, the press has billed it as a study by the prestigious LSE, lending it false legitimacy. Writing on RH Reality Check, Karen

Hardee and Kathleen Mogelgaard of Population Action International endorse the report's findings without even a blink of a critical eye.

Feminists need to rethink blaming

In fact, perhaps what is most distressing about the current population control resurgence is how many liberal feminists and progressive media outlets are jumping on board.

There's even an attempt by the Sierra Club and others to bring reproductive justice activists into the fold in the name of 'Population Justice.' The assumption is that we live in a win-win world, where there's no fundamental contradiction between placing disproportionate blame for the world's problems on poor women's fertility, and advocating for reproductive rights and health.

Fortunately, many feminists in the international reproductive health field understand that contradiction, because they see its negative consequences play out on the policy and program level. They spoke out strongly at the recent NGO Forum on Sexual and Reproductive Health and Development in Berlin, against linking reproductive health to population control. And within the USA, women of colour active in the fields of reproductive justice and environmental justice, are coming together to critique population control, and to find a much more progressive common ground than 'population justice.' As Loretta Ross, National Director of SisterSong Women of Colour Reproductive Justice Collective, writes, both reproductive justice and environmental justice movements share 'an understanding of the complexity and intersectionality of issues that include not only the right to have, or not have children, but the right to raise our children in healthy and safe communities'.

If there's one lesson to be learned from the current moment, it's that we have to remain ever vigilant about population control messaging. In the future, population rhetoric will shift from the environment to other areas, such as national security. Population agencies have long found it useful to deploy narratives about population growth breeding terrorism to grab media attention and appeal to conservatives in Congress. Women, especially in the Middle East, supposedly produce 'youth bulges' of angry young men who then go on to become suicide bombers and terrorists. Already, prominent people in the population field are claiming that Afghanistan's problems are primarily driven by rapid population growth, and that family planning should be a vital part of US strategy there.

Along with vigilance, there needs to be a major effort to re-educate people about population, development and environment concerns. Many Americans fall prey to overpopulation rhetoric because it's all they've ever been taught. Unlike Europe, US schools provide virtually no education about international development, and many environmental studies textbooks repeat myths, and employ racist images of starving, Third World people overshooting the carrying capacity of the environment.

Addressing these issues also means challenging the peculiar brand of American capitalist individualism, that continually shifts the burden for economic, social and environmental breakdown from powerful corporations and militarism, onto the shoulders of individuals, especially poor people of colour. I for one am getting tired of reading about individual carbon footprints. Sure, it's vitally important for well-off people to reduce their energy consumption, but how about the heavy carbon boot-prints of the fossil fuel industry and the military-industrial complex? They are grinding us all into the ground.

Laurie Mazur

Betsy Hartmann implies that everyone working on population-environment issues is part of a misogynistic plot to bring back 'population control.'

I'm here to tell you she is wrong.

I am a lifelong, card-carrying feminist and political progressive. I am passionately committed to sexual and reproductive health and rights, to environmental sustainability, and to closing the inequitable divide between men and women, rich and poor. And I believe that slowing population growth – ensuring that all people have the means and the power to make their own decisions about childbearing – will contribute to those ends.

I'm not alone. Over the last couple of years, I have helped bring together feminists, environmentalists, and reproductive health activists, to develop an approach to population and environment issues that is grounded in human rights and social justice. Our efforts culminated in a new book, *A Pivotal Moment: Population, Justice and the Environmental Challenge.*

We also helped launch a new campus movement. The 'population justice' effort is a partnership of the Sierra Club, the International Women's Health Coalition, the Feminist Majority Foundation, and others. Our goals are to increase US funding for family planning and reproductive health; to provide comprehensive sexuality education in the US; and to pass the *Global Poverty Act* and implement the Millennium Development Goals. Population control is not on the agenda.

There are many points on which Betsy Hartmann and I are in complete agreement. For example, I agree that the relationship between population dynamics and environmental issues is best viewed through the prism of inequity. It is the affluent countries' unsustainable drive for production and consumption – not population growth in the Global South – that have caused most of the environmental crises we face.

And we do face environmental crises. Human-induced climate change is threatening the very habitability of our planet. From acidifying oceans to depleted aquifers, the natural systems we depend upon are nearing 'tipping points,' beyond which they may not recover.

The United Nations Development Program says that for the world's most marginalised citizens, the consequences of environmental crises 'could be apocalyptic.' Women are on the front lines of the crisis – walking farther to collect water, working harder to coax crops from dry soil, coping with plagues of drought, flood and disease.

Against that backdrop, consider our demographic future. World population now stands at 6.8 billion. While the rate of growth has slowed in most parts of the world, our numbers still increase by 75 million to 80 million every year, the numerical equivalent of adding another USA to the world every four years or so. A certain amount of future growth is inevitable, but choices made today will determine whether world population reaches anywhere between 8 billion and 11 billion by the middle of the century.

If we take seriously the need to protect the planet and distribute its resources more equitably, it becomes clear that it would be easier to provide a good life – at less environmental cost – for 8 billion rather than 11 billion people. This is especially true for climate change: an analysis by Brian O'Neill at the National Centre for Atmospheric Research estimates that stabilising world population at 8 billion, rather than 9 billion or more, would eliminate one billion tons of CO_2 per year by 2050 – as much as completely ending deforestation.

Of course, slowing population growth is not all we must do. Continued reliance on fossil fuels could easily overwhelm any carbon emission reductions from slower growth. Still, slowing population growth is part of what we must do to avert catastrophic climate change.

Does that justify a new program of coercive population control? Absolutely not.

The last two decades have seen a seismic shift in thinking about population issues. Feminist reformers fought for – and won – a ground breaking international agreement on population at a 1994 UN meeting in Cairo. The Cairo agreement says that the best way to achieve a sustainable world is by making sure that all people can make real choices about childbearing. That means access to voluntary family planning and other reproductive-health information and services. It means education and employment opportunities, especially for women. And it means tackling the deep inequities – gender and economic – that limit choices for many. It is possible that growing concern about climate change and other environmental issues could help mobilise funds for sexual and reproductive health and rights, women's empowerment and other elements of the Cairo agreement.

But I agree with Hartmann that it could easily go the other way. As the connection between population growth and the environment becomes clear, we are hearing more unacceptable calls for 'population control.' For example, a book by an environmental journalist proposes a mandatory 'one child per human mother' policy.

How should we respond to these dangerous proposals – as feminists, as people who care about the environment and human well-being? We can acknowledge that slowing population growth is one of many things we can do to build a sustainable, equitable future. And – most importantly – we can fight for population policies that are firmly grounded in human rights and social justice.

Ian Angus, Simon Butler and myself debate *Too Many People?*

This debate comprises a review by myself of Ian Angus' and Simon Butler's *Too Many People? Population, Immigration and the Environmental Crisis*, published by *Socialist Resistance* in January 2012, and a reply by the authors published on the website *Climate and Capitalism* in January 2012. Ian Angus is editor of *Climate and Capitalism* and Simon Butler is co-editor of *Green Left Weekly*.

Alan Thornett:

As a long-time comrade of Ian Angus, a fellow ecosocialist, and as an admirer of his work on Marxism and ecology, I am disappointed by the tone he has adopted in his new book on population *Too Many People?*, which he has authored jointly with Simon Butler, co-editor of the Australian publication *Green Left Weekly*.

The thesis they advance is that the population of the planet is irrelevant to its ecology, and that even discussing it is a dangerous or even reactionary diversion – a taboo subject. The book appears to be a response to Laurie Mazur's very useful book published last year *A Pivotal Moment: Population, Justice and the Environmental Challenge*. This was reviewed by Sheila Malone in *Socialist Resistance* magazine, in July 2010, as part of a debate on the issue.

Mazur argues that it is not a matter of choosing between reactionary policies from the past but that 'we can fight for population policies that are firmly grounded in human rights and social justice'. I agree with her on this, though not with everything in her book.

I didn't expect to agree with *Too Many People?*, since I had differed with Ian on population for some time. I did expect, however, an objective presentation of the debates without the ideas of fellow ecosocialists being lumped together with those of reactionaries and despots.

The book brands (in heavy polemical tones) anyone with a contrary view to the authors' as 'Malthusianist' – supporters of the eighteenth-century population theorist the Reverend Thomas Malthus, who advocated starving the poor to stop them breeding. Or more precisely as 'populationist', by which the authors mean neo-Malthusianist. They explain it this way:

> Throughout the book we use the term 'populationism' to refer to ideologies that attribute social and ecological ills to human numbers, and 'populationist' to people who support such ideas. We prefer those terms to the more traditional 'Malthusianism' and 'Malthusian', for two reasons. First, because in our experience not everyone is familiar with Thomas Robert Malthus, so labels based on his name aren't informative. And second because most modern populationists don't actually agree with what Malthus wrote 200 years ago.[320]

The 'more traditional term', however, never goes away. This leaves the book stuck in the past, more concerned with rehashing the polarised conflicts from 200 years ago than engaging with the contemporary debates.

The authors are right to say that population is not the root cause of the environmental problems of the planet. It is capitalism. They are also right to say that stabilising the population would not in itself resolve them. But they are wrong to say that it is irrelevant. The fact is that current rate of population increase is unsustainable were it to continue – and whether it will continue no one knows. What we do know is that it has almost tripled in just over 60 years – from 2.5 billion in 1950 to the recently reached figure of 7 billion.

According to UN figures it will reach between 8 and 11 billion (with 9.5 billion as the median figure) by 2050. After that it could begin to stabilise – possibly doing so by the end of the twenty-first century. Even this, however, is highly speculative. Long-term population predictions, as the authors themselves acknowledge, are notoriously inaccurate. Meanwhile, nearly half the current world population is under 25 – which is a huge base for further growth.

Yet throughout the book the charge of 'Malthusianism' or 'populationism' is aggressively levelled against anyone who suggests that rising population is a legitimate, let alone important, subject for discussion.

This is reinforced by a sleight of hand over the term population 'control'. The authors refuse to draw any distinction between control and empowerment and then brand those they polemicise against – including fellow ecosocialists who advocate empowerment – as being in favour of population 'control'. This allows them to create an amalgam between every reactionary advocate of population control they can find – and there is no shortage of them, including Malthusians – and those who are opposed to such control. This is then referred to throughout the book as 'the populationist establishment'.

My own views would certainly fall within this so-called establishment. Yet I am opposed to population control and support policies based on empowerment – policies based on human rights and social justice, socially progressive in and of themselves, which can at the same time start to stabilise the population of the planet.

Such policies involve lifting people out of poverty in the poorest parts of the globe. They involve enabling women to control their own fertility through the provision of contraception and abortion services. They include challenging the influence of religion and other conservative influences such as patriarchal pressure. They involve giving women in impoverished communities access to education.

These are major strategic objectives in their own right, but the issue of rising population gives them an additional urgency. It reflects the fact that the book has nothing at all to say on the substantive (and huge) issue of women and population.

Important progress towards empowerment policies was made at the UN Conference on Population and Development held in Cairo in 1994. This, for the first time, pointed to the stabilisation of the global population through the elimination of poverty, the empowerment of women, and the effective implementation of basic human rights. That its proposals were side-lined by a vicious pro-life backlash and the arrival of George W Bush on the world stage does not invalidate the contribution it made.

This approach, however, along with the Cairo conference itself, is heavily slapped down in the book. Empowerment is presented as the slippery slope to not only population control but 'at its most extreme' to programs, human rights abuses, enforced or coercive sterilisation, sex-selective abortion, female infanticide, and even to ethnic cleansing![321] The authors put it this way:

Most supporters of population control today say that it is meant as a kindness – a benevolent measure that can empower women, help climate change, and lift people out of poverty, hunger, and underdevelopment. But population control has a dark past that must be taken into account by anyone seeking solutions to the ecological crisis.[322]

They go on:

At its most extreme, this logic has led to sterilisation of the 'unfit' or ethnic cleansing. But even family planning could be a form of population control when the proponents aim to plan other people's families.[323]

The term population 'control' is again perversely attributed to anyone with contrary views and we are again warned of the 'dark past' of population debates and the dangers of engaging in them – and anything can be abused, of course, including family planning. But only enforced contraception and or sterilisation, which we all oppose, could rationally be seen population control – not the extension to women of the ability to control their own fertility.

Equally mistaken is the crass assertion that to raise the issue of population under conditions where fertility levels are highest in the global south and declining in the north is in some way to target the women of the south and to blame them for the situation. Fred Pearce, who endorses the book, makes advocates of empowerment into 'people haters': 'How did apparently progressive greens and defenders of the underprivileged turn into people-haters, convinced of the evils of overbreeding amongst the world's poor'.

What the empowerment approach actually targets, of course, is the appalling conditions under which women of the global south are forced to live and the denial basic human rights to which they are subjected. It demands that they have the same opportunities and resources as the women of the global north.

Even more confused is the allegation that the provision of contraception to women in the global south is in some way an attack on their reproductive rights; an attempt to stop them having the family size they would otherwise want – a view which appears to be endorsed in the *Socialist Review* assessment of the book. If that were the case, it would of course be, not the right to choose, but enforced contraception.

In any case the proposition that most women in the global south, given genuine choice, would choose to have the large families of today, is not supported by the evidence. Over 200 million women in the global south are currently denied such services and there are between 70m and 80m unintended pregnancies a year – of which 46m end in abortions. 74,000 women die every year as a result of failed back-street abortions – a disproportionate number of these in the global south.

After attacking empowerment from every conceivable angle the authors then appear to accept at least the possibility that not all of us who think population is an important issue to discuss, support enforced sterilisation and human rights abuses:

> We are not suggesting that everyone who thinks population growth is an ecological issue would support compulsory sterilisation or human rights abuses. Most modern-day populationists reject the coercive programmes of the 20th century, but that does not mean that they have drawn the necessary lessons from those experiences.[324]

Unfortunately, it is the authors themselves who continue to draw false lessons from the past: *i.e.* that the left should leave this subject alone, keep out of the debates, and insist that there is nothing to discuss.

The problem with this is that it is not just wrong but dangerous. If socialists have nothing to say about the population of the planet, the field is left open to the reactionaries, and they will be very pleased to fill it. And one thing the authors are certainly right about is that there are plenty of such people out there, with some very nasty solutions indeed.

Ian Angus and Simon Butler

We were pleased to learn that Alan Thornett, whose record as a working class and socialist leader we respect, had reviewed our book, *Too Many People? Population, Immigration, and the Environmental Crisis*. We didn't expect him to agree with all of it, but we were looking forward to an open and comradely discussion.

Unfortunately, his review misrepresents our views and issues a sweeping condemnation that ignores most of what we wrote. No one who read only his article would have any idea what the book is about.

As a result, our reply has to focus on setting the record straight, rather than, as we would prefer, on deepening and extending the debate on population and the environment.

Since our book is about population and the environment, we were surprised to read, in the second paragraph of Thornett's review, that we believe the subject is irrelevant. In fact, the word "irrelevant" appears in regard to population growth only once in our book – in the foreword by noted ecosocialist Joel Kovel: 'while *population is by no means irrelevant*, giving it conceptual pride of place not only inflates its explanatory value but also obscures the essential factors that make for ecological degradation and makes it impossible to begin the hard work of overcoming them.'[325] (emphasis added)

That sentence, which says just the opposite of what Thornett claims, concisely sums up our core argument – an argument that Thornett never mentions in his review. We wish that were the only case where he grossly misrepresents our views, but it isn't.

For example, he accuses us of lumping everyone who disagrees with us – from some ecosocialists to reactionaries and despots – into 'a highly objectionable amalgam… referred to throughout the book as 'the populationist establishment'.

In fact, we use the term 'population [*not* populationist] establishment' just twice – pages 98-103 – *not* 'throughout the book.' And contrary to Thornett's charge, in both cases it refers to the rich Western foundations and agencies that finance Third World population reduction programs, not to environmentalists of any political stripe.

But more important than specific phrases is the fact that in *Too Many People?* we consistently 'distinguish between the reactionaries who promote population control to protect the status quo and the green activists who sincerely view population growth as a cause of environmental problems.' Thornett offers no evidence that we failed to make that important distinction.

We could continue, but even a summary list of his miss-readings would require too much space. We'd rather discuss political issues.

Numbers versus social analysis

Thornett's most important disagreement with our book is evident in his warning that world population 'has almost tripled in just over 60 years –

from 2.5bn in 1950 to the recently reached figure of 7bn. According to UN figures it will reach between 8bn and 11bn (with 9.5bn as the median figure) by 2050.' Such growth, he says categorically, is 'unsustainable.'

In other words, he agrees with the populationist view that where human numbers are concerned, *big is bad and bigger is worse*. Although he says that capitalism is the real environmental problem, he accepts an argument that separates population growth from its historical, social, and economic context, reducing humanity's complex relationship with nature to simple numbers.

We, on the other hand, agree with Mexican feminist and human rights activist Lourdes Arizpe in her 2014 book *A Mexican Pioneer in Anthropology*:

> The concept of population as numbers of human bodies is of very limited use in understanding the future of societies in a global context. It is what these bodies do, what they extract and give back to the environment, what use they make of land, trees, and water, and what impact their commerce and industry have on their social and ecological systems, that are crucial.[326]

Thornett's simplistic number-slinging is particularly problematic in a review of a book that explains why such statistics are misleading and unhelpful. Simply re-stating some *big is bad* numbers, while refusing to respond to or even mention our criticisms and counter-arguments, doesn't advance the discussion one inch.

Is birth control an environmental issue?

But what seems to upset Thornett most is our criticism of environmentalists who believe it is possible to reverse decades of horrendous experience by combining Third World population reduction programs with respect for human rights. He endorses the argument of liberal feminist Laurie Mazur, that 'We can fight for population policies that are firmly grounded in human rights and social justice.'

We, on the contrary, argue that 'population policies not only don't pave the way for progressive social and economic transformation, they raise barriers to it.'[327]

To Thornett, that means that we oppose empowering Third World women, and that we unfairly label supporters of voluntary family planning programs as advocates of 'population control.'

In what he seems to think is a challenge to our views, Thornett describes the oppression and restrictions faced by Third World women who want to control their fertility. He insists that ecosocialists must support the provision of contraception and birth control, and oppose any measures or policies that would restrict women's reproductive rights.

You'd never know from his account that we make the same point several times in *Too Many People?* Far from considering these, as Thornett claims, 'as secondary, as issues already dealt with', our book explicitly includes 'ensuring universal availability of high-quality health services, including birth control and abortion' as priority measures that ecosocialists should fight for. Once again, what we actually wrote was the opposite of his charge.

Thornett's false claim that we oppose empowering Third World women avoids our real argument: that Third World birth control programs are not an appropriate or effective way to fight the environmental crisis.

In the first place, as we show in *Too Many People?*, Third World population growth is not a significant cause of the environmental crisis – so focusing on population reduction would divert the environmental movement's limited resources into programs that just won't work.

And, as supporters of women's rights, we oppose birth control programs that are motivated by population-reduction goals because they so often undermine the very empowerment they are said to promote. In Chapter 8, we discuss coercive measures found in supposedly voluntary programs around the world, ranging from the crude (denial of financial, medical or social benefits to women who refuse to be sterilised) to the relatively subtle (mandatory attendance at population-reduction lectures as a condition of receiving health care).

A recent article by noted feminist and population expert Betsy Hartmann explained the dangers of population-motivated birth control programs this way:

> Equally troubling about overpopulation propaganda is the way it undermines reproductive rights. While its purveyors claim that they support family planning, they view it more as a means to an end – reducing population growth, rather than as a right in and of itself. The distinction may seem subtle, but it is not. Family planning programs designed to limit birth rates treat women, especially poor women and women of colour, as targets rather than as individuals worthy of respect. Quality of care loses out to an obsession with the quantity of births averted.[328]

Sadly, Thornett brushes these important concerns aside, calling them 'sleight of hand', and insisting that the term 'population control' only applies when there is 'enforced contraception.' That's an astonishing statement for any supporter of women's rights to make.

Formally speaking, there is no 'enforced contraception' in the United States, but, as feminist lawyer Mondana Nikoukari points out, there are 'gradations of coercion' that cause women of colour to be sterilised twice or even three times as often as white women.

Our comment: 'If that's true in the United States, how can we imagine that in countries where legal protections are much weaker, population-environment programs will truly respect women's rights?'[329]

We don't doubt the sincerity of those who support what Thornett calls an 'empowerment' approach to limiting population growth. We know that they oppose coercive population control. Unfortunately, their sincerity won't protect poor women from the unintended consequences of the policies they advocate. Nor will it address the real causes of our mounting ecological crises, which – although Thornett doesn't mention it – are discussed at some length in *Too Many People?*

Should we discuss population ... or adapt to populationism? In the Introduction to *Too Many People?*, we explained why we wrote the book: 'Our goal is to promote debate within environmental movements about the real causes of environmental destruction, poverty, food shortages, and resource depletion. To that end, we contribute this ecosocialist response to the new wave of green populationism...'[330]

So once more we were surprised to be accused of opposing discussion of population and its relationship to ecology. We clearly call for more debate, but Thornett claims we believe 'that even discussing it is a dangerous or even reactionary diversion – a taboo subject,' and that 'the left should leave this subject alone, keep out of the debates, and insist that there is nothing to discuss.'

On its face, this is an improbable charge. We have written an entire book and dozens of articles on population and the environment. We have spoken at public meetings, debated populationists in person and on radio, and participated in innumerable online discussions. Would we have done any of that if we thought the left should leave the subject alone?

Only in the very last paragraph of his review does it become clear that he doesn't really think we oppose discussion. Rather, he wants us to stop criticising the 'too many people' argument – the discussion he wants is not about *whether* overpopulation is a major environmental problem, but about *how to reduce birth rates.*

Our failure to do this, he says, is 'not only wrong but dangerous,' because 'the field is left open to reactionaries' who will use our absence from intra-populationist debates as an opportunity to promote 'some very nasty solutions indeed.'

Liberals often urge socialists to moderate their political views, to avoid strengthening the right. We did not expect to hear such an argument from Alan Thornett. In reply, we can only repeat what we said in *Too Many People?*

> The real danger is that liberal environmentalists and feminists will strengthen the right by lending credibility to reactionary arguments. Adopting the argument that population growth causes global warming endorses the strongest argument the right has against the social and economic changes that are really needed to stop climate change and environmental destruction.
>
> If environmentalists and others believe that population growth is causing climate change, then our responsibility is to show them why that's wrong, not to adapt to their errors.[331]

Derek Wall and Alan Thornett debate population

This debate takes the form of two articles on population published in the *Morning Star* in October in November 2014. The first was by Derek Wall and the second by Alan Thornett, putting the alternative point of view.

Derek Wall:

Wherever you look, it seems that overpopulation is in the news or projected by popular culture. David Attenborough has called for lower human numbers and the Channel 4 thriller Utopia, which aired a second series this summer, is about a plot to release a killer virus that would reduce the global population by 95 per cent to 500 million.

Overpopulation is often cited as the cause of environmental problems, and reduction in human numbers suggested as essential if we are serious about climate change, deforestation and other ecological challenges. It is a straightforward argument, apparently, that if there are more of us, we will do more damage to planet Earth. While many on the left often dismiss the idea of zero population growth as reactionary, population concern is shared by many people. More people equals more consumption, which in turn equals more pollution.

Sometimes population growth is linked to anti-immigration statements – the notion that England's green and pleasant land is under threat from a growing population arriving on our small island. If population concern is often about 'foreigners' and hints at the purity of the traditional British countryside, it is also linked to other reactionary traits.

The population lobby is inspired by the economist Malthus. The nineteenth-century vicar and classical economist famously argued that populations tend to grow geometrically, doubling in size, whereas food supply only grows arithmetically, by a small percentage each year. Thus, famine was almost inevitable, with population numbers increasing too fast to meet the supply of food. Malthus used his theory, not to defend the environment, but to attack the working class and peasants in England. He argued for the abolition of systems of welfare because he felt that poverty was caused not by inequality and exploitation, but by overpopulation.

A safety net for the unemployed, or other forms of help to reduce poverty, were doomed because, if the poor were given aid, they would simply have more children. Such a rise in family size with limited resources would lead back to misery.

He was using his Malthusian case to attack early socialists and proto-socialists, who thought a better, more equal society was possible. The rich and powerful, scared by the effects of the French revolution in 1789, needed theorists to justify their dominance. Hence any Malthusian concern with population is rooted in a reactionary creed. Malthus opposed the Speenhamland system, introduced in 1795, to alleviate poverty caused by high grain prices, and he would have hated the idea of a minimum wage today.

In fact, since Malthus's death, food supply has risen faster than human numbers. Lack of democracy and inequality create famine, as the economist Amartya Sen has shown, which in the capitalist era occurred because of lack of purchasing power and lack of political power over food distribution, not lack of food. The Irish famine, for example, was a product not simply of potato blight but of the English occupation of Ireland which blocked aid to those who were hungry, justified by Malthusian sentiments.

Where population control has been attempted it has often created oppression. Indira Gandhi's population control in India in the 1970s saw men being sterilised in return for radios. Women have been forcibly sterilised or hoodwinked into losing their fertility.

However, population control can have good motives as well as bad. Pointing to reactionary examples should not blind us to the fact that many people who want to reduce poverty and environmental destruction advocate population control.

Population advocates argue that empowerment of women and education can be used to cut population without violence or repression. It is important to listen to population control arguments and not to dismiss their advocates as knaves and nasty folk. Nonetheless population control arguments are flawed. The notion of population control is very problematic, and the idea that one group of people should decide the fertility of another group is unacceptable.

Education about population sounds innocent but often ends up being patronising and perceived as abuse. Population concern seems to speak to a worsening environmental crisis, in a mathematically persuasive way. More humans multiplied by more energy and resource use leads to greater environmental impact – QED: have fewer kids if you love your planet.

However, environmental problems, when examined, are a little more complex than immediate appearances. Climate change is produced by using fossil fuels, but we have many opportunities to use less, from affordable public transport to making sure new homes are insulated.

The tragic truth here is that we have influential groups like UKIP which campaign against measures for clean energy.

We consume too many resources not because population is rising but because the capitalist economy depends on us consuming more. There is a $9 trillion advertising industry urging us to buy more, to use more energy, to keep consuming. This seems a more immediate target for green action – zero advertising growth might be a better target than zero population growth. However, too much green action is about lifestyle choice and sacrifice, and we could consume without wrecking the environment if we had a rational rather than capitalist economy.

Goods could be made to last longer – think of say mobile phones or computers, which could be made so they could be upgraded rather than thrown. A green economy demands social change so that production can be made sustainable, but at present, with profit as our god, this is impossible.

In 1798 in the first edition of his *An Essay on the Principle of Population,* Malthus argued that poverty was caused by overpopulation, but we know today that poverty is a product of an unequal society. His followers today say population is the cause of climate change. However, from the actions of the Koch brothers, who defend fossil fuels, to the imperative to produce more, consume more and waste more in capitalism, there are more pressing forces driving the degradation of the environment.

In the 19th century the Malthusian League called for contraceptives to be openly available, and campaigned against sexual repression.

The League was right to do so and helped create a better society. However, the League also opposed workers going on strike because they said socialism was impossible and poverty was caused not by inequality but family size.

Twenty-first century Malthusians who challenge barriers to the availability of contraception promote common good; however, their wider ideology can be repressive, and distracts from the most important source of ecological disaster, which is capitalism.

Control and restraint for the 'multitude' by a self-defined elite has too often been the goal for advocates of zero population growth. Population control is also moralistic, and we often love the moralism of telling other people what we think they should do.

Population lobbyists are often from prosperous parts of the world and increasingly target not just human numbers but human movement. It's worth asking whether population lobbyists want to see a world with fewer people or specifically, a world with fewer people who are different from themselves?

Alan Thornett

I don't agree with the position of Derek Wall – a long time and respected comrade of mine in the ecological struggle – on the rising population of the planet in *The Morning Star* of Wednesday 29 October entitled 'It's Capitalism, Not Overpopulation, That Causes Inequality'.

I agree with some of the things he says. I agree with the title of his article, since it is indeed capitalism that causes inequality. I agree that rising population is not the key driver of the ecological crisis; which is capitalism and its thirst for profit. I agree that rising population is not a big contributor to global warming since (at the moment) the highest birthrates are in the impoverished South where the carbon footprint is small. I also agree that any attempt to link the rising global population to anti-foreigner or anti-immigrant racism is reactionary and should be condemned.

The problem is that these points do not resolve the problem, which is that the rate of increase of the global population is unsustainable. It has almost tripled in the last 60 years – from 2.5 billion in 1950 to over 7 billion today – an annual increase of 80 million a year (the population of Germany) and shows no sign of slowing down. In fact, this rate of increase has been remarkably stable for the past 50 years.

According to the UN, the global population will reach somewhere between 8 and 11 billion by mid-century. Meanwhile nearly half of the current global population is under twenty-five. This is the biggest new generation ever, and a huge potential for further growth. At the same time the per capita consumption of food, water, and manufactured goods is increasing even faster than the population itself.

Predictions that it will stabilise by the end of the century may be right or wrong (population is notoriously difficult to predict) but the question remains as to whether the resulting 10, 11, or 12 billion is sustainable even if it does stabilise.

Nor is this resolved by attacking the writings of the eighteenth-century economist Thomas Malthus in line with the polemics of Marx and Engels against him. Marx and Engels were entirely right. The ideas of Malthus were indeed reactionary. They are also, in my view, irrelevant to the issue of rising population today, and focusing on them leaves the left trapped in the past.

Rising population today is not an economic issue of the eighteenth century, it is an environmental issue of the twentieth and twenty-first century.

Today enough food can be produced by industrialised agriculture to feed the planet's 7bn inhabitants if it was efficiently and equitably distributed and not subject to the inequalities of the market, with its hugely wasteful distribution systems. The problem is not whether enough food can be produced by ever-bigger agribusiness, using ever more chemical fertilisers, pesticides, and mono-cropping techniques, but whether it can be produced and distributed without destroying the ecology of the planet in the process.

Rising population is most importantly an issue of biodiversity or the mass extinction of species – which Derek fails to mention. This (increasingly known as the sixth extinction) is the greatest extinction of species since the demise of the dinosaurs – and it is taking place in front of our eyes. It is due to habitat destruction, pollution, and the effect of carbon emissions and global warming, that not only causes the sea level to rise, but is the driving force behind the acidification of the oceans – one of the biggest single biodiversity disasters currently taking place.

The ecosocialist approach cannot be that none of this matters, or that all will be well after the revolution. There may be little left by then if destruction continues at the current rate. Modern humans are a part of nature and have both a need and an obligation to live in harmony with it. We share with other species a fragile and interrelated biosphere, and we should look to a situation where we can exist alongside other species without threatening their very existence and thereby ultimately our own. Such an approach, in my view, is not anti-people but entirely pro-people.

The left needs a radically new approach to the whole issue of population and the environment. Such an approach, which has had the support of many on the left including myself, is based on the empowerment of women and the rejection of any form of coercive population control, such as a limitation on families and any form of contraception that is not based on the right to choose.

This approach is based on the view that most women, if they had free choice, would be unlikely have the large families that prevail in much of the Global South. Some would, most would not. It argues that if women are able to control their own fertility, get access to education and jobs, and shed the influences of patriarchy and religion, fertility rates would fall further and the global population would stabilise. And it would improve the lives of millions of women in the process. It is a real win-win situation and, along with a wider understanding of the nature of the problem, would start to stabilise the global population.

PART V

APPENDICES

An ecosocialist manifesto

The idea for this ecosocialist manifesto was jointly launched by Joel Kovel and Michael Lowy at a workshop on ecology and socialism, held in September 2001 at Vincennes, near Paris.

The twenty-first century opens on a catastrophic note, with an unprecedented degree of ecological breakdown and a chaotic world order, beset with terror and clusters of low-grade, disintegrative warfare that spread like gangrene across great swathes of the planet: central Africa, the Middle East and North-western South America, and reverberate throughout the nations. In our view, the crises of ecology and of societal breakdown are profoundly interrelated and should be seen as different manifestations of the same structural forces.

The former broadly stems from rampant industrialisation that overwhelms the Earth's capacity to buffer and contain ecological destabilisation. The latter stems from the form of imperialism known as globalisation, with its disintegrative effects on societies that stand in its path. Moreover, these underlying forces are essentially different aspects of the same drive, which must be identified as the central dynamic that moves the whole: the expansion of the world capitalist system.

We reject all euphemisms or propagandistic softening of the brutality of this regime: all greenwashing of its ecological costs, all mystification of the human costs under the names of democracy and human rights. We insist instead upon looking at capital from the standpoint of what it has really done. Acting on nature and its ecological balance, the regime, with its imperative to constantly expand profitability, exposes ecosystems to destabilising pollutants, fragments habitats that have evolved over aeons to allow the flourishing of organisms, squanders resources, and reduces the sensuous vitality of nature to the cold exchangeability required for the accumulation of capital. From the side of humanity, with its requirements for self-determination, community, and a meaningful existence, capital reduces the majority of the world's people to a mere reservoir of labour power, while discarding much of the remainder as useless nuisances. It has invaded and undermined the integrity of communities through its global mass culture of consumerism and depoliticisation. It has expanded disparities in wealth and power to levels unprecedented in human history. It has worked hand in glove with a network of corrupt and subservient client states whose local elites carry out the work of repression while sparing the centre of its opprobrium. And it has set going a network of translational organisations under the overall supervision of the Western powers and the superpower United States, to undermine the autonomy of the periphery and bind it into indebtedness, while maintaining a huge military apparatus to enforce compliance to the capitalist centre.

We believe the present capitalist system cannot regulate, much less overcome, the crises it has set going. It cannot solve the ecological crisis, because to do so requires setting limits upon accumulation – an unacceptable option for a system predicated upon the rule: Grow or Die! And it cannot solve the crisis posed by terror and other forms of violent rebellion, because to do so would mean abandoning the logic of empire, which would impose unacceptable limits on growth and the whole 'way of life' sustained by empire. Its only remaining option is to resort to brutal force, thereby increasing alienation and sowing the seed of further terrorism … and further counter-terrorism, evolving into a new and malignant variation of fascism. In sum, the capitalist world system is historically bankrupt. It has become an empire unable to adapt, whose very gigantism exposes its underlying weakness. It is, in the language of ecology, profoundly unsustainable, and must be changed fundamentally, nay, replaced, if there is to be a future worth living. Thus the stark choice once posed by Rosa Luxemburg returns: Socialism or Barbarism!, where the face of the latter now reflects the imprint of the intervening century and assumes the countenance of ecocatastrophe, terror counterterror, and their fascist degeneration.

But why socialism, why revive this word seemingly consigned to the rubbish-heap of history by the failings of its twentieth-century interpretations? For this reason only: that however beaten down and unrealised, the notion of socialism still stands for the supersession of capital. If capital is to be overcome, a task now given the urgency of the survival of civilisation itself, the outcome will perforce be 'socialist', for that is the term which signifies the breakthrough into a post-capitalist society. If we say that capital is radically unsustainable and breaks down into the barbarism outlined above, then we are also saying that we need to build a 'socialism' capable of overcoming the crises capital has set going. And if socialisms past have failed to do so, then it is our obligation, if we choose against submitting to a barbarous end, to struggle for one that succeeds. And just as barbarism has changed in a manner reflective of the century since Luxemburg enunciated her fateful alternative, so too must the name and the reality of a socialism become adequate for this time.

It is for these reasons that we choose to name our interpretation of socialism as an ecosocialism, and dedicate ourselves to its realisation.

Why ecosocialism?

We see ecosocialism not as the denial but as the realisation of the 'first-epoch' socialisms of the twentieth century, in the context of the ecological crisis. Like them, it builds on the insight that capital is objectified past labour, and grounds itself in the free development of all producers, or to use another way of saying this, an undoing of the separation of the producers from the means of production. We understand that this goal was not able to be implemented by first-epoch socialism, for reasons too complex to take up here, except to summarise as various effects of underdevelopment in the context of hostility by existing capitalist powers.

This conjuncture had numerous deleterious effects on existing socialisms, chiefly, the denial of internal democracy, along with an emulation of capitalist productivism, and led eventually to the collapse of these societies and the ruin of their natural environments. Ecosocialism retains the emancipatory goals of first-epoch socialism, and rejects both the attenuated, reformist aims of social democracy and the productivist structures of the bureaucratic variations of socialism. It insists, rather, upon redefining both the path and the goal of socialist production in an ecological framework. It does so specifically in respect to the 'limits on growth' essential for the sustainability of society. These are embraced not, however, in the sense of imposing scarcity, hardship and repression. The goal, rather, is a transformation of needs, and a profound shift toward the qualitative dimension and away from the quantitative. From the standpoint of commodity production, this translates into a valorisation of use-values over exchange-values – a project of far-reaching significance grounded in immediate economic activity.

The generalisation of ecological production under socialist conditions can provide the ground for the overcoming of the present crises. A society of freely associated producers does not stop at its own democratisation. It must, rather, insist on the freeing of all beings as its ground and goal. It overcomes thereby the imperialist impulse both subjectively and objectively. In realising such a goal, it struggles to overcome all forms of domination, including, especially, those of gender and race. And it surpasses the conditions leading to fundamentalist distortions and their terrorist manifestations. In sum, a world society is posited in a degree of ecological harmony with nature, unthinkable under present conditions. A practical outcome of these tendencies would be expressed, for example, in a withering away of the dependency upon fossil fuels integral to industrial capitalism. And this in turn can provide the material point of release of the lands subjugated by oil imperialism, while enabling the containment of global warming, along with other afflictions of the ecological crisis.

No one can read these prescriptions without thinking, first, of how many practical and theoretical questions they raise, and second and more dishearteningly, of how remote they are from the present configuration of the world, both as this is anchored in institutions and as it is registered in consciousness. We need not elaborate these points, which should be instantly recognisable to all. But we would insist that they be taken in their proper perspective. Our project is neither to lay out every step of this way nor to yield to the adversary because of the preponderance of power he holds. It is, rather, to develop the logic of a sufficient and necessary transformation of the current order, and to begin developing the intermediate steps towards this goal. We do so in order to think more deeply into these possibilities, and at the same moment, begin the work of drawing together with all those of like mind. If there is any merit in these arguments, then it must be the case that similar thoughts, and practices to realise these thoughts, will be coordinatively germinating at innumerable points around the world. Ecosocialism will be international, and universal, or it will be nothing. The crises of our time can and must be seen as revolutionary opportunities, which it is our obligation to affirm and bring into existence.

Joel Kovel and Michael Lowy

Paris, September 2001

The Belém
Ecosocialist Declaration

The text of this declaration was prepared by a committee elected at the Paris Ecosocialist Conference of 2007 comprised of Ian Angus, Joel Kovel and Michael Löwy. It was distributed at the World Social Forum in Belém, Brazil, in January 2009.

'*The world is suffering from a fever due to climate change, and the disease is the capitalist development model.*' – Evo Morales, president of Bolivia, September 2007

Humanity's choice

Humanity today faces a stark choice: ecosocialism or barbarism.

We need no more proof of the barbarity of capitalism, the parasitical system that exploits humanity and nature alike. Its sole motor is the imperative toward profit and thus the need for constant growth. It wastefully creates unnecessary products, squandering the environment's limited resources and returning to it only toxins and pollutants. Under capitalism, the only measure of success is how much more is sold every day, every week, every year – involving the creation of vast quantities of products that are directly harmful to both humans and nature, commodities that cannot be produced without spreading disease, destroying the forests that produce the oxygen we breathe, demolishing ecosystems, and treating our water, air and soil like sewers for the disposal of industrial waste.

Capitalism's need for growth exists on every level, from the individual enterprise to the system as a whole. The insatiable hunger of corporations is facilitated by imperialist expansion in search of ever greater access to natural resources, cheap labour and new markets. Capitalism has always been ecologically destructive, but in our lifetimes these assaults on the

Earth have accelerated. Quantitative change is giving way to qualitative transformation, bringing the world to a tipping point, to the edge of disaster. A growing body of scientific research has identified many ways in which small temperature increases could trigger irreversible, runaway effects – such as rapid melting of the Greenland ice sheet or the release of methane buried in permafrost and beneath the ocean – that would make catastrophic climate change inevitable.

Left unchecked, global warming will have devastating effects on human, animal and plant life. Crop yields will drop drastically, leading to famine on a broad scale. Hundreds of millions of people will be displaced by droughts in some areas and by rising ocean levels in others. Chaotic, unpredictable weather will become the norm. Air, water and soil will be poisoned. Epidemics of malaria, cholera and even deadlier diseases will hit the poorest and most vulnerable members of every society.

The impact of the ecological crisis is felt most severely by those whose lives have already been ravaged by imperialism in Asia, Africa, and Latin America, and indigenous peoples everywhere are especially vulnerable. Environmental destruction and climate change constitute an act of aggression by the rich against the poor.

Ecological devastation, resulting from the insatiable need to increase profits, is not an accidental feature of capitalism: it is built into the system's DNA and cannot be reformed away. Profit-oriented production only considers a short-term horizon in its investment decisions, and cannot take into account the long-term health and stability of the environment. Infinite economic expansion is incompatible with finite and fragile ecosystems, but the capitalist economic system cannot tolerate limits on growth; its constant need to expand will subvert any limits that might be imposed in the name of 'sustainable development'. Thus, the inherently unstable capitalist system cannot regulate its own activity, much less overcome the crises caused by its chaotic and parasitical growth, because to do so would require setting limits upon accumulation – an unacceptable option for a system predicated upon the rule: Grow or Die!

If capitalism remains the dominant social order, the best we can expect is unbearable climate conditions, an intensification of social crises and the spread of the most barbaric forms of class rule, as the imperialist powers fight among themselves and with the global south for continued control of the world's diminishing resources.

At worst, human life may not survive.

Capitalist strategies for change

There is no lack of proposed strategies for contending with ecological ruin, including the crisis of global warming looming as a result of the reckless increase of atmospheric carbon dioxide. The great majority of these strategies share one common feature: they are devised by and on behalf of the dominant global system, capitalism.

It is no surprise that the dominant global system which is responsible for the ecological crisis also sets the terms of the debate about this crisis, for capital commands the means of production of knowledge, as much as that of atmospheric carbon dioxide. Accordingly, its politicians, bureaucrats, economists and professors send forth an endless stream of proposals, all variations on the theme that the world's ecological damage can be repaired without disruption of market mechanisms and of the system of accumulation that commands the world economy.

But a person cannot serve two masters – the integrity of the Earth and the profitability of capitalism. One must be abandoned, and history leaves little question about the allegiances of the vast majority of policy-makers. There is every reason, therefore, to radically doubt the capacity of established measures to check the slide to ecological catastrophe.

And indeed, beyond a cosmetic veneer, the reforms over the past 35 years have been a monstrous failure. Isolated improvements do of course occur, but they are inevitably overwhelmed and swept away by the ruthless expansion of the system and the chaotic character of its production.

One example demonstrates the failure: in the first four years of the twenty-first century, global carbon emissions were nearly three times as great per annum as those of the decade of the 1990s, despite the appearance of the Kyoto Protocols in 1997.

Kyoto employs two devices: the 'cap and trade' system of trading pollution credits to achieve certain reductions in emissions, and projects in the Global South – the so-called clean development mechanism

(CDM) – to offset emissions in the highly industrialised nations. These instruments all rely upon market mechanisms, which means, first of all, that atmospheric carbon dioxide becomes a commodity under the control of the same interests that created global warming. Polluters are not compelled to reduce their carbon emissions, but allowed to use their power over money to control the carbon market for their own ends, which include the devastating exploration for yet more carbon-based fuels. Nor is there a limit to the amount of emission credits which can be issued by compliant governments.

Since verification and evaluation of results are impossible, the Kyoto regime is not only incapable of controlling emissions, it also provides ample opportunities for evasion and fraud of all kinds. As even the *Wall Street Journal* put it in March, 2007, emissions trading 'would make money for some very large corporations, but don't believe for a minute that this charade would do much about global warming.'

The Bali climate meetings in 2007 opened the way for even greater abuses in the period ahead. Bali avoided any mention of the goals for drastic carbon reduction put forth by the best climate science (90 per cent by 2050); it abandoned the peoples of the global south to the mercy of capital by giving jurisdiction over the process to the World Bank; and made offsetting of carbon pollution even easier.

In order to affirm and sustain our human future, a revolutionary transformation is needed, where all particular struggles take part in a greater struggle against capital itself. This larger struggle cannot remain merely negative and anti-capitalist. It must announce and build a different kind of society, and this is ecosocialism.

The ecosocialist alternative

The ecosocialist movement aims to stop and to reverse the disastrous process of global warming in particular and of capitalist ecocide in general, and to construct a radical and practical alternative to the capitalist system. Ecosocialism is grounded in a transformed economy founded on the non-monetary values of social justice and ecological balance. It criticises both capitalist 'market ecology' and productivist socialism, which ignored the

Earth's equilibrium and limits. It redefines the path and goal of socialism within an ecological and democratic framework.

Ecosocialism involves a revolutionary social transformation, which will imply the limitation of growth and the transformation of needs by a profound shift away from quantitative and toward qualitative economic criteria, an emphasis on use-value instead of exchange-value.

These aims require both democratic decision-making in the economic sphere, enabling society to collectively define its goals of investment and production, and the collectivisation of the means of production. Only collective decision-making and ownership of production can offer the longer-term perspective that is necessary for the balance and sustainability of our social and natural systems.

The rejection of productivism and the shift away from quantitative and toward qualitative economic criteria involve rethinking the nature and goals of production and economic activity in general. Essential creative, non-productive and reproductive human activities, such as householding, child-rearing, care, child and adult education, and the arts, will be key values in an ecosocialist economy.

Clean air and water and fertile soil, as well as universal access to chemical-free food and renewable, non-polluting energy sources, are basic human and natural rights defended by ecosocialism. Far from being 'despotic', collective policy-making on the local, regional, national and international levels amounts to society's exercise of communal freedom and responsibility. This freedom of decision constitutes a liberation from the alienating economic 'laws' of the growth-oriented capitalist system.

To avoid global warming and other dangers threatening human and ecological survival, entire sectors of industry and agriculture must be suppressed, reduced, or restructured and others must be developed, while providing full employment for all. Such a radical transformation is impossible without collective control of the means of production and democratic planning of production and exchange. Democratic decisions on investment and technological development must replace control by capitalist enterprises, investors and banks, in order to serve the long-term horizon of society's and nature's common good.

The most oppressed elements of human society, the poor and indigenous peoples, must take full part in the ecosocialist revolution, in order to revitalise ecologically sustainable traditions and give voice to those whom the capitalist system cannot hear. Because the peoples of the global south and the poor in general are the first victims of capitalist destruction, their struggles and demands will help define the contours of the ecologically and economically sustainable society in creation. Similarly, gender equality is integral to ecosocialism, and women's movements have been among the most active and vocal opponents of capitalist oppression. Other potential agents of ecosocialist revolutionary change exist in all societies.

Such a process cannot begin without a revolutionary transformation of social and political structures based on the active support, by the majority of the population, of an ecosocialist programme. The struggle of labour – workers, farmers, the landless and the unemployed – for social justice is inseparable from the struggle for environmental justice. Capitalism, socially and ecologically exploitative and polluting, is the enemy of nature and of labour alike.

Ecosocialism proposes radical transformations in:

a the energy system, by replacing carbon-based fuels and biofuels with clean sources of power under community control: wind, geothermal, wave, and above all, solar power.

b the transportation system, by drastically reducing the use of private trucks and cars, replacing them with free and efficient public transportation;

c present patterns of production, consumption, and building, which are based on waste, inbuilt obsolescence, competition and pollution, by producing only sustainable and recyclable goods and developing green architecture;

d food production and distribution, by defending local food sovereignty as far as this is possible, eliminating polluting industrial agribusinesses, creating sustainable agro-ecosystems and working actively to renew soil fertility.

To theorise and to work toward realising the goal of green socialism does not mean that we should not also fight for concrete and urgent reforms right now. Without any illusions about 'clean capitalism', we must work to impose on the powers that be – governments, corporations, international institutions – some elementary but essential immediate changes:

- drastic and enforceable reduction in the emission of greenhouse gases,
- development of clean energy sources,
- provision of an extensive free public transportation system,
- progressive replacement of trucks by trains,
- creation of pollution clean-up programs,
- elimination of nuclear energy, and war spending.

These and similar demands are at the heart of the agenda of the Global Justice movement and the World Social Forums, which have promoted, since Seattle in 1999, the convergence of social and environmental movements in a common struggle against the capitalist system.

Environmental devastation will not be stopped in conference rooms and treaty negotiations: only mass action can make a difference. Urban and rural workers, peoples of the global south and indigenous peoples everywhere are at the forefront of this struggle against environmental and social injustice, fighting exploitative and polluting multinationals, poisonous and disenfranchising agribusinesses, invasive genetically modified seeds, biofuels that only aggravate the current food crisis. We must further these social-environmental movements and build solidarity between anti-capitalist ecological mobilisations in the North and the South.

This Ecosocialist Declaration is a call to action. The entrenched ruling classes are powerful, yet the capitalist system reveals itself every day more financially and ideologically bankrupt, unable to overcome the economic, ecological, social, food and other crises it engenders. And the forces of radical opposition are alive and vital. On all levels, local, regional and international, we are fighting to create an alternative system based in social and ecological justice.

Universal Declaration of the Rights of Mother Earth

This Declaration was adopted by the World People's Conference on Climate Change and the Rights of Mother Earth, in Bolivia.

Preamble

WE, THE PEOPLES AND NATIONS OF EARTH: considering that we are all part of Mother Earth, an indivisible, living community of interrelated and interdependent beings with a common destiny; gratefully acknowledging that Mother Earth is the source of life, nourishment and learning and provides everything we need to live well; recognising that the capitalist system and all forms of depredation, exploitation, abuse and contamination have caused great destruction, degradation and disruption of Mother Earth, putting life as we know it today at risk through phenomena such as climate change; convinced that in an interdependent living community it is not possible to recognise the rights of only human beings without causing an imbalance within Mother Earth; affirming that to guarantee human rights it is necessary to recognise and defend the rights of Mother Earth and all beings in her and that there are existing cultures, practices and laws that do so; conscious of the urgency of taking decisive, collective action to transform structures and systems that cause climate change and other threats to Mother Earth; proclaim this Universal Declaration of the Rights of Mother Earth, and call on the General Assembly of the United Nations to adopt it, as a common standard of achievement for all peoples and all nations of the world, and to the end that every individual and institution takes responsibility for promoting through teaching, education, and consciousness raising, respect for the rights recognised in this Declaration and ensure through prompt and progressive measures and mechanisms, national and international, their universal and effective recognition and observance among all peoples and States in the world.

Article 1. Mother Earth

1 Mother Earth is a living being.

2 Mother Earth is a unique, indivisible, self-regulating community of interrelated beings that sustains, contains and reproduces all beings.

3 Each being is defined by its relationships as an integral part of Mother Earth.

4 The inherent rights of Mother Earth are inalienable in that they arise from the same source as existence.

5 Mother Earth and all beings are entitled to all the inherent rights recognised in this Declaration without distinction of any kind, such as may be made between organic and inorganic beings, species, origin, use to human beings, or any other status.

6 Just as human beings have rights, all other beings also have rights which are specific to their species or kind and appropriate for their role and function in the communities within which they exist.

7 The rights of each being are limited by the rights of other beings and any conflict between their rights must be resolved in a way that maintains the integrity, balance and health of Mother Earth.

Article 2. Inherent rights of Mother Earth

1 Mother Earth and all beings of which she is composed have the following inherent rights:

a the right to life and to exist;

b the right to be respected;

c   the right to regenerate its bio-capacity and to continue its vital cycles and processes free from human disruptions;

d   the right to maintain its identity and integrity as a distinct, self-regulating and interrelated being;

e   the right to water as a source of life;

f   the right to clean air;

g   the right to integral health;

h   the right to be free from contamination, pollution and toxic or radioactive waste;

i   the right to not have its genetic structure modified or disrupted in a manner that threatens it integrity or vital and healthy functioning;

j   the right to full and prompt restoration following the violation of the rights recognised in this Declaration caused by human activities.

2   Each being has the right to a place and to play its role in Mother Earth for her harmonious functioning.

3   Every being has the right to wellbeing and to live free from torture or cruel treatment by human beings.

Article 3. Obligations of human beings to Mother Earth

1   Every human being is responsible for respecting and living in harmony with Mother Earth.

2   Human beings, all States, and all public and private institutions must:

a   act in accordance with the rights and obligations recognised in this Declaration;

b   recognise and promote the full implementation and enforcement of the rights and obligations recognised in this Declaration;

c   promote and participate in learning, analysis, interpretation and communication about how to live in harmony with Mother Earth in accordance with this Declaration;

d ensure that the pursuit of human wellbeing contributes to the wellbeing of Mother Earth, now and in the future;

e establish and apply effective norms and laws for the defence, protection and conservation of the rights of Mother Earth;

f respect, protect, conserve and where necessary, restore the integrity, of the vital ecological cycles, processes and balances of Mother Earth;

g guarantee that the damages caused by human violations of the inherent rights recognised in this Declaration are rectified and that those responsible are held accountable for restoring the integrity and health of Mother Earth;

h empower human beings and institutions to defend the rights of Mother Earth and of all beings;

i establish precautionary and restrictive measures to prevent human activities from causing species extinction, the destruction of ecosystems or the disruption of ecological cycles;

j guarantee peace and eliminate nuclear, chemical and biological weapons;

k in accordance with their own cultures, traditions and customs;

l promote economic systems that are in harmony with Mother Earth and in accordance with the rights recognised in this Declaration.

Article 4. Definitions

1 The term 'being' includes ecosystems, natural communities, species and all other natural entities which exist as part of Mother Earth.

2 Nothing in this Declaration restricts the recognition of other inherent rights of all beings or specified beings.

27 April 2010

Endnotes

1   Alan Thornett, *Militant Years — car workers' struggles in Britain in the 1960s and 1970s*, Resistance Books, 2011.

2   Its original name is the Socialist Environment and Resources Association (SERA) and the acronym is still used but the full original name is not.

3   Found at *redgreenlabour.org*

4   JB Foster, *Marx's Ecology: Materialism and Nature*, MRP, 2000.

5   Paul Burkett, *Marx and Nature*, 1999, second edition, Haymarket, 2014.

6   JB Foster is a professor of sociology at the University of Oregon. Paul Burkett is professor of economics at Indiana State University in Terre Haute.

7   William Morris on Art and Socialism,page 91, Google Books.

8   Philip Lymbery, *Dead Zone: Where the Wild Things Were*, Bloomsbury, 2017.

9   Ibid. pp xi-xiii.

10 Found at: *www.theguardian.com/environment/2018/jun/11/chris-packham-springwatch-warns-of-ecological-apocalypse-britain*

11 Philip Lymbery, *Dead Zone: Where the Wild Things Were*, Bloomsbury, 2017, p. xiii-xiv.

12 Rachel Carson, *Silent Spring*, first published in 1962.

13 Michael McCarthy has been environmental correspondent of *The Times* and *The Guardian*. He won the RSPB medal for outstanding contribution to the environment.

14 Michael McCarthy, *Say Goodbye to the Cuckoo*, John Murray, 2009.

15 Ibid. On the cover.

16 Elizabeth Kolbert, *The Sixth Extinction: An Unnatural History*, Bloomsbury, 2014.

17 Joel Kovel, *The Enemy of Nature: The End of Capitalism or the End of the World*, 2007 edition, p. 131.

18 Edward O Wilson, *The Diversity of Life*, Penguin, 1992.

19 Ibid. p. 241.

20 Read more at: *https://www.brainyquote.com/topics/environmental*

21 Can be found at: *https://www.ecologyandsociety.org/vol14/iss2/art32/*

22   Found at *http://eschooltoday.com/ozone-depletion/effects-of-ozone-depletion.html*

23   Fred Pearce, *When the Rivers Run Dry*, Eden Project, 2006, p.23.

24   Fred Pearce, *When the Rivers Run Dry*, Eden Project, 2006. Fred Pearce is an author and journalist focusing on the environment and popular science.

25   This can found at *www.palestinelink.eu/palestine/facts-and-figures/water*

26   Fred Pearce, *When the Rivers Run Dry*, p. 35.

27   Ibid. p. 58 and 59.

28   Vandana Shiva, *Soil Not Oil: Climate Change, Peak Oil and Food Insecurity*, Zed Books, 2008.

29   Ibid. p. 87.

30   Vandana Shiva, *Water Wars: Privatisation, Pollution and Profit*, Southend Press, p.2002.

31   Ibid. p. 2.

32   Review available at: *http://socialistresistance.org/dead-zone-where-the-wind-things-were/10040*

33   James Honeyborne and Mark Brownlow, *Blue Planet II*, BBC Books, 2017, p. 284.

34   More info at: *http://news.nationalgeographic.com/2017/05/henderson-island-pitcairn-trash-plastic-pollution/*

35   *Blue Planet II*, p. 285.

36   Ibid. p. 286.

37   Edward O Wilson, *The Diversity of Life*, Penguin, second edition 2001, p. xxii.

38   Ibid. p.125.

39   BA Woodcock et al. (2017), 'Country-specific Effects of Neonicotinoid Pesticides on Honeybees and Wild Bees', Science, 356 / 6345, June 29, pp.1393-5.

40   A four-month survey published by *Mammal Review* in 2003 found that 'a British population of approximately 9 million cats was estimated to have brought home in the order of 92 (85–100) million prey items in the period of this survey, including 57 (52–63) million mammals, 27 (25–29) million birds and 5 (4–6) million reptiles and amphibians.'

41   Can be found at: *https://www.nature.com/articles/ncomms2380*

42   *https://www.globalwitness.org/en/press-releases/deadliest-year-record-land-and-environmental-defenders-agribusiness-shown-be-industry-most-linked-killings/*

43 *Global Warming and Recurrent Mass Bleaching of Corals*, TP Hughes, JT Kerry, and M Álvarez-Noriega, *Nature*, 2017, vol. 543, p. 373-7.

44 This was confirmed at the 11th International Seagrass Biology Workshop held in Sanya, China in 2014, where 100 leading seagrass scientists and conservationists met to discuss and update the global status of this critical habitat.

45 Elizabeth Kolbert, *The Sixth Extinction: An Unnatural History*, Bloomsbury, 2014.

46 A book with the same title was published in 1996 by Richard Leakey and the British science writer Roger Lewin. Richard Leaky is a palaeontologist and naturalist who became the director of the Kenyan Wildlife Conservation department.

47 Ibid. p. 94.

48 The UN agency dealing with biodiversity in the 2012 Intergovernmental Science-Policy Platform on Biodiversity and Ecosystem Services (IPBES) was established by the UN member states as an independent intergovernmental body. It is supposed to provide policymakers with objective scientific assessments about the state of knowledge regarding the planet's biodiversity, ecosystems and the benefits they provide to people, as well as the tools and methods to protect and sustainably use these vital natural assets.

49 *The Guardian*, 27 October 2016.

50 Available at: *www.livingplanetindex.org/projects?main_page_ project=ReportSummariesMain&home_flag=1*

51 *The State of the World's Plants Report*, Kew Gardens 2017.

52 Karl Marx, *Critique of the Gotha Programme* 1875.

53 Wikipedia describes it this way: Epicureanism is a system of philosophy based upon the teachings of the ancient Greek philosopher Epicurus, founded around 307 BC. Epicurus was an atomic materialist, following in the steps of Democritus. His materialism led him to a general attack on superstition and divine intervention. Following Aristippus—about whom very little is known—Epicurus believed that what he called 'pleasure' (ἡδονή) was the greatest good, but that the way to attain such pleasure was to live modestly, to gain knowledge of the workings of the world, and to limit one's desires. *https://en.wikipedia.org/wiki/Epicureanism*.

54 Its full title was: *On the Origin of Species by Means of Natural Selection, or*

the Preservation of Favoured Races in the Struggle for Life.

55   JB Foster, Brett Clarke, and Richard York, *The Ecological Rift: Capitalism's War on the Earth*, MRP, 2010.

56   Ibid. p. 123.

57   Karl Marx, *Grundrisse*, Vintage, 1973, p. 489.

58   Quoted in JB Foster, *Marx's Ecology*, MRP, 2000, p. 112.

59   Found at: *https://www.marxists.org/archive/marx/works/1844/manuscripts/labour.htm*

60   Translates as: good fathers of their families.

61   Vol. 3, p.   911. Found at: *https://www.marxists.org/archive/marx/works/download/pdf/Capital-Volume-III.pdf*

62   Available   at: *http://www.columbia.edu/~lnp3/mydocs/ecology/diamat_ecology.htm*

63   Available at: *https://www.marxists.org/archive/morris/works/1884/useful.htm*

64   Available at: *https://www.marxists.org/archive/morris/works/1884/as/as.htm*

65   *https://www.marxists.org/archive/morris/works/1884/hwl/hwl.htm*

66   *https://www.marxists.org/archive/morris/works/1894/make.htm*

67   William Morris, *News from Nowhere*, Google edition p. 252.

68   Sheila Rowbotham, *Edward Carpenter: A Life of Liberty and Love*, Verso, 2008, p.442.

69   Edward Carpenter, *The Smoke Dragon and How to Destroy It*, Bristol Radical History Group, 2017.

70   *The Clarion* was published between 1891 and 1934 with a circulation of around 80,000 at the turn of the century. Carpenter was one of the founders of the paper along with Robert Blatchford and Bernard Shaw.

71   *The Clarion*, 28 April 1894.

72   Sheila Rowbotham, *Edward Carpenter: A life of Liberty and Love*, Verso, 2008.

73   Ibid. p. 55.

74   Scott Nearing, *Economics for the Power Age*, John Day, first edition 1952, p. 2.

75   Ibid. p. 4.

76   Ibid. p. 43.

77   A good account of this can be found in *The Life of Murray Bookchin* by Janet Biehl, published in 2015 by Oxford University Press, chapter 1.

78   Murray Bookchin ('Lewis Herber'), *Ecology and Revolutionary Thought*, Comment Newsletter, 1964, p. 2.

79   Rachel Carson, Silent Spring, Penguin Books edition, 1999, p.257.

80   The largest species of diving duck found in the USA.

81   Rachel Carson, *Lost Woods*, p. 15.

82   Roderick Frazier Nash, *Wilderness and the American Mind*, Yale, first published 1967.

83   Roderick Frazier Nash, *The Rights of Nature: A History of Environmental Ethics*, University of Wisconsin Press, 1989.

84   Barry Commoner, *The Closing Circle*, New York, 1972.

85   Ibid. p. 56.

86   Ibid. pp. 33-46.

87   Ibid. p. 14.

88   Ibid. p. 274.

89   Ibid. p. 49.

90   Christopher Caudwell, *Heredity and Development*, Lawrence and Wishart, 1986.

91   Richard Levins and Richard Lewontin, *The Dialectical Biologist*, Harvard University Press, 1985.

92   *Christopher Caudwell: A Critical Evaluation*, Keith MacDonald, dissertation, 2013, p. 96; available at *https://orca.cf.ac.uk/55411/1/U202275.pdf*

93   Christos Efstathiou, *EP Thompson: A Twentieth-century Romantic*, Merlin, 2015, p. 24.

94   EP Thompson, *William Morris—Romantic to Revolutionary*, Merlin, 1955.

95   Ibid. second edition, p. 170.

96   Ibid. p. 769.

97   Ibid. p. 810.

98   Raymond Williams, *Socialism and Ecology*, pp. 7-8.

99   Stan Rosenthal, *Eco-Socialism in a Nutshell*, SERA, 1980.

100 Ibid p. 3.

101 Stephen Croall and Kaianders Sempler, *Nuclear Power for Beginners*, Beginners Books, 1978.

102 Official title: The Federal Republic of Germany.

103 From Klaus Engert's account.

104 Mayer, Margit and John Ely, *The German Greens: Paradox between Movement*

and Party, Temple University Press, 1998, p. 35.

105 Derek Wall, *Earth First! – and the anti-roads movement*, Routledge, 1999, p.36.

106 Hugo Blanco (2018), *We the Indians: The Indigenous Peoples of Peru and the Struggle for Land*, Resistance Books, Merlin Press and then IIRE, p. 82.

107 *The Environmentalism of the People, Against the Current*, edition 42, 1993.

108 Ibid. p. 103.

109 Derek Wall, *Hugo Blanco: a Revolutionary for Life*, Merlin and Resistance Books, 2018, p.50.

110 Ibid, p.51.

111 Maria Mies and Vandana Shiva, *Ecofeminism*, 1993, republished in 2014.

112 Fred Pearce, *Water Wars*, p. 64.

113 Michael Löwy, *From Marx to Ecosocialism, Capitalism Nature Socialism*, 2010, 13/1, p. 121-33.

114 *Monthly Review*, vol. 64, no. 9 pp. 1-19.

115 He is also a professor of economics and government and chair of the Grantham Institute on Climate Change and the Environment at the London School of Economics.

116 The Stern Review, 2007, p.xiii.

117 Ibid. p.27.

118 Derek Wall, *The Rise of the Green Left*, Verso p. 32.

119 Derek Wall joined the Ecology Party in 1980, was the International Coordinator of the Green Party of England and Wales for many years, and a member of the Green Left.

120 Derek Wall's recent books include: *Economics after Capitalism* (Pluto, 2015), *The Sustainable Economics of Elinor Ostrom* (Routledge, 2014) and *The Commons in History: Culture, Commons, Conflict and Ecology*, MIT Press, 2014.

121 Paris Accord, article 2, point a).

122 Reported at: *https://350.org/press-release/thousands-worldwide-take-part-in-largest-global-civil-disobedience-in-the-history-of-the-climate-movement*

123 The Atlas can be accessed at *info@maplecroft.com*

124 Raymond Williams, *Socialism and Ecology*, SERA, 1982.

125 Ibid. p.3.

126 *New Left Review*, 1/178, December 1989, p. 1.

127 Jonathan Porritt, *Seeing Green: Politics of Ecology Explained*, OUP, 1984.

128 Ibid. p. 44.

129 Martin Ryle, *Ecology and Socialism*, Radius, 1988.

130 Ibid. p.45.

131 Ibid. p.13

132 Vandana Shiva is a leader of the International Forum on Globalization along with Ralph Nader and the environmentalist Jeremy Rifkin and also of the Slow Food movement. She won the Alternative Nobel Peace Prize in 1993. Books by Shiva include: *Staying Alive* (1989), *The Violence of the Green Revolution* (1991), *Biodiversity* (1995), *Monocultures of the Mind* (1993), *Stolen Harvest* (2001), *Protect or Plunder* (2001), *Earth Democracy* (2005), and *Soil Not Oil* (2008).

133 'Savage Capitalism' was published in *Ecosocialism Or Barbarism*, edited by Jane Kelly and Sheila Malone, Resistance Books, 2006.

134 More information at *http://www.internationalviewpoint.org/spip.php?article5019*

135 Michael Löwy, *Ecosocialism: A Radical Alternative to Capitalist Catastrophe*, Haymarket, 2015, p. 3.

136 Joel Kovel, *The Enemy of Nature: The End of Capitalism or the End of the World*, conclusion to Chapter 4.

137 Ibid. p. 91.

138 Fred Magdoff and Chris Williams, *Creating an Ecological Society—towards a revolutionary transformation*, Monthly Review Press, 2017.

139 *Creating an Ecological Society – towards a revolutionary transformation*, p.18.

140 JB Foster, *The Ecological Revolution: Making Peace with the Planet*, MRP, 2009, p. 7.

141 MRP, New York, 2009, p. 288.

142 JB Foster, *The Ecological Revolution*, p. 8.

143 Michael Löwy, *Ecosocialism: A Radical Alternative to Capitalist Catastrophe*, p.11-12.

144 Derek Wall, *The Rise of the Green Left*, p. 68.

145 James Hansen, *Storms of my Grandchildren*, 2009, p.172.

146 Dick North, *Environment, Capitalism and Socialism*, Australian DSP, p.134.

147 Daniel Tanuro, *Green Capitalism: Why It Can't Work*, p.68.

148 Can be found at *www.vox.com/2016/10/18/13012394/i-732-carbon-tax-washington*

149 James Hansen, *Storms of My Grandchildren*, p.205.

150 Ibid. p.209.

151 Ibid. p.209.

152 Ibid. p.221.

153 JB Foster, Brett Clarke, and Richard York, *The Ecological Rift: Capitalism's War on the Earth*, p.116.

154 Ibid. p.117.

155 Ibid. p.118.

156 JB Foster, *James Hansen and the Climate Exit Strategy*, Monthly Review, 64/9, February, 2013.

157 Found at: *https://jacobinmag.com/2018/09/carbon-tax-divided-peoples-policy-project*

158 *https://www.quotetab.com/quotes/by-barry-commoner#WcTRCBfIJp71HPfA.97*

159 *The Alternative Economic Strategy: A Labour Movement Response to the Economic Crisis*, CSE Books, 1980. Published by the Conference of Socialist Economists.

160 Ibid. p. 35, chapter 4.

161 Derek Wall, *Earth First! – and the anti-roads movement*, Routledge, 1999, p. 8.

162 *The Stern Review*, summary of conclusions.

163 Naomi Klein, *This Changes Everything*, Simon and Schuster, 2014, p. 161.

164 Found at: *https://www.unenvironment.org/news-and-stories/press-release/ipcc-presents-assessment-measures-mitigate-climate-change*

165 Kate Raworth, *Doughnut Economics – Seven Ways to Think Like a 21st-Century Economist*, Business Books, 2017.

166 *The Limits to Growth* was written by Dennis Meadows, Donella Meadows, Jørgen Randers, and William Behrens III. Published by Universe Books NY. First edition 1972 second edition 1974. Dennis Meadows is an American scientist and professor of systems management, and former director of the Institute for Policy and Social Science Research at the University of New Hampshire. Donella Meadows (d. 2001) was an American environmental scientist, teacher, and writer.

167 The Club of Rome describes itself as: 'an organization of individuals who share a common concern for the future of humanity and strive to make a difference. Our members are notable scientists, economists, businessmen

and businesswomen, high level civil servants and former heads of state from around the world' (https://www.clubofrome.org).

168 Andre Gorz, *Ecology as Politics*, Southend Press, 1980, p. 84.

169 Jackson is a professor of sustainable development at the University of Surrey and director of the Centre for the Understanding of Sustainable Prosperity.

170 Tim Jackson, *Prosperity Without Growth: Economics for a Finite Planet*, Earthscan/Routledge, 2009.

171 Ibid. p. 8.

172 Ibid. pp. 13-14.

173 Al Gore, *The Future*, p. 142.

174 Ibid. p. 161.

175 Speaking at the SWP's Marxism 2016 event

176 The second edition.

177 Socialist Resistance website, 27 December 2010.

178 The Stakhanovite movement began with the Soviet second 5-year plan in 1935 as a new stage of 'socialist competition'. It took its name from Aleksei Grigorievich Stakhanov, who had mined 102 tonnes of coal in less than six hours (fourteen times his quota) on 31 August 1935. However, Stakhanovite followers would soon 'break' his record. On 1 February 1936, it was reported that Nikita Izotov had mined 640 tonnes of coal in a single shift. The Stakhanovite movement, supported and led by the Communist Party, soon spread over other industries of the Soviet Union.

179 Speaking at the SWP's Marxism event in 2016.

180 Derek Wall is a prominent ecosocialist, previously the principal speaker of the Green Party in England and Wales, and has been active in the ecology movement since 1979. He joined the Ecology Party in the early 1980s and was one of a small number of greens who took the role of capitalism seriously and analysed it in his writings.

181 Derek Wall, *The Rise of the Green Left*, Pluto, 2010, p. 79.

182 Ibid. p. 80.

183 Victor Serge, *From Lenin to Stalin*.

184 Some socialists put forward a theory of 'state capitalism' about these countries, that claimed that capitalism continue to exist there. In my view this was wrong.

185 The Chernobyl Disaster was a catastrophic nuclear accident on 25-28 April 1986 in a reactor at the Chernobyl nuclear power plant near the now abandoned town of Pripyat some 100 km north of Kiev (now Ukraine).

186 Douglas R Weiner, *A Little Corner of Freedom: Russian Nature Protection from Stalin to Gorbachev*, California, 1988, p.188

187 Douglas R Weiner, *Models of Nature: Ecology, Conservation and Cultural Revolution in Soviet Russia*, Pittsburgh,1988.

188 *The Biosphere* was first published in 1926 in Leningrad in the USSR. Three years later it was published in Paris as *La Biosphère*. Today there is available an abridged version of the second French edition published in 1986 by Synergetic Press, Arizona.

189 Ibid. p. 19.

190 It can found here: https://climateandcapitalism.com/2014/11/03/rise-fall-environmentalism-early-soviet-union/

191 Laurie Mazur, *A Pivotal Moment*, 2010, p. xii.

192 Joseph Hansen, *Too Many Babies: The Myth of the Population Explosion*, Pathfinder Press, 1960.

193 Ibid. p. 40.

194 UN DESA report, 'World Population Prospects: 2015 Revision', published in June 2015.

195 Worldometers population calculator can be found at: http://www.worldometers.info/world-population/

196 *What Every Environmentalist Needs to Know About Capitalism*, p. 12.

197 Al Gore, *The Future*, p.166.

198 *UN News* July 2015: https://news.un.org/en/story/2015/07/505352-un-projects-world-population-reach-85-billion-2030-driven-growth-developing

199 First published in *The Conversation*.

200 Thomas Malthus, *An Essay on the Principles of Population*, first published 1798 by Johnson.

201 *Quoted in John Cunningham Wood (ed.), Karl Marx's Economics*, second series, vol. 8, Routledge NY, 1959, p. 102.

202 This can be found at: *https://www.marxists.org/archive/marx/works/1881/letters/81_02_01.htm*

203 *Ecology Against Capitalism, Monthly Review Press, 2002, chapter 11.*

204 *Ibid. p.151.*

205 Donella and Dennis Meadows, *Limits to Growth*, p. 24.

206 Ibid. p.260.

207 Paul Ehrlich, *The Population Bomb*, Ballantine, 1968, p. xi.

208 Murray Bookchin, *Which Way for the Ecology Movement?*, AK Press, 1994, p.31.

209 Joel Kovel, *The Enemy of Nature, 2007 second edition, 2007, p.198.*

210 *Fred Pearce, Peoplequake: Mass Migration, Aging Nations, and the Coming Population Crash*, Eden Project Books, 2011, p.67.

211 Tanuro, Daniel, *Green Capitalism: Why It Can't Work*, Merlin and Resistance Books, 2013, p. 17.

212 Martin Empson, *Land and Labour: Marxism, Ecology and Human History*, Bookmarks, 2014, p. 193.

213 Jonathan Neale, *Stop Global Warming: Change the World*, Bookmarks, 2008, p.31.

214 Wally Seccombe, *Marxism and Demography, New Left Review*, 1/137, 1983.

215 Ibid. p. 22.

216 Ibid. p. 24.

217 Laurie Mazur is director of the Population Justice Project and as an independent author and consultant to non-profit organizations. She has written extensively on population and environmental issues.

218 Laurie Mazur, *A Pivotal Moment: Population, Justice and the Environmental Challenge*, Island Press, 2010.

219 The UN International Conference on Population and Development, Cairo,1994.

220 The POA can be found at https://www.unfpa.org/sites/default/files/event-pdf/PoA_en.pdf

221 Laurie Mazur, *'A Neglected Climate Strategy: Empower Women, Slow Population Growth', Bulletin of the Atomic Scientists*, October, 2009.

222 Population Matters can be found at: https://www.populationmatters.org/

223 Al Gore, *The Future*, p. 168.

224 Jenny Hawley and Friends of the Earth, *Why Women Will Save the Planet*, Zed Books; 2015, second edition, 2018.

225 Ibid. second edition, p. 187.

226 Her report can be found at *http://www.mail-archive.com/ecofem@csf. colorado.edu/msg06397*.html

227 Cairo conference *Programme of Action*, para 3.16.

228 Ibid. para 3.13.

229 Ibid. para 7.12.

230 Betsy Hartmann, *Reproductive Rights and Reproductive Wrongs—the global politics of population control and contraceptive choice*, Perennial Library, 1987.

231 *Too Many People?*, p. 37.

232 Ibid. p. 38.

233 Ibid. p. 25.

234 Paul Ehrlich was a professor of biology at Stanford University and has written over 80 papers and several books on this subject.

235 Barry Commoner, *The Closing Circle: Nature, Man, and Technology*, p. 235

236 Ibid. p.242.

237 Angus and Butler, *Too Many People?*, p.27.

238 Ibid. p.27.

239 Maria Mies and Vandana Shiva, *Ecofeminism*, p.188.

240 Ibid. p.66.

241 Published by Third World Network, Penang, Malaysia. Can be found at http://enb.iisd.org/Cairo/twnpop.txt

242 The 'carrying capacity' of an individual species is calculated as the highest population level of that species that can be supported indefinitely in a given habitat without permanently damaging the ecosystem upon which it is dependent.

243 Can be found at *https://www.marxists.org/archive/marx/works/1883/don/ ch09.htm*

244 *The Guardian*, 29 August 2016.

245 George Monbiot, *How Did We Get into This Mess?*, p.81.

246 Simon Lewis and Mark Maslin, *The Human Planet and How We Created the Anthropocene*, p.104-7.

247 Ibid. p.112.

248 Andreas Malm, *Fossil Capital*, p. 391.

249 Ibid. p.267.

250 Ibid. p.272.

251 Ibid. p.48.

252 Jason W Moore, *Capitalism in the Web of Life: Ecology and the Accumulation of Capital*.

253 Found at *http://climateandcapitalism.com/2016/06/23/two-views-on-marxist-ecology-and-jason-w-moore/*

254 Philip Lymbery, *Farmageddon – the true cost of cheap meat*, 2014, p. ix.

255 David Adam, *The Guardian*, May 31st 2009.

256 Colin Tudge, *Feeding People Is Easy*, p. 3.

257 Via Campesina's seven principles of food sovereignty established in 2005 can be found at: *http://www.nfu.ca/sites/www.nfu.ca/files/Principles%20 of%20Food%20Sovereignty.pdf*

258 Philip Lymbery, *Dead Zone: Where the Wild Things Were*, p. 52.

259 Fred Pearce, *When the Rivers Run Dry*, Eden Project, 2006, p. 23.

260 *The Guardian*, 21 July 2017.

261 *http://www.dailymotion.com/video/x24ieya*

262 Ibid. p. 91.

263 Ibid. p. 92.

264 Ibid. p. 264.

265 Martin Empson, *Land and Labour*, p. 193.

266 Ibid. p. 194.

267 Ibid. p. 194.

268 Markegard is a grass-feeding ranch and research project.

269 Anderson, Kip and Kuhn, Keegan, *Cowspiracy*, Earthaware, 2016, p. 62.

270 Ian Angus (ed.), *The Global Fight for Climate Justice*, Resistance Books, 2009, p.110-111.

271 Joel Kovel, *The Enemy of Nature: The End of Capitalism or the End of the World*, p.167-9.

272 Al Gore, *An Inconvenient Truth*, p.305.

273 Winfried Wolf, *Car Mania*, revised English edition,1966, p.x.

274 Robert J. Samuelson, *Washington Post*, 10 July 2016.

275 Marc Fisher, *Chicago Tribune*, 11 September 2015.

276 Wang, Yunshi, Jacob Teter and Daniel Sperling, *'Will China's Vehicle Population Grow Even Faster than Forecasted?'*, Access Magazine, 1/41, pp. 29-33.

277 Climate camps started 2006 in Britain at Drax power station, North Yorkshire and in 2007 near London against the extension of Heathrow airport.

278 Can be found at *https://www.cacctu.org.uk/tuc2017climatemotion*

279 Paul Hampton, *Workers and Trade Unions for Climate Solidarity*, Routledge, 2016, p. 68.

280 CSE Books, *Alternative Economic Strategy*, 1980.

281 Hilary Wainwright and Dave Elliot, *The Lucas Plan: New Trade Unionism in the Making*, Allison and Busby, 1982, p. 107.

282 *https://redgreenlabour.org/*

283 *www.facebook.com/clara.paillard/videos/ pcb.10157186647010931/10157186645395931/?type=3&theater*

284 *https://redgreenlabour.org/bolsonaro-environmental-holocaust-brazil/*

285 *https://rebellion.earth/*

286 Prometheanism is a term popularized by the political theorist John Dryzek to describe an environmental orientation which perceives the Earth as a resource whose utility is determined primarily by human needs and interests and whose environmental problems are overcome through human innovation.

287 Alfred Schmidt, *The Concept of Nature in Marx*, first published 1962; Verso, 2014.

288 JB Foster and Brett Clark, *Marx's Ecology and the Left*, Monthly Review, June 2016.

289 The laws of thermodynamics dictate energy behaviour, for example, how and why heat, which is a form of energy, transfers between different objects. The first law of thermodynamics is the law of conservation of energy and matter. In essence, energy can neither be created nor destroyed; it can however be transformed from one form to another. The second law states that isolated systems gravitate towards thermodynamic equilibrium, also known as a state of maximum entropy, or disorder; it also states that heat energy will flow from an area of low temperature to an area of high temperature.

290 Joan Martinez-Alier is also the author of *The Environmentalism of the Poor: A Study of Ecological Conflicts and Valuation* (2001).

291 Foster and Burkett, *Marx and the Earth: An Anti-critique*, 2016.

292 Sergei Andreević Podolinsky (1850-1891) was a pioneer of ecological economics. He set out to reconcile socialist thought and the second law of thermodynamics by synthesizing the approaches of Karl Marx, Charles Darwin and Sadi Carnot.

293 James O'Connor the director of the Centre for Political Ecology Studies in Santa Cruz, California.

294 *Capitalism Nature Socialism* volume 2,1991- issue 3.

295 *Capitalism, Nature and Socialism* became an increasingly important vehicle for debate and discussion around ecological and ecosocialist ideas and remained so after Joel Kovel followed him as its editor.

296 Daniel Bensaïd, *Marx for Our Times*, Verso, 2002.

297 *Organization and Environment*, 21/1, March 2008.

298 JB Foster and Paul Burkett, *Marx and the Earth*, Brill, 2016.

299 Paul Hampton, *Marxism and Entropy*, May, 2010.

300 JB Foster and Paul Burkett, *Marx and the Earth*, p. 90.

301 Daniel Bensaïd, *Marx for Our Times*, Verso, 2002, p. 324.

302 Ibid. p. 324.

303 Ibid. p. 324.

304 Ted Benton, *Marx & Philosophy Review of Books*, 23 March 2010, available at: *https://marxandphilosophy.org.uk/reviews/7570_the-ecological-revolution-review-by-ted-benton/*

305 Joel Kovel, *The Enemy of Nature: The End of Capitalism or the End of the World*, Zed Books, 2002.

306 JB Foster and Paul Burkett, *Marx and the Earth*, Brill, 2016, p.35.

307 *Monthly Review*, 65/7, December 2013.

308 Published in French in 2010, and in English in 2013 by Resistance Books and Merlin.

309 Review available at: *http://socialistresistance.org/a-book-to-stimulate-discussion/6630*

310 Ibid. p. 139.

311 Ibid. p. 138.

312 Ibid. p. 139.

313 JB Foster and Paul Burkett, *Marx and the Earth: An Anti-Critique*, Brill, 2016.

314 Ibid. p. 16.

315 Ibid. p. 17.

316 John Bellamy Foster and Paul Burkett, *Marx and the Earth*, Brill, 2016, p.102.

317 Michael Löwy, *Ecosocialism: A Radical Alternative to Capitalist Catastrophe*, Haymarket, 2015.

318 Ibid. p. 2.

319 Danial Tanuro, *The Impossibility of Green Capitalism*, p. 138.

320 Angus and Butler, *Too Many People?* p.xxi.

321 Ibid. p. 94.

322 Ibid. p. 83.

323 Ibid. p. 84.

324 Ibid. p .95.

325 Ibid. p. xvi.

326 Lourdes Arizpe, *A Mexican Pioneer in Anthropology*, p.193.

327 Angus and Butler, *Too Many People?*, p.105.

328 *Climate and Capitalism* online magazine, 31 August 2011.

329 Angus and Butler, *Too Many People?* p.102.

330 Ibid. pp. 4-5.

331 Ibid. p. 104.

Bibliography

This bibliography includes books and articles referenced in the text and also books related to the subject.

Albert, Michael, *Parecon: Life After Capitalism*, Verso, 2003.

Altieri, Miguel, *Agroecology, Small Farms, and Food Sovereignty*, Monthly Review, Volume 61, Issue 03, July-August 2009.

Anderson, Kip and Keegan Kuhn, *Cowspiracy*, Earthaware, 2016.

Angus, Ian (ed.) *The Global Fight for Climate Justice*, Resistance Books, 2009.

Angus, Ian, *Facing the Anthropocene: Fossil Capitalism and the Crisis of the Earth System*, Monthly Review Press, 2016.

Angus, Ian and Simon Butler, *Too Many People? Population, Immigration, and the Environmental Crisis*, Haymarket, 2014.

Arizpe, Lourdes, *A Mexican Pioneer in Anthropology*, Springer, 2014.

Bahro, Rudolf, *Socialism and Survival*, Heretic Books, 1982.

Bahro, Rudolf, *From Red to Green*, Verso, 1984.

Bahro, Rudolf, *Building the Green Movement*, Gay Men's Press, 1986.

Bahro, Rudolf, *Avoiding Social and Ecological Disaster*, Gateway, 1994.

Bello, Walden, *The Food Wars*, Verso, 2009.

Benjamin, Walter, *One-Way Street and Other Writings*, Penguin, 2009.

Bensaïd, Daniel, *Marx for Our Times*, Verso, 2002.

Benton Ted, 'Marxism and Natural Limits: An Ecological Critique and Reconstruction', New Left Review, 1/178, 1989.

Benton, Ted, *Natural Relations: Ecology, Animal Rights and Social Justice*, Verso, 1993.

Benton, Ted, *Solitary Bees*, Pelagic Publishing, 2017.

Biehl, Janet, *The Life of Murray Bookchin*, Oxford, 2015.

Biro, Andrew, *Critical Ecologies: The Frankfurt School and Contemporary Environmental Crises*, University of Toronto Press, 2011.

Blanco, Hugo, *Land or Death: The Peasant Struggle in Peru*, Pathfinder, 1972.

Blanco, Hugo, *Workers and Peasants to Power*, Pathfinder, 1978.

Blanco Hugo, *We the Indians: The Indigenous Peoples of Peru and the Struggle for Land*, Resistance Books, Merlin Press and the IIRE, 2018.

Blewitt, John (ed.), *The Post Growth Project*, Greenhouse, 2014.

Bonneuil, Christophe and Jean-Baptiste Fressoz, *The Shock of the Anthropocene*, Verso, 2016.

Bookchin, Murray (Lewis Herber), 'Ecology and Revolutionary Thought', *Comment* newsletter, 1964.

Bookchin, Murray, *Which Way for the Ecology Movement?*, AK Press, 1994.

Burkett, Paul, *Marx and Nature*, 1999, 2nd edition, Haymarket, 2014.

Caldicott, Helen, *Nuclear Power is not the Answer*, The New Press, 2006.

Campaign against Climate Change Trade Union Group, *One Million Climate Jobs*, 3rd edition, 2013.

Carpenter, Edward, *The Smoke-Dragon and How to Destroy It (1894)*, Bristol Radical History Group: Radical Pamphleteers pamphlet 38, 2017.

Carson, Rachel, *The Sea Around Us*, New Yorker 1950; Oxford University Press 1989.

Carson, Rachel, *The Edge of the Sea*, Houghton Mifflin, 1955.

Carson, Rachel, *Silent Spring*, first published in the USA by Houghton Mifflin in 1962.

Carson, Rachel, *Lost Woods: The Discovered writings of Rachel Carson*, Beacon Press Books, 1998.

Caudwell, Christopher, *Illusion and Reality*, Lawrence and Wishart, 1937.

Caudwell, Christopher, Studies in a Dying Culture, first published posthumously by Bodley Head in 1938.

Caudwell, Christopher, *The Concept of Freedom*, first published by Lawrence and Wishart in 1965.

Caudwell Christopher, *Heredity and Development*, Lawrence and Wishart, 1986.

Chattopadhyay, Kunal, *Early Soviet Commitment to Environment Protection and its Decline*, Climate and Capitalism post, 3 November 2014.

Chivers, Danny, *Renewable Energy: Cleaner, Fairer Ways to Power the Planet*, New International, 2015.

Clarke, John (ed.), *Nature in Question*, Earthscan, 1993.

Cohen, Joel, *How Many People Can the Earth Support?*, Norton, 1995.

Commoner, Barry, *Science and Survival*, Viking, 1963.

Commoner, Barry, *The Closing Circle*, New York, 1972.

Commoner, Barry, *Making Peace with the Planet*, New Press, 1975.

Commoner, Barry, *The Poverty of Power*, Bantam Books, 1976.

Cooley, Mike, *The Human Price of Technology*, 1st edition 1980, Spokesman, 2016.

Cowsill, John, *Safe Planet: Renewable Energy Plus Workers' Power*, Earth Books, 2014.

Cunningham Wood, John (ed.), *Karl Marx's Economics*, second series, vol. 8, Routledge, 1959, p.102.

Crane, Nicholas, *The Making of the British Landscape – from the ice age to the present*, W&N Frist edition 2016 second edition 2017.

Croall, Stephen and Kaianders Sempler, *Nuclear Power for Beginners*, Beginners Books, 1978.

Craig, Dilworth, *Too Smart for our Own Good: The Ecological Predicament of Humankind*, Cambridge University Press, 2009.

Dawson, Ashley, *Extreme Cities: The Peril and Promise of Urban Life in the Age of Climate Change*, Verso, 2017.

Diamond, Jared, *Guns Germs and Steel – a short history of everybody for the last 13,000 years*, Vintage 1997.

Dorling, Danny, *Population 10 Billion: The Coming Demographic Crisis and How to Survive It*, Constable, 2013.

Economy, Elizabeth C., *The River Runs Black*, Cornell University Press, 2004.

Efstathiou, Christos, *E.P. Thompson: A Twentieth-century Romantic*, Merlin, 2015.

Ehrlich, Paul, *The Population Bomb*, Ballantine, 1968.

Elder, Charlie, *While Flocks Last*, Corgi Books, 2009.

Emmott, Stephen, *10 Billion*, Penguin, 2013.

Empson, Martin, *Climate Change: Why Nuclear Power Is Not the Answer*, SWP, 2006.

Empson, Martin, *Marxism and Ecology: Capitalism, Socialism and the Future of the Planet*, Socialist Workers Party, 2009.

Empson, Martin, *Land and Labour: Marxism, Ecology and Human History*, Bookmarks, 2014.

Engels, Friedrich, *The Condition of the Working Class in England*, Penguin, 1987.

Engels, Friedrich, *The Dialectics of Nature*, in Russian, 1925; Lawrence and Wishart, 1939.

Faulkner, Peter, *Against the Age: And Introduction to William Morris*, George Allen and Unwin, 1980.

Food and Agriculture Organization (FAO), *Livestock's Long Shadow: Environmental Issues and Options*, Rome, 2006.

Foreman, Dave, *Man Swarm and the Killing of Wildlife*, Raven's Eye Press, 2011.

Foster, John Bellamy, *The Vulnerable Planet,* Monthly Review Press, 1999.

Foster, John Bellamy, *Marx's Ecology: Materialism and Nature*, Monthly Review Press, 2000.

Foster, John Bellamy, *Ecology Against Capitalism*, Monthly Review Press, 2002.

Foster, John Bellamy, *The Ecological Revolution: Making Peace with the Planet*, Monthly Review Press, 2009.

Foster, John Bellamy, *'James Hansen and the Climate Exits Strategy'*, Monthly Review, 64/9, February 2013.

Foster, John Bellamy, *'Marxism and the Rift in the Universal Metabolism of Nature'*, Monthly Review, December 2013.

Foster, John Bellamy and Brett Clark, *Marx's Ecology and the Left*, Monthly Review, June 2016.

Foster, John Bellamy, Brett Clark, and Richard York, *The Ecological Rift: Capitalism's War on the Earth*, Monthly Review Press, 2010.

Foster, John Bellamy and Paul Burkett, *'Classical Marxism and the Second Law of Thermodynamics: Marx/Engels, the Heat Death of the Universe Hypothesis, and the Origins of Ecological Economics'*, Organisation and Environment, 21/1, 3-37, 2008.

Foster, John Bellamy and Paul Burkett, *Marx and the Earth*, Brill, 2016.

Foster, John Bellamy and Fred Magdoff, *What Every Environmentalist Needs to Know About Capitalism*, Monthly Review Press, 2011.

Friends of the Earth and C40 Cities, *Why Women Will Save the Planet*, Zed Books, 2015, 2nd edition, 2018.

Gilding Paul, *The Great Disruption: How the Climate Crisis Will Transform the Global Economy*, Bloomsbury, 2011.

Gore, Al, *Earth in the Balance*, Houghton, 1992.

Gore, Al, *The Future*, W.H. Allen, 2013

Gore, Al, *Inconvenient Truth*, documentary, 2006.

Haila, Yrjö and Richard Levins, *Humanity and Nature: Ecology, Science and Society*, Pluto, 1992.

Hamilton, Clive (ed.), *The Anthropocene and the Global Environmental Crisis*, Routledge, 2015.

Hamilton, Clive, Bonneuil, Christophe and Gemenne, François, *The Anthropocene and the Global Environmental Crisis*, Routledge, 2015.

Hampton, Paul, *Workers and Trade Unions for Climate Solidarity*, Routledge, 2016.

Hansen, James, *Storms of My Grandchildren: The Truth About the Coming Climate Catastrophe and Our Last Chance to Save Humanity*, Bloomsbury, 2009.

Hansen Joseph, *Too Many Babies: The Myth of the Population Explosion*, Pathfinder Press, 1960.

Jackson, Tim, *Prosperity Without Growth—Economics for a Finite Planet*, Earthscan/Routledge, 2009.

Hartmann, Betsy, *Reproductive Rights and Reproductive Wrongs*, Perennial Library, 1987.

Hartmann, Betsy, '*The 'New' Population Control Craze: Retro, Racist, Wrong Way to Go*', On the Issues Magazine, fall 2009.

Hill, Christopher, *A Nation of Change and Novelty*, Routledge, 1990.

Honeyborne, James and Mark Brownlow, *Blue Planet II*, BBC Books, 2017.

House of Commons Environment, Food and Rural Affairs, Environmental Audit, Health and Social Care, and Transport select committees, *Improving Air Quality*, March 2018.

Hughes, T.P., Kerry, J.T., Álvarez-Noriega, M. et al. '*Global Warming and Recurrent Mass Bleaching of Corals*', Nature, vol. 543, March 2017.

Hulsberg, Werner, *The Greens at the Crossroads*, New Left Review, 1/152, August 1985.

Jackson Tim, *Prosperity without Growth: Economics for a Finite Planet*, Earthscan / Routledge, 2009.

Jomo, K.S. *Tigers in Trouble*, Zed Books, 1998.

Kelly Jane and Sheila Malone, *Ecosocialism or Barbarism*, Resistance Books, 2006.

Kew Gardens, *The State of the World's Plants Report*, 2017.

Klein, Naomi, *This Changes Everything: Capitalism vs The Climate*, Simon and Schuster, 2014.

Kolbert, Elizabeth, *The Sixth Extinction: An Unnatural History*, Bloomsbury, 2014.

Kovel, Joel, *The Enemy of Nature: The End of Capitalism or the End of the World*, Zed Books, 2002. Second, expanded edition, Zed Books, 2007.

Kumar, Ashok and Dibya Lochan Mohanta, '*Population, Environment and Development in India*', *Journal of Human Ecology*, October 2017.

Labour Party, *In Trust for Tomorrow*, 1994.

Lappé, Frances Moore and Anna Lappé, *Hope's Edge: The Next Diet for a Small Planet*, Penguin, 2003.

Leakey, Richard and Roger Lewin, *The Sixth Extinction*, Weidenfeld and Nicolson, 1996.

Lear, Linda, *Rachel Carson: Witness for Nature*, Penguin, 1997.

Levins, Richard and Richard Lewontin, *The Dialectical Biologist*, Harvard University Press, 1985.

Lewis, Simon L. and Mark A. Maslin, *The Human Planet and How We Created the Anthropocene*, Pelican, 2018.

Lohmann, Larry, *Carbon Trading: A Critical Conversation on Climate Change, Privatisation and Power*, Corner House, 2006.

Löwy, Michael, *Ecosocialism: A Radical Alternative to Capitalist Catastrophe*, Haymarket, 2015.

Lymbery, Philip, *Farmageddon: The True Cost of Cheap Meat*, Bloomsbury, 2014.

Lymbery, Philip, *Dead Zone: Where the Wild Things Were*, Bloomsbury, 2017.

Lynas, Mark, *Six Degrees: Our Future on a Hotter Planet*, Harper Perennial, 2008.

Lynas, Mark, *The God Species: How Humans Really Can Save the Planet*, Fourth Estate, 2011.

Magdoff, Fred and Chris Williams, *Creating an Ecological Society—towards a revolutionary transformation*, Monthly Review Press, 2017.

Malm, Andreas, *Fossil Capital: The Rise of Steam Power and the Roots of Global Warming*, Verso, 2016.

Malthus, Thomas, *An Essay on the Principles of Population*, 1798; Dover, 2007.

Mayer Margit and John Ely, *The German Greens—paradox between movement and party*, Temple University Press Philadelphia, 1998.

Mamdani, Mahmood, *The Myth of Population Control: Family, Caste, and Class in an Indian Village*, Monthly Review Press, 1972.

Margolies, David, *Selected Writings of Christopher Caudwell*, Pluto, 2017.

Marx, Karl, *Grundrisse*, Penguin Books, 1971; Vintage, 1973.

Marx, Karl and Friedrich Engels, *The Communist Manifesto*, Penguin classics 2015.

Marx, Karl and Friedrich Engels, *The German Ideology*, International Publishers, 1947.

Mayer, Margit and John Ely, *The German Greens: Paradox between Movement and Party*, Temple University Press, 1998.

Mazur, Laurie (ed.), *A Pivotal Moment: Population, Justice and the Environmental Challenge*, Island Press, 2009.

Mazur, Laurie, 'Population and Environment: A Progressive, Feminist Approach', *Climate and Capitalism*, 17 January 2010.

McCarthy, Michael, *Say Goodbye to the Cuckoo*, John Murray, 2009.

McKibben, Bill, *The End of Nature*, Viking, 1990.

Meadows, Donella H and Dennis L, *The Limits to Growth. A report for the Club of Rome's Project on the Predicament of Mankind*. Second edition, 1974, First published by Universe Books, 1972.

Merchant, Carolyn, *The Death of Nature: Women, Ecology and the Scientific Revolution*, Harper, 1980.

Mies, Maria and Vandana Shiva, *Ecofeminism*, Zed Books, 1993. This edition by Zed 2014.

Monbiot, George, *Heat*, Penguin, 2006.

Monbiot, George, *Feral: Searching for Enchantment on the Frontiers of Rewilding*, Allen Lane, 2013.

Monbiot, George, *How Did We Get into This Mess?*, Verso, 2017.

Moore, Charles, *Plastic Ocean*, Avery, 2011. Convention on Biological Diversity, Global Diversity Outlook 3, Montréal, 2010.

Moore, W. Jason, *Capitalism and the Web of Life: Ecology and the Accumulation of Capital*, Verso, 2015.

Moore, W. Jason (ed.), *Anthropocene or Capitalocene*, Kairos, 2016.

Morris, William, *News from Nowhere and Other Writings*, Penguin, 1993.

Morton, A.L., *Political Writings of William Morris*, Lawrence and Wishart, 1984.

Nash, Roderick Frazier, *Wilderness and the American Mind*, Yale University Press, 1967.

Nash, Roderick Frazier, *The Rights of Nature: A History of Environmental Ethics*, University of Wisconsin Press, 1989.

Neale, Jonathan, *Stop Global Warming: Change the World*, Bookmarks, 2008.

Nearing, Scott, *Economics for the Power Age*, John Day, 1952.

Nearing, Scott, *The Good Life*, Schocken Books, 1970.

Nearing, Scott, *The Making of a Radical: A Political Autobiography*, Chelsea Green Publishing, 2002.

New Economics Foundation, *Growth Isn't Working: Why We Need a New Economic Direction*, 2006.

Nikiforuk, Andrew, *Tar Sands*, Greystone Books, first published 2010.

Nore, Petter and Turner Terisa (ed.) *Oil and the Class Struggle*, Zed, 1980.

O'Connor James, *On the Two Contradictions of Capitalism*, published in *Capitalism Nature Socialism*, Vol 2, 1991 – issue 3.

Paddock, William and Paul, *Famine 1975! America's Decision: Who Will Survive*, Little Brown, 1967.

Pearce, Fred, *When the Rivers Run Dry*, Eden Project, 2006.

Pearce, Fred, *Peoplequake: Mass Migration, Aging Nations, and the Coming Population Crash*, Eden Project Books, 2011.

Pepper, David, *Ecosocialism: From Deep Ecology to Social Justice*, Routledge, 1993.

Pirani, Simon, *Burning Up – a global history of fossil fuel consumption*, Pluto, 2018.

Place, Francis, *Illustrations and Proofs of the Principles of Population*, Augustus M. Kelly Publications, 1967.

Porritt, Jonathan, *Seeing Green: Politics of Ecology Explained*, OUP, 1984.

Pugh, Cedric, *Sustainability, the Environment and Urbanisation*, Earthscan, 1996.

Raworth, Kate, *Doughnut Economics – Seven Ways to Think Like a 21st-Century Economist*, Business Books, 2017.

Red Green Study Group, *What on Earth is to be Done?*, RGSG, 1995.

Riftkin Jeremy, *Beyond Beef: The Rise and Fall of the Cattle Culture*, Plume, 1992.

Riftkin, Jeremy, *Rain Forest in your Kitchen*, Island Press, 1992.

Robins, Paul, *Political Ecology: A Critical Introduction*, Wiley Blackwell, 2012.

Roberts, Alan, *The Phantom Solution: Climate Change and Nuclear Power*, Arena, 23, 2005.

Rockström et al., '*Planetary Boundaries: Exploring the Safe Operating Space for Humanity*', Ecology and Society, 14/2, 2009.

Rosenthal, Stan, *Eco-Socialism in a Nutshell*, SERA, 1980; republished by *Climate and Capitalism*, 2013.

Rowbotham, Sheila, *Edward Carpenter: A Life of Liberty and Love*, Verso, 2008.

Roy, Arundhati, *The Greater Common Good*, essay reprinted in *The Cost of Living*, Flamingo, 1999.

Ryle, Martin, *The Politics of Nuclear Disarmament*, Pluto, 1981.

Ryle, Martin, *Ecology and Socialism*, Radius, 1988.

Sagan, Carl, *Billions and Billions: Thoughts of Life and Death at the Brink of the Millennium*, Ballantine Books, 1998.

Saito, Kohei, *Karl Marx's Ecosocialism*, Monthly Review Press, 2017.

Sandom, Christopher, Søren Faurby, Brody Sandel and Jens-Christian Svenning, *Global Late Quaternary Megafauna Extinctions Linked to Humans, Not Climate Change*, Proceedings of the Royal Society B. Published 4 June 2014.DOI: 10.1098/rspb.2013.3254

Salleh, Ariel, *Eco-feminism as Politics—nature, Marx and the postmodernism*, Zed, 1997.

Sarkar, Saral, Eco-socialism or Eco-capitalism, Zed, 1999.

Schmidt, Alfred, *The Concept of Nature in Marx*, first published 1962; Verso, 2014.

Schwagerl, Christian, *The Anthropocene: The Human Era and How It Shapes the Planet*, Synergetic Press, 2014.

Seccombe, Wally, *Marxism and Demography, New Left Review, 1/137, 1983.*

Seccombe, Wally, *Weathering the Storm—working class families from the industrial revolution to the fertility decline.* Verso, 1993.

Shapiro, Judith, *Mao's War Against Nature: Politics and the Environment in Revolutionary China*, Cambridge University Press, 2001.

Simpson, Tony (ed.), *Socially Useful Production*, Forest Stewardship Council, 2016.

Sinclair, Upton, *The Jungle*, 1906; Penguin, 1985.

Sharzer, Greg, *No Local: Why Small-scale Alternatives Won't Change the World*, Zero Books, 2011.

Shiva, Vandana, *The Violence of the Green Revolution: Ecological Degradation and Political Conflict in Punjab*, Natraj Publishers, 1981.

Shiva, Vandana, *Staying Alive: Women, Ecology and Development*, Zed Books, 1989.

Shiva, Vandana (ed.), *Biodiversity: Social and Ecological Perspectives*, Zed Books, 1992.

Shiva, Vandana and Maria Mies, *Ecofeminism*, Fernwood, 1993.

Shiva, Vandana, *Monocultures of the Mind: Biodiversity, Biotechnology and Agriculture*, Zed Books, 1993.

Shiva, Vandana, *Stolen Harvest: The Hijacking of the Global Food Supply*, South End Press, 2000.

Shiva, Vandana, *Protect or Plunder: Understanding Intellectual Property Rights*, Zed Books, 2001.

Shiva, Vandana, *Water Wars: Privatisation, Pollution and Profit*, South End Press, 2002.

Shiva, Vandana, *Earth Democracy: Justice, Sustainability, and Peace*, South End Press, 2005

Shiva, Vandana, *Soil Not Oil: Climate Change, Peak Oil and Food Insecurity*, Zed Books, 2008.

Shiva, Vandana, *Staying Alive*, South End Press, 2010.

Shiva, Vandana, *Biopiracy: The Plunder of Nature and Knowledge*, Natraj, 2011.

Shiva, Vandana, *Who Really Feeds the World*, North Atlantic Books, 2015.

Simms, Andrew, *A New Path to Prosperity: Cancel the Apocalypse*, Little Brown, 2013.

Smith, Dai, *Raymond William: A Warrior's Tail*, Parthian, 2008.

Soper, Kate, *What Is Nature? Culture, Politics and the Non-Human*, Blackwell, 1988.

Soper, Kate, Greening Prometheus: *Marxism and Ecology in the Greening of Marxism*, New York, 1996.

Sperling, Daniel and Deborah Gordon, *Two Billion Cars*, Oxford University Press, 2010.

Spicer, John, *Biodiversity: A Beginner's Guide*, Oneworld, 2006.

Steinbeck John, *The Log from the Sea of Cortez*, Penguin, 1941.

Stern, Nicholas, *The Economics of Climate Change*, Cambridge University Press, 2006.

Stern, Nicholas, *A Blueprint for a Safer Planet*, Bodley Head, 2009.

Stretton Hugh, *Capitalism, Socialism and the environment*, Cambridge, 1976.

Tal, Alon, *The Land is Full*, Yale University Press, 2016.

Tanuro, Daniel, *Green Capitalism: Why It Can't Work*, Merlin, Resistance Books, and IIRE, 2013.

The Alternative Economic Strategy: A Labour Movement Response to the Economic Crisis, CSE Books, 1980.

Thompson, E.P., *William Morris: Romantic to Revolutionary*, Merlin, 1955.

Thompson, Ken, *Do We Need Pandas?: The Uncomfortable Truth about Biodiversity*, Green Books, 2010.

Trades Union Congress, *Unlocking Green Enterprise*, 2009.

Trades Union Congress, *Powering Ahead*, 2016.

Trotsky, Leon, *Literature and Revolution*, 1924.

Tudge, Colin, *So Shall We Reap: What's Gone Wrong with the World's Food – And How to Fix It*. Penguin, 2003.

Tudge, Colin, *Feeding People Is Easy*, Pari Publishing, 2007.

Tyndall, John, *Heat Considered as a Law of Motion*, Longman 1863.

UN Environment Programme (2000), Report of the Governing Council, sixth special session, 29-31 May.

Vernadsky, Vladimir, *The Biosphere*, Synergetic Press, 1986, first published Leningrad, 1926.

Wadhams, Peter, *A Farewell to Ice: A Report from the Artic*, Alan Lane, 2016.

Wainwright, Hillary and Dave Elliot, *The Lucas Plan: New Trade Unionism in the Making*, Allison and Busby, 1982.

Wall, Derek, *Earth First! – and the anti-roads movement*, Routledge, 1999.

Wall, Derek, *The Rise of the Green Left*, Pluto, 2010.

Wall, Derek, *Green Politics*, No-Nonsense Guides, New Internationalist Publications.

Wall, Derek, *The Commons in History: Culture, Commons, Conflict and Ecology*, MIT Press, 2014.

Wall, Derek *The Sustainable Economics of Elinor Ostram*, Routledge, 2014.

Wall, Derek *Economics after Capitalism*, Pluto, 2015.

Wall, Derek, *Elinor Ostrom's Rules for Radicals*, Pluto, 2018.

Wall, Derek, *Hugo Blanco: a Revolutionary for Life*, Merlin and Resistance Books, 2018.

Wallis, Victor, *Red-Green Revolution – the politics and technology of ecosocialism*, Political Animal Press, Toronto, 2018.

Williams, Chris, Ecology and Socialism – solutions to capitalist ecological crisis, Haymarket, 2010.

Wang, Yunshi, Jacob Teter and Daniel Sperling, *Will China's Vehicle Population Grow Even Faster than Forecasted?*, Access Magazine, 1/41, pp.29-33.

Waters, Colin N, Jan A Zalasiewicz, Mark Williams, Michael A Ellis and Andrea A Snelling, *A Stratigraphical Basis for the Anthropocene*, Geological Society of London, Lyell Special Publications 395 March 2014.

Weiner, Douglas R., *Models of Nature: Ecology, Conservation and Cultural Revolution in Soviet Russia*, Pittsburgh, 1988.

Weiner, Douglas R., *A Little Corner of Freedom: Russian Nature Protection from Stalin to Gorbachev*, California, 1999.

Wilkinson, Richard and Pickett Kate, *The Spirit Level: Why Equality Is Better for Everyone*, Penguin, 2009.

Wilson, Edward O., *The Diversity of Life*, Penguin, first edition 1992 second edition 2001.

Wilson, Edward O., Half-Earth: Our Planet's Fight for Life, Liveright Publishing, 2016.

Williams, Chris, *Ecology of Socialism—Capitalism and the Environment*, Haymarket, 2010.

Williams, Raymond, *Culture and Society 1780-1950*, Pelican, 1958.

Williams, Raymond, *The Long Revolution*, Chatto and Fakenham, 1961.

Williams, Raymond, *Socialism and Ecology*, SERA, 1982.

Wolf, Winfried, *Car Mania: A Critical History of Transport*, revised English edition, Pluto, 1996.

Woodcock, B.A. et al., *Country-specific Effects of Neonicotinoid Pesticides on Honeybees and Wild Bees, Science*, 356/6345, June 2017, pp.1393-5.

Woodin, Michael and Caroline Lucas, *Green Alternatives to Globalisation: A Manifesto*, Pluto, 2004.

World Bank, *Climate Change Report*, 2012.

World Wildlife Fund, *Living Planet Report 2016*.

Wrigley, E.A., *Energy and the English Industrial Revolution*, Cambridge, 2010.

Zimmerman, Michael E. (ed.), *Environmental Philosophy from Animal Rights to Radical Ecology*, Prentice Hall, 1993.

Index

About Resistance Books and the IIRE

Resistance Books is the publishing arm of Socialist Resistance. We publish books independently, and also jointly with Merlin Press (London) and the International Institute for Research and Education (Amsterdam). Further information about Resistance Books, including a full list of titles available and how to order them, can be obtained at www.resistancebooks.org.

To contact Resistance Books:
Email: info@resistancebooks.org;
Website: www.resistancebooks.org;
Post: Resistance Books, PO Box 62732, London, SW2 9GQ.

Socialist Resistance is a revolutionary Marxist, internationalist, ecosocialist and feminist organisation. Analysis and news from Socialist Resistance can be read online at:
www.socialistresistance.org

To contact Socialist Resistance:
Email contact@socialistresistance.org;
Website: www.socialistresistance.org;
Post: Socialist Resistance, PO Box 62732, London, SW2 9GQ.

Socialist Resistance collaborates with the Fourth International, whose online magazine, International Viewpoint, is available at www.internationalviewpoint.org.

The International Institute for Research and Education

is a centre for the development of critical thought and the exchange of experiences and ideas between people engaged in their struggles. Since 1982, when the Institute opened in Amsterdam, its main activity has been the organisation of courses for progressive forces around the world. The seminars, courses and study groups deal with all subjects related to the emancipation of the oppressed and exploited around the world. It has welcomed participants from across the world, most of them from developing countries. The IIRE provides activists and academics opportunities for research and education in three locations: Amsterdam, Islamabad and Manila.

The IIRE publishes Notebooks for Study and Research, which focus on contemporary political debates, as well as themes of historical and theoretical importance. The Notebooks have appeared in several languages besides English and French. All the Notebooks are available by going to http://iire.org/en/resources/notebooks-for-study-and-research.html. Other publications and audio files of the events held at the IIRE are available in several languages and can be freely downloaded from www.iire.org.

To contact the International Institute for Research and Education:
Email: iire@iire.org;
Website: www.iire.org;
Phone: 00 31 20 671 7263;
Post: International Institute for Research and Education,
Lombokstraat 40, Amsterdam, 1094 AL, The Netherlands

Lightning Source UK Ltd.
Milton Keynes UK
UKHW011552070519
342241UK00004B/399/P

9 780902 869912